K Today

Teaching and Learning in the Kindergarten Year

Dominic F. Gullo, editor

National Association for the Education of Young Children
Washington, DC

National Association for the Education of Young Children
1313 L Street, NW, Washington, DC 20005-4101
202-232-8777 or 800-424-2460
www.naeyc.org

Through its publications program the National Association for the Education of Young Children (NAEYC) provides a forum for discussion of major issues and ideas in the early childhood field, with the hope of provoking thought and promoting professional growth. The views expressed or implied are not necessarily those of the Association.

Carol Copple, *publications director.* Bry Pollack, *senior editor.* Malini Dominey, *production and design.* Lisa Bowles, *editorial associate.* Leah Pike, *editorial assistant.* Natalie Cavanagh, *photo editor.* Cynthia Bond, *copyeditor.* Laura Power, *indexer.*

Library of Congress Control Number: 2006927200
ISBN 13: 978-1-928896-39-5
ISBN 10: 1-928896-39-1
NAEYC Item #155

Did you know . . . ?

In the course of working on this book, we learned many interesting things about kindergarten and kindergartners. Among them were a multitude of "factoids" that we found particularly intriguing. Here's a small sampling of them for your enjoyment.

—Eds.

Not long after kindergartens were introduced in mid 19th-century Germany, they came to be seen as products of the socialist movement and were banned.

The brain of a kindergarten child has 1,000 trillion synapses, about twice as many as her pediatrician's.

By the time they enter kindergarten, children in the U.S. have watched an average of 4,000 hours of television.

Children age 6 or under frequently believe that fluttering leaves make the wind, and that the moon follows you as you walk.

Dyslexia affects one out of every five children—10 million in America alone.

American children prefer being outdoors to indoors, yet they may spend as much as 90% of their childhood inside.

By age 7, about two-thirds of children say they have played with imaginary companions, and one-third say they still do.

Only 1% of kindergarten classrooms have desks for each child but no activity centers, whereas 79% have activity centers but no desks.

Children who show resilience in difficult life circumstances often identify a favorite teacher as being an important role model.

For sources, see p. 173

Contents

Part IV. Kindergarten in a Policy Context

Preface

by Dominic F. Gullo

In recent years, issues and changes affecting kindergarten have stirred many animated discussions among educators. Standards, packaged curriculum, standardized testing, scientifically based instruction, computers and other electronic media, changes in families—these and many other topics have churned up plenty of confusion and controversy. We have asked ourselves: What is happening and why? Within this shifting scene, what are the opportunities for making kindergarten education better? And in the transformation of kindergarten, are things of value also being lost? How, we have wondered, can we prepare and support teachers to be effective in today's kindergarten classrooms with today's kindergartners?

National leaders, including those in the National Association for the Education of Young Children (NAEYC), have been asking these questions, too. In my recent term on the Governing Board, I heard a lot about the issues confronting kindergarten teachers and teacher educators. In the course of discussions with NAEYC staff, particularly with then director of professional development Marilou Hyson and publications director Carol Copple, a recognition surfaced that the time was ripe for a book to address such questions.

In helping to develop this volume, I was delighted to collaborate with NAEYC because of the organization's focus on the broad span of development from birth through age 8. Also important to me for this book was that NAEYC ensures all its publications are both firmly grounded in the early childhood knowledge base and highly accessible to all levels of readers.

It is my hope that this resource not only gives those readers important information but also encourages them to reflect and promotes well-informed, thoughtful teaching and leadership at the kindergarten level.

About this volume

K Today: Teaching and Learning in the Kindergarten Year is a compilation of 15 chapters by highly respected early childhood educators, each an expert in his or her field. Individually and across the chapters, we have strived to paint a realistic picture of the challenges and roles of today's kindergarten educators, especially given state and district mandates, families' expectations, and the everyday world of children.

The volume is divided into four parts, each approaching kindergarten from a slightly different angle. Together, the chapters offer an illuminating picture of teaching and learning in the kindergarten year. In Part I, **Off to Kindergarten,** three chapters consider today's kindergartens in all their variety, the children who are in them, and the families these children come from. In Chapter 1, **Beth Graue** examines various aspects of the contemporary kindergarten milieu, including the shifts in kindergarten's format and focus, and how social changes and pressures have resulted in changes in kindergarten and the children who attend.

In Chapter 2, **Laura Berk** introduces us to the kindergarten child. She examines what we know about kindergartners—how are they different from preschoolers and from first-graders?—describes major trajectories in their learning and development, and highlights significant variations in these characteristics and trajectories. The families of kindergarten children are the focus of Chapter 3, authored by **Doug Powell** and **Hope Gerde**. They discuss the diverse characteristics of today's families in relation to the impact on children's development and learning and on home-school connections.

Part II, **Developing Foundations in the Kindergarten Year,** examines what might be considered the real basics that underlie all young children's learning and development in all areas of the curriculum. **Susan Golbeck** (Chapter 4) describes important features of kindergartners' cognitive development and suggests how teachers can foster these cognitive skills through interactions, materials, and environments. In Chapter 5, **Martha Bronson** takes a look at the fundamental social and emotional skills developing in the kindergarten year and describes the role of the kindergarten teacher in promoting social and emotional competence.

The focus of Part III is **Teaching, Curriculum, and Assessment in Kindergarten.** This part of the book outlines what children should know and be able to do in each of eight areas, as well as how effective teachers ensure that such learning and skill development occurs. In Chapter 6, **Cate Heroman** and **Carol Copple** discuss key aspects of teaching in the kindergarten year, from setting up the learning environment and schedule to making decisions about curriculum and using effective teaching strategies.

In Chapters 7 through 12, the authors examine six curriculum areas and for each emphasize the "big ideas" and skills that kindergartners should acquire, as well as the state of standards setting, in that domain. These authors are **Dorothy Strickland** (language and literacy); **Julie Sarama** and **Doug Clements** (mathematics); **Ingrid Chalufour** and **Karen Worth** (science); **Gayle Mindes** (social studies); **Mary Jalongo** and **Joan Isenberg** (creative thought and expression); and **Steve Sanders** (physical education). Each of these chapters also sketches a picture of how effective teachers promote children's learning in that

particular domain of the kindergarten curriculum. Part III concludes with my own chapter (Chapter 13), which discusses how to use assessment to inform decisions about promoting kindergartners' learning and development. In it I describe a variety of assessment strategies, with an emphasis on matching the assessment to the curriculum, using assessment information to make instructional decisions, and sharing assessment information with families.

Part IV, **Kindergarten in a Policy Context,** examines issues that extend beyond the kindergarten classroom. Transition from kindergarten to first grade is the focus of Chapter 14, contributed by **Jason Downer, Kate Driscoll,** and **Robert Pianta.** The authors emphasize how kindergarten teachers can partner with families and with first grade teachers to ensure children's success. In the final chapter (Chapter 15), **Lynn Kagan** and **Kristie Kauerz** consider major trends and policy issues of the present and future.

Dominic F. Gullo is a professor and deputy chair in the elementary and early childhood education department at Queens College, City University of New York. He served on the NAEYC Governing Board from 2001 to 2005. Dr. Gullo is interested in the relationship between preschool experiences and children's social and academic competence in kindergarten and the primary grades, and investigates the effects of various curriculum models on children's development and learning. He writes about assessment in early childhood education and early childhood school reform and consults with school districts around the country in early childhood education, language and literacy, and assessment.

Part I

Off to Kindergarten

This Thing Called Kindergarten

1

M. Elizabeth Graue

Imagine that an alien from a distant planet comes to Earth to study our culture and comes across the word *kindergarten*. "What does this mean?" the alien wonders. First he tries the dictionary: "A program or class for 4- to 6-year-old children that serves as an introduction to school." The alien is puzzled by the word's origins from the German *kinder* ("children") and *garten* ("garden"). Is fertilizer involved?

Next the alien tries popular culture. He sees that humans are enamored with something called *All I Really Need to Know I Learned in Kindergarten,* by Robert Fulghum. There is a book, plays, even a poster—all focusing on sharing, playing, cleaning up messes, saying you're sorry, cookies, napping. The poster ends with the line, "And it is still true, no matter how old you are, when you go out in the world, it is best to hold hands and stick together." Switching media, the alien watches a movie called *Kindergarten Cop,* in which a man with huge biceps and an Austrian accent playing an undercover police officer staggers under the weight of shrieking children hanging from his every limb. The alien wonders why the idea of this man teaching kindergarten is seen as so darned funny. Particularly puzzling is when one of the characters warns

another, "Kindergarten is like the ocean; you don't want to turn your back on it." Here, kindergarten sounds dangerous, hardly the caring context described by Fulghum. Later the alien notes that saying "He's so dumb he flunked kindergarten" about someone is considered a great insult.

An introduction to school, a child's garden, a warm and fuzzy place, playtime with an undercurrent of danger, something with the lowest standards. What *is* this thing called kindergarten?

That extraterrestrial is rightfully confused. Things do not get much clearer when we look at the data ourselves. In 2002, some 96 percent of America's four million age-eligible children were enrolled in kindergarten (U.S. Department of Commerce 2002). Yet only 14 states mandate kindergarten attendance, and 7 states do not even require school districts to make kindergarten available. (For more on this, see the box on the next page.) How can kindergarten be so valued as to be nearly universal, but not important enough to be required?

Most adults remember kindergarten as a time of play and transition from home to school. But kindergarten today is more structured and likely follows one or more years in group settings. Researchers, too, are caught up in the puzzle of defining kindergarten. Pointing to the variability in policies and a lack of research on specific classroom practice, scholars of kindergarten highlight its muddled image (McMaken 2001; Vecchiotti

M. Elizabeth Graue, a former kindergarten teacher, is a professor of early childhood education at the University of Wisconsin–Madison. Teacher "Mrs. Kastenbach" (a pseudonym) shared her classroom with the author during the 2004–05 school year.

the optimal tool for keeping the best of its past and leveraging its potential in the future.

Goals and purposes of kindergarten

On this first morning of her last year of teaching, Mrs. Kastenbach looks around with satisfaction at her brightly colored classroom. The room will soon buzz with the energy of a new group of 5- and 6-year-olds. Observing this 40-year teaching veteran offers a window on kindergarten's past and into its future. Her experience and knowledge point her toward supporting the children's social and emotional development through play, while the school district's standards and curriculum guide her to focus on developing their academic skills. It is a delicate balancing act. As the first of the children arrive, Mrs. K. greets them with warmth and enthusiasm in joyful support of their transition to "real school."

It seems that more than any other elementary grade, kindergarten is all about the children, linking its practices and expectations to the needs of 5-year-olds. Like most veteran teachers, Mrs. Kastenbach has seen those needs defined in different ways. In her early days of teaching, her classes were half-day sessions of 31 children each. At that time, children were thought to be too immature to be in school all day, but mature enough to be herded through 2½ hours of activities in a crowd. The curriculum focused on social and institutional practices—learning to line up, sit in a circle, listen to other children talk, and share.

Over the years, the sessions expanded to school-day length, and the number of children in a class decreased. Now, working in a state-sponsored class-size reduction program, Mrs. Kastenbach teaches 15 children in a school-day program of 6½ hours daily. With this shift came specific demands on her time and expertise: a plethora of assessments to gauge children's individual gains and ultimately program efficacy, a more intensive curriculum focused on literacy and mathematics, and a sense of accountability for learning. But it is a life she loves: "I feel really fortunate to be able to do this. No day is the same.

2003; West, Denton, & Germino-Hausken 2000; West, Denton, & Reaney 2001). Sara Vecchiotti says it best, "Kindergarten suffers from the middle-child syndrome, [it is] caught between early education and public education, because it shares features of both educational levels" (2003, 6).

Kindergarten is also caught between our emotions and our intellect—a prisoner of dichotomies too powerful to escape. It is a place of nostalgic memory and powerful ritual imagery, as well as curriculum foundations for later school success. This chapter will explore this tension—highlighting kindergarten's unique position in education and arguing that exploiting its liminal qualities is i go home tired and fall asleep in the chair with the cat. But it's the greatest job in the world."

Mrs. Kastenbach considers the children sitting before her on the rug. Fifteen little bodies bursting with energy, some entirely at ease, others hanging back to see what rules to follow. Danton and Dulce attended the district's early childhood program for children with potential delays. Because their old classroom was across the hall, they already know where the bathroom is and how to open a locker. Omar and Arturo chat in Spanish; Mrs. K. taught their older sisters and worries whether they are fluent enough in English to get by without ESL services.

Sherice and Maya jostle for Mrs. K.'s attention; theirs is a long-standing competition, since they entered infant care together. Tatum's parents both have developmental disabilities; he would have benefited from preschool but didn't go. He's wearing his dad's T-shirt, big rubber boots, and shorts that drag on the ground. Adam was old enough to go to kindergarten last year, but his mom didn't think he was ready. Shelley ambles in a bit later than the rest—her grandmother had a hard time getting her out the door.

Fifteen children, all excited about school. Some are away from home for the first time, while some are already old hands at child care. A few are beginning to read, and others have little clue about how to find their nametag on the table. They all have strengths, challenges, and families who sent the best child they had to school.

The mix of children in Mrs. Kastenbach's group only hints at the variation in almost every dimension that characterizes kindergarten classrooms today. Some children are living in grinding poverty, others in affluent comfort. There are tiny boys wearing size 4T and BIG girls who would not look out of place in third grade. There is the child who only turned 5 the week before school started and the one held out a year ("redshirted") who turned 6 that same week. There are children who are computer savvy and those who have no books at home, much less a computer. Some children fit into the group dynamic with little effort, others sit on the sidelines for weeks, waiting for a moment of comfort to begin social interaction. There are first-time kindergarten parents and parents whose older children have passed through already. Some

children will eventually receive special education services and others will always be in the center of the developmental distribution.

The variation is huge—the natural developmental variability of a group of young children sharing a 12-month age span linked to a school's kindergarten cutoff date (for more on this, see the box **Kindergarten Entrance Age** in the Kagan and Kauerz chapter in this volume). That variation is extended by another year through redshirting and retention, plus the factor of socioeconomic status that shapes the opportunities of children well before they come to school (Lee & Burkam 2002). How is Mrs. Kastenbach supposed to get them all to the same level of literacy preparation and other important kindergarten benchmarks by the following June? Much of her success—and our understanding of that success—has to do with how we conceptualize kindergarten.

Kindergarten's place in the elementary school

Kindergarten has a long and vital history in the United States. The first kindergarten was located in Watertown, Wisconsin, during the mid 19th century; over time, private and public settings developed programs designed to meet the varied needs of the nation's citizens. Some kindergartens served primarily middle-class children and reflected the play-oriented emphasis of Friedrich Froebel, the founder of "the children's garden," or *kindergarten*. Other free/charity kindergartens worked to socialize the children of immigrants and the poor. The first public school kindergarten opened in 1870 in St. Louis and served 3- to 6-year-olds.

Over the years, kindergartens were housed in public and private schools, church facilities, and for-profit child care centers. But by the mid 20th century, the majority of kindergartners were educated in public-school settings (Vecchiotti 2003). This history, with its mix of purposes, sponsors, and structures, has made kindergarten's functions and relationships to schooling and preschool a wonderful, but sometimes troubled, hybrid of early childhood and elementary education.

Unlike the buzzing hive of an early childhood program, the elementary school has a penchant for quiet, orderly structure. Kindergarten's noisy gaggle, so constitutionally unsuited to marching in elementary school's much valued line, caused it to stick out there like a clown in a bank. Kindergarten teachers typically had a specialized educational credential, and the kindergarten was housed in special rooms with entrances and restrooms separate from the rest of the elementary school. Kindergarten's blocks, paints, rhythm instruments, and housekeeping corner meant its classrooms were filled with supplies and equipment quite unlike the usual elementary school fare. These differences in design reflected kindergarten's function as the official transition from home to school. Kindergartens even looked more like home than school, often with large bay windows, fireplaces, and cozy furniture.

The curriculum for kindergarten built on its historical purposes of socializing young immigrants and supporting social development (Bloch 1987). Kindergarten was viewed as the place to get children ready for school. The focus was on social development—what it meant to be a student and to be part of the institution of the school. The mode of teaching was play—diverse child-oriented activities of interacting socially, sharing materials, and managing space. The content consisted of topics such as "my family," "my community," "animals," "transportation"—topics that built on what children already knew and had experienced, and focused on the very important social lessons that were the core of kindergarten at that time.

But as more women have entered the workforce, more families have enrolled their children in preschool or child care at earlier ages. Too, the promise of early intervention provides increasing numbers of children with publicly supported pre-K programs, including Head Start. It has become much more likely that an incoming kindergartner has had some kind of prior educational or group experience. In fact, some 80 percent of children entering kindergarten have had at least one year of preschool, and half have had two years (U.S. Department of Commerce 2002).

This has led to a shift in curriculum. Children typically come to kindergarten having done thematic units on the post office, having played in the sand and water tables, having learned to line up to go to the playground, to listen to directions, and to work and play with others. So kindergarten curriculum has begun to include more academic content. Units on shapes and colors have morphed into the "Letter of the Week." Educational publishers have discovered the kindergarten market, developing textbooks and curriculum kits for 5-year-olds. Most teacher-education programs have not prepared early childhood teachers for this new world. In the name of "alignment" and "standards," report cards, assessments, and content from higher grades have been pushed down onto kindergarten. The kindergarten day has gotten longer.

Kindergarten's mission has changed from helping children get used to school to preparing them to achieve in first grade. This is not a subtle change. Rather than having intrinsic worth, kindergarten is being redefined in terms of its ability to set up children's academic success at the *next* level.

On one hand, this assimilation of kindergarten into the elementary school culture has given kindergarten new relevance and status in the broader educational system. Certainly it is unrealistic to expect, as society changes and schools evolve, that children would forever attend the kindergarten of the past. But are we losing too many of the characteristics that have traditionally made kindergarten unique? Are we giving sufficient thought and attention to the intended—and unintended—outcomes of this assimilation? How does the new kindergarten support *all* children's developmental needs and experiences?

Social or academic? A false dichotomy

To think about how kindergarten fits into the school of the 21st century means asking questions about goals and means. But it makes no sense to ask, "Is kindergarten for social development, as in its earlier days, *or* is its focus academics, like the

M. Elizabeth Graue

rest of the elementary curriculum?" "Is kindergarten about play *or* is it a place of learning?" To anyone who understands kindergarten and kindergartners, that is like asking whether life is about work *or* family, or whether water *or* air is more important.

To suppose that one must choose a single focus for teaching 5- and 6-year-olds is to forget the integrated manner in which children of this age experience the world. And it assumes that the world operates in an either/or mode. Returning to Mrs. Kastenbach's classroom helps to see how kindergarten is all about *both*. It is absolutely reasonable to expect that kindergarten is about playful learning *and* learningful play, and about academic socialization *and* social academics. To make the most of the kindergarten experience, a teacher must be a master of knowledge about specific curriculum content, about children in general, and about her students in particular.

It's mid winter in Mrs. Kastenbach's classroom. As always, the learning focus changes as the day progresses. The beginning of class is all about connecting—Mrs. K. finds out who's absent, makes sure that she knows what's going on with each child at home, and determines who's having hot lunch. There's also group sharing of the mundane news that's exciting to 5-year-olds. Next comes the calendar ritual—weather, day of the week, number of days in school, and multiple ways to represent the notion of *now* in the passage of time.

An extended literacy period follows. Mrs. K. initially wrote each "morning message," but the children are gradually taking over that role. The group writing follows general patterns, but has come to reflect the children's lives and their emerging knowledge of written language. Shared reading revolves around a book chosen to illustrate the classroom theme.

This relatively quiet time gives way to more conversation and movement during center time, but the children remain engaged in experiences through which they learn and develop. Mrs. K. has set up a variety of centers, including blocks, writing, dramatic play, puzzles and games, and computers. She moves around the room as the children play, sometimes pulling students aside to complete one of the many assessments required by her district, sometimes cleaning up a bit, and at other times managing social interactions. A whole-group activity involving listening

and following directions makes for a smooth transition for the children to their scheduled music, physical education, or art class. Singing and dancing helps the group segue to lunch.

A parallel afternoon schedule emphasizes math in place of literacy, with science and social studies woven in. After a final center time, the children head home at 3:00.

In many ways, Mrs. K.'s room is every kindergarten across the United States: a brightly colored space filled with child artwork; surfaces sticky with glue; and a place where friendships form and fracture, where tears come and go, and where hugs and kind words are an appropriate response to most situations. It is also the quintessentially 21st-century kindergarten, designed to address both sides of the social/academic divide. It is a program that balances all kinds of diverse needs. Across the kindergarten day, Mrs. K. blends attention to groups and individuals, to child choice and teacher-guided instruction, to social and academic skills, to physical and intellectual needs, and to quiet and noisy activities. Through skillful environmental design, a well-planned curriculum, and attention to the particular needs of the children each day, Mrs. Kastenbach supports the broad development goals and specific learning outcomes that are important for them.

Mrs. K.'s classroom is a wonderful example of teaching that is *responsive* to the needs of the specific children in the given class, guided by planned curriculum and knowledge of development (Graue, Kroeger, & Brown 2003). This kind of teaching is similar to putting together a very complex puzzle that changes daily. Mrs. Kastenbach brings with her a career's worth of knowledge about children—knowledge about child development and learning and its patterns and processes, her experiences as a mother of three very different children, and her knowledge of the families and children in her community. She draws on this rich store of knowledge to support her students.

To be a good teacher "you need to know them here," she says, pointing to her heart and smiling. This kind of knowledge needs to be constantly refreshed through interaction—through conversations with individuals and groups, observations of children's relationships, and assessments that guide instruction. Knowing children as a group is one thing, but knowing them individually, day by day, is very hard work. Such knowledge requires care, attention, and vigilance that the teacher is keyed into *today's* child, not the one she thought she knew yesterday. And the teacher who knows the children well views each individual child in relation to that child's unique cultural and social context and relationships.

Knowing children "with one's heart" must be combined with knowing them intellectually. That intellectual part attends to knowledge of the content, and the content of kindergarten is hugely complex. The classic kindergarten curriculum consists of child-centered, environmentally mediated content supported during center or choice time—highly social in nature and created on the spot by the children in the class. The teacher may be out of the children's immediate sight, but she plays an integral role in supporting children in their social interactions. Rather than being a ringleader of the class circus, the teacher spends time learning about children as they interact, and teaching them in context.

> You can have standards for learning without "standardizing" your teaching.

Mrs. Kastenbach sits at a table with Keira, going over letter-sound correspondence. Then she goes quietly to the block area to help Shelley talk through her issue with Joshua, following up on yesterday's discussion of negotiating play space and materials. Mrs. K. doesn't make pronouncements. Instead she comes in respectfully, waiting for an opportune moment to build on the children's existing conversation. She has been listening with one ear for quite a while, so she understands where and how to intervene. She joins in their play, modeling with Shelley and Joshua the kinds of behavior she is trying to support. It is subtle, playful, and full of teaching.

To do this kind of work, Mrs. K. must be wholly present in these social contexts, mindfully filling them with places for the children to teach her what to teach. Paperwork, straightening the book corner, and snack preparation can be handled later—this is prime teaching time.

The knowledge needed for teaching content in literacy, mathematics, science, and so on, has received much attention recently, and many teachers have received focused professional development from their districts. The standards movement has had the effect of providing a roadmap for the academic content of the kindergarten curriculum and its relation to the other grades. Most districts now require a series of individual assessments during the year to document each child's learning.

It would be easy for Mrs. Kastenbach to end up focusing all her attention on what gets assessed. But Mrs. K. understands that you can have standards for learning without "standardizing" your teaching. She uses the content knowledge in literacy, mathematics, etc., as a general plan, a set of hopeful expectations to guide but not determine her practice. It helps her with the big-picture elements of her teaching that she uses in conjunction with her knowledge of the social development of her students. With these rich sources of knowledge, she has a strong sense of where the class is going and the confidence to make the sidetrips that can make teaching come alive. She can respond to the children's needs and interests.

One way teachers such as Mrs. Kastenbach keep their teaching responsive is by carefully balancing teacher-guided learning experiences with those that children choose and pursue primarily on their own initiative. Rather than seeing their teaching as one or the other, they recognize that a responsive classroom has the teacher and children engaged in a carefully choreographed but always somewhat improvisational dance—one in which they all actively share teaching and learning. A good example in Mrs. Kastenbach's class is how the generation of "morning message" shifts over the year from her to the children:

Each morning the children write a morning message. In the fall, Mrs. K. wrote the message herself. But as the year has progressed, the children have gained the confidence and skills to record their thoughts in writing. Mrs. K. has moved from modeling to guiding to supporting. Now, as the end of the year draws near, she's able to hand over the marker and make only occasional comments to help them when they are stuck.

M. Elizabeth Graue

Another example is Mrs. Kastenbach's work with Shelley in the block corner. On that occasion, both teacher and child were active participants in the social learning that took place.

This balance ensures that both the teacher and children are engaged in the learning process, a process that represents the interests and knowledge of all participants. This kind of teaching is based in a solid knowledge of children and content, a teacher's commitment to both the social and academic aspects of kindergarten curriculum, and the ability to trust her class to share the direction their learning will take.

When a child does not fit the curriculum map

A question that has challenged kindergarten teachers for as long as kindergarten has existed is what to do with children who are not matching up with the norm. Teachers see three types of lags. The first—what I call *pokey maturation*—is the one most frequently associated with readiness in the broad sense. These children are seen as immature and less developed than their classmates. Sometimes it is a rate problem: the child's maturational timetable is just a bit slower than his peers'. Or it can be a comparison problem: the child is young in the cohort because of a birthday right before the entrance cutoff date. Or it is comparative in a different way: a less assertive child is seen as immature because the child's parent hopes that she will be a leader.

The second lag occurs when children *lack the experiences* on which the kindergarten curriculum is based. Many kindergarten teachers feel that children are less well prepared for kindergarten today than they were 15 years ago (West, Germino-Hausken, & Collins 1993). But with the escalation of the curriculum in the primary grades, what used to be first grade work is now work for the kindergarten. Are these increased expectations somehow related to the perceptions of students as deficient?

The final type is the result of a *disability*. But how does a teacher tell whether a lag in development comes from maturation, experience, or a learning problem that would be supported through special education services? When is intervention warranted, and when is waiting the strategy of choice? Increasingly, schools are following the directives of key national organizations (e.g., NAECS/SDE 2000) and responding to differences in development with programs that keep children in their regular classroom.

Recognizing that it is very difficult to differentiate among the three causes of developmental lags, kindergarten teachers are asked to respond to children's differences by doing careful assessment, focused instruction, and balanced teaching. This careful work by kindergarten teachers takes place in a context in which some parents are making decisions to delay their children's kindergarten entry, larger numbers of children are experiencing publicly funded pre-K programming that is advocated for its preventative effects, and the downward pressure of accountability systems is creating a ripple effect on the kindergarten.

This results in an interesting chicken-and-egg problem. Are more children being identified as unready or as having learning problems because of a curriculum escalation? Or, is the curriculum escalating because kindergartners have changed as the result of social shifts, such as increases in preschool attendance, early intervention programs, redshirting, and retention? These questions may never be answered with certainty. But they are worth asking because they force us to pay attention to shifts that have important implications for students and teachers.

Effective kindergarten curriculum and practice take their shape in relation to a particular set of children at a particular time and place—that is, in response to those children's needs, experiences, strengths, and weaknesses. A kindergarten program cannot be child-proofed. There is no guarantee that it will be uniformly effective for every child, through standards language or the simple desire that "every child be reading by the end of the year." Kindergarten must not be turned into first grade by quietly moving the young 5-year-olds into an additional year of preschool. Instead, the children's garden has to be a place for *every* child to grow and learn, in every dimension of development. That means a place in kindergarten for every child regardless of how close he is to the age cutoff, the curriculum chosen, or the ideas about who is "typically developing."

To get there, though, kindergarten teachers must recognize their own contributions to the system. They must become powerful advocates—for themselves, their students, and their programs—by making sure they are adequately knowledgeable about children's development in their local social and cultural contexts. This knowledge enables teachers to evaluate proposed changes in curriculum and other practices that might put children's development at risk.

Kindergarten at a crossroads

So much is expected of kindergarten. It is a transition between home and school, a bridge between early childhood education and elementary school, and a foundation for social and academic skill development. Lately, more than ever, kindergarten teachers need to know who they are, what their role is, and what the goals for their program are. Without this clarity of purpose, kindergarten risks being driven off course by the winds that periodically blow through the education establishment. More purposeful advocacy for kindergarten must articulate its historical strengths and potential contributions to children. Kindergarten is too important not to protect and nurture.

Mrs. Kastenbach stands at the doorway of her classroom for the last time, a lump in her throat. Everything is packed up. She has given away much of her considerable accumulated teaching materials, and moved things so that the room can be cleaned over the summer. She imagines that she can still hear the voices of all the children across the years who told her they loved her, the cries over fallen block structures, and the cheers of accomplishment. She chuckles to herself, thinking of the fourth grade teacher who is taking her place—a woman nearing retirement who thinks that teaching fifteen 5- and 6-year-olds has to be easier than twenty-five 9-year-olds.

Mrs. K. has left her books and toys and her files about thematic units. She has also left her heart and soul in this room, a place filled with joy for so many children. "After being a mom, teaching kindergarten was the best thing I ever did," she thinks, smiling a satisfied smile. Then she walks through the doorway and down the hall, heading off to a new adventure.

References

Bloch, M.N. 1987. Becoming scientific and professional: An historical perspective on the aims and effects of early education. In *The formation of the school subjects,* ed. T.S. Popkewitz, 25–62. London: Falmer.

Graue, M.E., J. Kroeger, & C. Brown. 2003, Spring. The gift of time: Enactments of developmental thought in early childhood practice. *Early Childhood Research & Practice* 5 (1). Online: http://ecrp.uiuc.edu/v5n1/graue.html.

Lee, V.E., & D.T. Burkam. 2002. *Inequality at the starting gate: Social background differences in achievement as children begin school.* Washington, DC: Economic Policy Institute.

McMaken, J. 2001. *ECS state notes: State statutes regarding kindergarten.* Accessed at www.ecs.org/clearinghouse/29/21/2921.pdf.

NAECS/SDE (National Association of Early Childhood Specialists in State Departments of Education). 2000. *Still! Unacceptable trends in kindergarten entry & placement.* Position statement. Chicago: Author. Online: http://naecs.crc.uiuc.edu/position/trends2000.html.

U.S. Department of Commerce, Bureau of the Census, National Center for Education Statistics. 2002. *Percent of population 3 to 24 years old enrolled in school, by race/ethnicity, sex, and age: Selected years, October 1980 to 2001.* Washington, DC: Author.

Vecchiotti, S. 2003. Kindergarten: An overlooked educational policy priority. *Social Policy Report* 17 (2): 3–19.

West, J., K. Denton, & E. Germino-Hausken. 2000. *America's kindergartners* (NCES 2000-070). Washington, DC: National Center for Education Statistics, U.S. Department of Education.

West, J., K. Denton, & L. Reaney. 2001. *The kindergarten year* (NCES 2001-023). Washington, DC: National Center for Education Statistics, U.S. Department of Education.

West, J., E. Germino-Hausken, & M. Collins. 1993. *Readiness for kindergarten: Parent & teacher beliefs* (NCES 93–257). Washington, DC: National Center for Education Statistics, U.S. Department of Education.

M. Elizabeth Graue

Looking at Kindergarten Children

2

Laura E. Berk

Kindergartners' development—their characteristics, competencies, and needs—should be the foundation for all classroom experiences that teachers provide: curriculum, daily schedule, educational activities, and teaching practices. Asked to reflect on their new students, experienced kindergarten teachers often mention that kindergartners, despite wide individual variation, have common attributes that make them ready for a new phase in their education, which might be considered the beginning of formal schooling. David, a teacher who has taught kindergarten for three years, makes this observation:

> Kindergartners are more independent, self-confident, and exuberant about mastering new skills than they were just a year earlier. They're better-coordinated physically, eager to be entrusted with responsibility, on a more even keel emotionally, and more willing and able to work cooperatively with others.

As David's description suggests, as children enter school, they are also undergoing a transitional period in all domains of their development. From ancient times, societies have recognized that there is a momentous transformation in children's functioning between the ages of 5 and 7. Anthropological research reveals that most cultures

begin systematic teaching of children at about this age (Rogoff 1996). Almost universally, mature members of societies begin to guide these children toward tasks that increasingly resemble those they will perform as adults.

David's account is certainly not a precise description of what all kindergartners are like. But it gives a broad idea of what parents and teachers can expect. Each kindergarten child is unique, having been influenced by individual heredity and environment (and the interaction of the two) since the moment of conception. Moreover, kindergartners' variability is particularly great precisely because they are in developmental transition (McCall, Appelbaum, & Hogarty 1973).

Yet another reason for developmental diversity has to do with the spread of two to two and a half years in age in a typical kindergarten classroom—from about 4¾ to 7¼ years old. Cutoff dates for enrollment in kindergarten vary widely. At one extreme, five states (as of the 2006-07 school year) require that children turn 5 on or before August 15 to enter kindergarten. At the other extreme, four states have cutoff dates between November 30 and January 1 (Education Commission of the States 2004). Furthermore, about 9 percent of children eligible for kindergarten on the basis of their birthdates are held out a year (a practice called "redshirting")—a trend that has accelerated over the past two decades as academic expectations of kindergartners have

---

Laura E. Berk is a Distinguished Professor of Psychology at Illinois State University.

increased. Finally, about 5 to 6 percent of children repeat kindergarten (West, Denton, & Germino-Hausken 2000).

Illustrating the dramatic variation among kindergartners are two students in David's socio-economically diverse, Southern California class. Sammy, age 6, the only child of two professional parents, bounds into the classroom the first week of school and enthusiastically shows David several of his favorite picture books from home, all of which he can "read" by heart.

> Sammy quickly displays a terrific memory for facts and loves to spout off his knowledge of dinosaurs, addition, and subtraction. He has entered kindergarten after having attended a high-quality preschool for two years, and he has more than the expected literacy and numeracy knowledge, including an enthusiasm for books and telling stories, a knowledge of letters and many of their basic sounds, a few sight vocabulary words, and the capacity to print his name.

At the same time, Sammy struggles with cooperation and sharing.

> He is often overbearing during circle time; he has trouble understanding that others need chances to contribute their ideas, too. And during center time, he grabs from other children and tries to dominate when he doesn't get his way.

Then there is Jasmine, who lives in a low-income apartment with her large, extended family of three adults and seven other children ages 1 to 8—two are siblings, the rest are cousins. Since infancy, an aunt has cared for Jasmine when her parents were unavailable; she has no preschool experience. Jasmine's parents tell David that they want her to be a cooperative, well-behaved student. They also state that they rarely read to her, either in their native Spanish or in English. Here are David's thoughts about Jasmine at the start of the school year:

> Jasmine is compliant, but anxious and withdrawn. She rarely speaks unless spoken to, and when I ask her a question, she replies in a voice that is barely above a whisper. She is unfamiliar with certain frequently used English words, such as *ceiling* and *hammer,* and can name only a few letters. When I try to talk with her about a picture book, she shows little interest. Her drawings are completed in a hurry and restricted to the outlines of stick figures. Her descriptions of them are just as limited, such as, "A frog." Jasmine spends much time alone, watching other children and minimally involved in activities.

Although she is shy, David concludes that much of Jasmine's isolation stems from an inability to express herself, and from behavioral expectations at home that differ from those at school.

To be successful with Sammy and Jasmine, David has to provide for both their common and individual learning needs. He must use his knowledge of kindergartners' development—and the various factors known to influence their progress.

Major developmental milestones and individual variations

Kindergartners undergo a wide range of significant changes—physical, neurological, cognitive, emotional, and social. These changes are mutually influential: Every area of functioning contributes to the others.

Physical and motor development

Motor skills are the result of a dynamic developmental system: jointly contributing are kindergarten children's longer, leaner body; their motivation to attain new goals; their advancing cognition; their improved ability to cooperate with peers; and opportunities for extensive practice (Thelen & Smith 1998). As children participate in small-group games with reciprocal roles, they integrate previously acquired motor skills into more complex actions. In the gross motor area, for example, kindergartners run more quickly and smoothly, changing directions easily. They throw and catch with increasing involvement of their whole body, shifting their weight with the release of the ball and varying the force of their throw in accord with where they want the ball to land. When a ball is thrown to them, kindergartners can anticipate its place of landing by moving forward, backward, and sideways, and "giving" with their body to

Laura E. Berk

absorb the force of the ball (Cratty 1986; Roberton 1984).

Fine motor skills advance with improved control of the hands and fingers and an increased desire to communicate through written expression. Most kindergarten children are adept at gripping a crayon or pencil as a result of experimentation during the preschool years. They have tried different forms of pencil holding, gradually discovering the grip and angle that maximize stability and writing efficiency (Greer & Lockman 1998). By age 5, children use an adult pencil grip when writing and drawing—a milestone that results from the child's own active reorganization of behavior. In their efforts to write, kindergartners gradually print recognizable letters as they make progress in differentiating them perceptually. Still, they continue for some time to confuse letters with similar features, such as *C* and *G,* and those that are mirror images of each other, such as *b* and *d* (Bornstein & Arteberry 1999). Consequently, letter reversals in the writing of 4- to 7-year-olds are common. Not until children learn to read do they find it useful to notice the difference between mirror-image forms.

Brain development

During the preschool period and the kindergarten year, the brain grows steadily, increasing from 70 percent to 90 percent of its eventual adult weight (Thatcher et al. 1996). In addition to gains in size, the brain undergoes much reshaping and refining. Among these modifications are profound changes in the frontal lobes—areas devoted to regulating thought and action. The frontal lobes govern the inhibition of impulse, orderly memory, and the integration of information—capacities that facilitate reasoning and problem solving. All these skills improve considerably in the kindergarten child.

Throughout the preschool years, the brain overproduces connections (called "synapses") between neurons. At about age 4 to 5, children have nearly double the number of synapses in some brain areas, such as the frontal lobes, that adults have. This overabundance of communication channels supports the brain's "plasticity," or high capacity for learning. It helps ensure that the child will be able to acquire basic human abilities even if some brain areas happen to be damaged. As the child interacts with the environment and learns, the synaptic connections of stimulated neurons become increasingly elaborate, committed to specific functions, and in need of space. Neurons that are seldom stimulated lose their connective fibers. This reduces the number of total synapses and makes room for the committed structures (Huttenlocher 2002; Nelson 2002).

> At about age 4 to 5, children have nearly double the number of synapses in some brain areas that adults have.

The first five to seven years of life are a sensitive period for brain development. During this time, the brain is especially responsive to stimulation, which prompts this massive wiring of neurons and sculpting of brain regions. The brain is more malleable than it will be later, making preschool and kindergarten an optimum time for learning and effective intervention with all children. The brain lays down its basic organization in two phases. Neuroscientists and child development researchers refer to the first as *experience-expectant brain growth,* underscoring that young children need a wide variety of ordinary experiences during this phase—opportunities to see and touch objects, hear language and other sounds, and move about and explore the environment. As a result of millions of years of evolution, the brain of a young child *expects* to encounter these experiences, and if it does, it will grow normally. A second phase, called *experience-dependent brain growth,* becomes increasingly prominent during the school years. It involves the refinement of established brain structures as a result of specific activities, which vary widely across individuals and cultures (Greenough & Black 1992). Learning to read and write, play computer games, weave an intricate rug, tend a garden, and play the violin are examples of such activities.

Experience-expectant brain growth tends to take place naturally, as adults offer young children age-appropriate play materials and stimulating, enjoyable daily routines and social interaction—a shared meal, a picture book to talk about, a song to sing, an outing at the park. The resulting growth readies the brain for experience-dependent development (Huttenlocher 2002; Shonkoff & Phillips 2000). Hurrying the young child into mastering skills that depend on extensive training, such as some aspects of reading, musical performance, or sports, risks overwhelming the brain's neural circuits, and reduces its sensitivity to the experiences it needs for healthy development (Bruer 1999).

The kindergarten year, as the following sections show, requires a nuanced balance: plenty of play, child choice, verbal interaction, and learning of foundational skills in classrooms rich in engaging activities that are adaptable to children's varying readiness for experience-dependent learning. Kindergartners learn best under conditions in which adults guide and support their active efforts, with gradual and measured introduction of more formal lessons.

Cognitive development

Kindergarten children's thinking is reorganizing—gradually becoming more systematic, accurate, and complex. Children's advancing reasoning and problem solving is supported by gains in attention, memory, language, and knowledge of the world. (For much more about children's cognitive development, see the Golbeck chapter in this volume.)

Reasoning. Piaget characterized the major change in reasoning around kindergarten age as a move from one-dimensional to *multidimensional* representations, which is reflected in the transition from preoperational to concrete operational thought. In Piaget's well-known conservation tasks, preschoolers typically focus on just one dimension. For example, they commonly say that the amount of lemonade changes when it is poured from a tall, thin container into a short, wide container; they fail to notice that all changes in the height of the liquid are compensated for by changes in its width. By contrast, many kindergartners are able to focus on two dimensions and

relate them. Similarly, preschoolers given shapes of different sizes and colors to sort have great difficulty shifting from one basis of sorting to another—from color to size, for example—but children age 5 and older can readily do so (Brooks et al. 2003; Zelazo, Frye, & Rapus 1996).

Major contemporary theorists of cognitive development agree with Piaget that a change in children's thinking occurs at about kindergarten age. But they characterize the transition, which Piaget described as sharply different stages, as taking place gradually. They believe that both brain development and experience contribute to give the older child a larger memory span, and thus the ability to hold in mind and consider two or more elements at once (Case 1992, 1998; Cowan et al. 1999). Kindergartners' advances in reasoning are initially fragile, and they occasionally fall back on earlier and more simplistic ways of thinking. Consequently, the kindergarten child's thinking sometimes seems limited and inflexible, and at other times remarkably advanced.

This move toward more complex thinking shows up not just in the "tabletop universe of test items, problems, and games" (White 1996, 28) that researchers often use to investigate children's thinking. In everyday situations such as drawing pictures, for example, a 4- or 5-year-old depicts people and objects separately, ignoring their spatial arrangement. At age 6 to 7, the child is able to coordinate these two aspects, and the drawing depicts both the features of objects and the objects' spatial relationship to one another. In creating stories, a similar progression takes place. Younger children focus on only a single character's action and emotion; older children combine two characters' actions and emotions in a single plot (Case & Okamoto 1996).

Because of variations in their experiences, interests, and goals, children display thinking that is better developed on some tasks than on others (Sternberg 2002). In this respect, culture is profoundly influential. For example, Jasmine, who comes from a family living in poverty, might have had limited exposure to books and other materials important to school learning. But she might well have impressive competence in areas where she

Laura E. Berk

has simple experience, such as sorting and counting household items, caring for younger siblings, or smoothly collaborating with an adult in preparing a family meal. Indeed, a growing body of multicultural and cross-cultural research shows that what is valued as "intelligent" behavior varies considerably from one cultural group to another (Sternberg & Grikorenko 2004).

Attention. Kindergartners' improved ability to focus and manage their attention contributes to transformations in their reasoning. Development of the frontal lobes of the cerebral cortex leads to greater *cognitive inhibition*—an improved ability, while engaged in a task, to prevent the mind from being distracted and straying to alternative thoughts. Although the capacity for cognitive inhibition increases throughout the preschool years, dramatic gains occur from the kindergarten year on. This enables children to focus more intently on the types of tasks they will encounter often in school. Still, kindergartners tend to have a limited attention span compared with older children or adults, unless they are pursuing self-chosen goals in play, which are highly motivating. With the support of adults, kindergartners are also increasingly capable of planning; they can think out a short, orderly sequence of actions ahead of time and allocate their attention accordingly.

Attentional problems, however, are an area of persistent difficulty for a substantial minority of young children. As many as 3 to 5 percent of school-age children are diagnosed with attention-deficit hyperactivity disorder (ADHD)—characterized by inattention, impulsivity, and excessive motor activity that cause serious academic and social problems. ADHD tends to run in families and is linked to abnormal brain functioning, including in the frontal lobes (Casellanos et al. 2003). Although a highly structured learning situation is often assumed to be useful in dealing with ADHD behavior, such classrooms actually result in children having greater difficulty with impulse control. Young children with ADHD learn best in situations with the same flexible features that benefit their peers without attentional issues—situations in which they are offered choices in activities, can collaborate in small groups on

projects, and can move about often (see, e.g., Berk 2001; Jacob, O'Leary, & Rosenblad 1978).

Memory. The combination of brain growth and improved use of memory strategies (such as rehearsing information and organizing it into categories) eventually benefit children's ability to recall information. However, kindergartners are not yet good at deliberate use of memory strategies. When asked to recall items, such as a list of toys or groceries, they might rehearse on one occasion but not on another; even when they do rehearse, their recall rarely improves. At this age, applying a memory strategy initially requires so much effort and attention that children have little attention left for the memory task itself (Schneider 2002).

> Major contemporary theorists of cognitive development agree with Piaget that a change in children's thinking occurs at about kindergarten age.

Despite kindergartners' limited memory for unrelated items, they show good memory for complex, narrative information that is meaningful to them. For example, at about age 4½ to 5, children can give chronologically organized, detailed, and evaluative accounts of personal experiences, as this kindergartner illustrates: "We went to the lake. Then we fished and waited. I caught a big catfish! Dad cooked it. It was so good we ate it all up!"

Children's narratives improve with age and with opportunities for elaborative conversations with others about personally significant events. Increased memory capacity and experiences with personal storytelling contribute to kindergartners' ability to generate clear oral narratives (Ely 2005). In turn, narrative ability contributes to children's literacy development by strengthening their language skills and preparing them to produce more explicit written narratives.

Because children pick up the narrative styles of parents and other significant adults in their lives, children's styles of personal storytelling vary widely across cultures. For example, instead of the topic-focused style expected in school, in which a single experience is related from beginning to end, many cultures use a topic-associating style, in which several similar experiences are blended (McCabe 1997). Yet, too often, teachers mistakenly criticize this culturally distinctive narrative form as "disorganized" rather than valuing it as another legitimate means of organizing experiences.

Language

By about age 6, the typical child's vocabulary reaches some 10,000 words (Bloom 1998). Children of this age use most of the grammatical structures of their native language competently and are skilled conversationalists who can maintain a topic of discussion over many speaker turns (Tager-Flusberg 2005). Furthermore, beginning at about age 4, children improve steadily in their ability to adapt to a listener's point of view and in their ability to communicate clearly—for example, to describe one object among a group of similar objects (Deutsch & Pechman 1982). As adults and peers ask children to clarify their meaning, children's messages become increasingly precise.

Although language gains are especially noticeable during the preschool years, certain aspects of language undergo more rapid change from kindergarten on. By the end of elementary school, the typical child's vocabulary has quadrupled to 40,000 words. On average, kindergarten and grade-school children learn about 20 new words each day (Anglin 1993). Kindergartners also become increasingly knowledgeable about the features of language. For example, they have a good sense of the concept of "word." When an adult reading a story stops to ask, "What was the last word I said?" they almost always answer correctly for all parts of speech (Karmiloff-Smith et al. 1996). Furthermore, between ages 5 and 8, children make great strides in *phonological awareness*—the ability to reflect on and manipulate the sound structure of language. This awareness is evident in their sensitivity to changes in sounds within words, to rhyming, and to incorrect pronunciation (Foy & Mann 2003). Children's consciousness of the features of language—phonological awareness in particular—is an excellent predictor of success at reading and spelling.

Children's language development is profoundly affected by early conversational and literacy experiences, and kindergartners vary greatly in such experiences. Before starting kindergarten, the average child from a middle-class family has been read to for a total of 1,000 hours; a child from a family living in poverty, for only 25 hours (Neuman 2003). As a result, kindergartners from economically disadvantaged families arrive at the starting gate of formal schooling behind in virtually all the cognitive, language, and literacy skills we have considered. As just one illustration, their vocabularies average only one-fourth the size of their middle-class peers' (Lee & Burkam 2002). Language- and literacy-rich kindergarten environments are crucial for narrowing these gaps and reducing low-income children's risk for academic failure.

Emotional development

In the years leading up to kindergarten entry, a variety of factors contribute to expansion of children's emotional experiences and to gains in their ability to interpret the emotional cues of others. These influences include the development of the frontal lobes of the cerebral cortex, cognitive and language development, a firmer self-concept, and the patient guidance and reasonable expectations of adults. (For much more about children's social-emotional development, see the Bronson chapter in this volume.)

Emotional self-regulation. Throughout the preschool years, children improve steadily in emotional *self-regulation*—the ability to adjust their emotional state to a comfortable level of intensity so they can engage productively in tasks and interact positively with others. Regulating emotion requires *effortful* management of strong feelings, and children benefit from gains in several cognitive capacities discussed earlier: the ability to shift attention away from frustrating experiences, to inhibit thoughts and behaviors, and to plan or actively take steps to relieve stressful situations (Eisenberg & Spinrad 2004). The

Laura E. Berk

warmth, patience, and verbal guidance of parents and teachers are vital in modeling emotional control and teaching children strategies for managing emotions.

By kindergarten age, children can verbalize a variety of effective emotional self-regulation strategies. Nevertheless, children with highly emotionally reactive temperaments have greater difficulty regulating their feelings, and they require extra adult support (Kochanska & Knaack 2003).

Emotional understanding, empathy, and sympathy. Understanding of emotion is generally well developed by kindergarten age. By age 5, children can correctly judge the causes of many emotions ("She's sad because her kitty is sick"). They also can predict the consequences of many emotions with reasonable accuracy (that an angry child might hit someone, that a happy child is more likely to share). Furthermore, 5-year-olds can come up with effective ways to relieve others' negative feelings, such as giving a hug to reduce sadness.

As with cognition, preschoolers and young kindergartners can consider only one aspect of emotion at a time; they staunchly deny that people can experience two feelings at once. But at about age 6 and older, children can better appreciate that a person can, for example, "feel happy that he got a lot of birthday presents but sad that he didn't get just what he wanted" (Pons et al. 2003).

The more that adults acknowledge children's emotional reactions and explain others' feelings, the better preschoolers and kindergartners become at "reading" others' emotions (Denham & Kochanoff 2002). Furthermore, preschoolers and kindergartners with a warm, relaxed relationship with a parent (a secure attachment bond) tend to better understand emotion, perhaps because secure attachment is related to richer parent-child conversations about feelings (Laible & Thompson 1998, 2002). Make-believe play also contributes to emotional understanding as children act out situations that induce strong emotion and resolve those feelings (Youngblade & Dunn 1995). Emotional understanding, in turn, greatly helps children get along with others. It is related to older

preschoolers' and kindergartners' friendly and considerate behavior, willingness to make amends after harming another, and peer acceptance (Dunn, Brown, & Maguire 1995; Fabes et al. 2001).

Gains in all these emotional capacities increase children's ability to experience *empathy*— to feel with others their emotional hurt or unhappiness. Empathy is an important motivator of *sympathetic concern* for another's plight, which increases the likelihood that children will respond with kind, helpful, and comforting behavior (Eisenberg & Fabes 1998). When parents are warm, encourage their children's emotional expressiveness, and show sensitive concern for their feelings (that is, model sympathy), their children are more likely to react in a concerned way to the distress of others (Koestner, Franz, & Weinberger 1990; Strayer & Roberts 2004). Parents who teach the importance of kindness and intervene when their child displays inappropriate emotion (e.g., taking pleasure in another's misfortune) have children who respond to others' distress with high levels of sympathy (Eisenberg 2003).

> Before starting kindergarten, the average child from a middle-class family has been read to for a total of 1,000 hours; a child from a family living in poverty, for only 25 hours.

About 3 percent of kindergartners, mostly boys, are highly aggressive. Children who strike out at others with verbal and physical hostility are limited in their ability to take another's perspective and are less empathic and sympathetic. Although these children may have inherited reactive, impulsive traits that predispose them to behave aggressively, biological risk factors are not sufficient to induce continuing aggression (Pettit 2004; Tremblay 2000). Rather, angry, punitive parenting transforms the children's undercontrolled style into persistent aggression and serious learning problems, which are evident by kindergarten age (Brame, Nagin, & Tremblay 2001; Broidy et al. 2003). Early treatment that includes both parent and child interventions is vital.

Self and social development

In early childhood, children come to understand that each person has a rich inner life of beliefs, opinions, and interpretations of reality different from their own (Wellman, Cross, & Watson 2001). This appreciation strengthens over the late preschool and early school years, as a result of cognitive and language development, conversations with adults and peers about mental states, and make-believe play, which is rich in mental-state talk. Kindergartners' knowledge of mental states subsequently contributes greatly to their developing self-concept and sociability.

Self-concept. When asked to describe themselves, kindergartners focus on observable characteristics: their name, physical appearance, possessions, and everyday behaviors (Harter 1996). They also mention typical emotions and attitudes, such as "I'm happy when we get to run outside" or "I don't like to be with kids I don't know"—statements that suggest a budding grasp of their own unique personality (Eder & Mangelsdorf 1997).

Because of cognitive limitations, kindergartners are unable to compare their accomplishments with those of more than one classmate at a time. In addition, they cannot yet sort out the precise causes of their successes and failures. Instead, they view all good things as going together: A person who tries hard is also a smart person who is going to succeed. As a result, most kindergartners are "learning optimists," who rate their own ability very highly, underestimate the difficulty of tasks, and are willing to exert effort when presented with new challenges (Harter 2003). These attitudes contribute greatly to kindergartners' initiative during a period in which they must master many new skills.

> Most kindergartners are "learning optimists," who rate their own ability very highly, underestimate the difficulty of tasks, and are willing to exert effort when presented with new challenges.

Nevertheless, kindergartners readily internalize adult evaluations. When these messages are repeatedly negative, children show early signs of self-criticism, anxiety about failing, and weakened motivation that can seriously interfere with learning and academic progress (Burhans & Dweck 1995).

Sociability. As children gain in verbal communication and in understanding of others' thoughts and feelings, their skill at interacting with peers improves. During the preschool years, *cooperative play* (in which children orient toward a common goal, such as building a block structure or acting out a make-believe theme together) increases. Nevertheless, *parallel play* (in which a child plays near other children with similar materials but does not interact) and *solitary play* remain common among kindergartners (Howes & Matheson 1992; Rubin, Fein, & Vandenberg 1983).

Parents and teachers may wonder whether a child who often plays alone is developing normally. Most kindergartners who tend to play by themselves enjoy it, and their solitary activities—painting, looking at books, working puzzles, building with blocks—are positive and constructive. Such children are usually well adjusted, and when they do play with peers they show socially skilled behavior (Coplan et al. 2004). A few children, however, do retreat into solitary activities when they would rather be playing with classmates but have been rejected by them. Some are temperamentally shy children whose social fearfulness causes them to withdraw (Rubin, Burgess, & Hastings 2002). Others are immature, impulsive children who find it difficult to regulate their anger and aggression.

Gender segregation. One of the most noticeable features of kindergartners' sociability is their preference for play with peers of their same sex, which strengthens over early childhood; by age 6, children spend 11 times as much time playing with same-sex peers as they do with other-sex peers (Maccoby & Jacklin 1987; Martin & Fabes 2001). Studies (animal and human) indicate that prenatal sex-hormone exposure affects play styles, promoting more-active play among boys and calmer, gentler actions among girls (Hines 2004). Then, as

Laura E. Berk

children interact with peers, they choose play partners whose interests and behaviors are compatible with their own. Social pressures for "gender-appropriate" play and cognitive influences also contribute to gender segregation. Children pick up a wealth of gender stereotypes in early childhood ("Trucks are for boys!" "Only girls can be nurses!"). Only after their capacity for two-dimensional reasoning develops do they gradually come to understand that body differences, not activities and superficial aspects of appearance (hairstyle or clothing), determine a person's sex.

Friendships. Like older children, kindergartners seek compatibility in their friendships, choosing friends who are similar not just in gender but also in age, socioeconomic status, ethnicity, personality (sociability, helpfulness, aggression), and school performance (Hartup 1996). However, when children attend ethnically diverse schools and live in integrated neighborhoods, they often form friendships with peers of other ethnicities—a powerful predictor of tolerant attitudes (Ellison & Powers 1994; Quillian & Campbell 2003).

Young children with gratifying friendships are more likely to become psychologically healthy and competent adolescents and young adults (Bagwell et al. 2001; Bukowski 2001). For most kindergartners, friendships involve sensitivity, caring, emotional expressiveness, sharing, cooperation, and joy—qualities that promote emotional understanding, empathy, sympathy, and positive social behavior (Hartup 1996; Vaughn et al. 2001). Close friendships also foster positive attitudes toward school. When children attend kindergarten with preschool friends, they adapt more quickly to classroom life. And kindergartners who easily make new friends perform better academically, perhaps because these rewarding relationships energize cooperation and initiative in the classroom (Ladd, Birch, & Buhs 1999; Ladd, Buhs, & Seid 2000).

However, friendships that are argumentative and aggressive interfere with children's adjustment. Kindergartners with conflict-ridden peer relationships are more likely to have friendships that do not last, to dislike school, and to achieve poorly. Shy or self-centered children also are likely to have few or no friends (Ladd 1999). It is vital to help these kindergartners form rewarding friendships. Without supportive friendships as a context for acquiring positive social skills, children's maladaptive behaviors tend to persist.

Major influences on the child

Brain development, temperament, interactions with adults (family members, caregivers, teachers), and appropriately stimulating experiences combine to influence kindergartners' many changing capacities. Among these factors, the involvement and guidance of adults and the quality of the learning environments those adults create have a profound impact (Berk 2001, 2005; Hart, Newell, & Olsen 2003).

Parenting

Parenting powerfully shapes children's development, and good parenting is a major protective factor for children who confront stressful life conditions—such as poverty or parental divorce—that predispose them to future problems (Masten 2001). Parental warmth, patience, explanations, and reasonable expectations for their children's maturity are linked to many aspects of kindergartners' competence. This combination of parental acceptance and control makes up the *authoritative* child-rearing style. Decades of research confirm that authoritative parenting tends to foster task-persistence, cooperativeness, high self-esteem, social and moral maturity, and favorable school performance in children of diverse temperaments, ethnic and socioeconomic backgrounds, and family structures (Bradford et al. 2003; Hart, Newell, & Olson 2004).

In contrast, children of parents who are coercive and punitive (have an *authoritarian* style) or who are overly indulgent or inattentive (have a *permissive* style) display a wide array of problems. These include poor impulse control, anger and defiance, retreat in the face of challenging tasks, and poor school achievement (Baumrind 1997; Hart, Newell, & Olson 2004).

Statistical analysis shows that parenting behavior accounts for 25 to 50 percent of the variation found between socioeconomic and ethnic groups in the academic, social, and behavioral indicators that contribute to kindergarten readiness. So early intervention programs that target parenting style can contribute greatly to kindergartners' school success (Brooks-Gunn & Markman 2005).

Home environment

An organized, stimulating home environment and parental affection, involvement, and encouragement of maturity promote children's mental development (Bradley et al. 2001). If these qualities of family life are present, children of all income levels and ethnic backgrounds will tend to have higher language and cognitive scores into their school years (Roberts, Burchinal, & Durham 1999; Smith, Duncan, & Lee 2003). In other words, low-income parents who manage, despite the stresses of their everyday lives, to create these favorable conditions at home contribute greatly to their children's success in school.

> The kindergarten child is still within the age range during which the brain is highly sensitive to educational intervention.

Activities in which parents interact verbally with their children are particularly powerful. The sheer amount that parents talk to preschoolers is a strong predictor of children's intelligence and academic achievement in elementary school (Hart & Risley 1995). When parents ask their children many and varied questions and volunteer their own recollections and evaluations, children produce more coherent and detailed personal stories (Farrant & Reese 2000), which improves their narrative ability and contributes to literacy development. Regular family mealtimes are impressive contributors to children's language and literacy progress in kindergarten and the early grades, perhaps because mealtimes are among the few routine occasions in which children—whether as participants or listeners—enter an adult conversational world (Beals 2001).

But research shows that not all children get such support. Surveys over the past two decades reveal a decline in family mealtimes and conversations, which has been attributed to increasingly hectic schedules (Hofferth & Sandberg 2000). Other research consistently indicates that low-income parents provide their children with less verbal stimulation than middle-income parents do, so that low-income children are exposed to 30 million fewer words by age 4 than are their middle-income peers (Hart & Risley 2003).

While family conversation has decreased, television viewing has increased. The average preschooler or kindergartner watches 1½ to 2 hours a day, with time devoted to TV especially high in low-income families (Scharrer & Comstock 2003). Educational television programs can strengthen children's academic and social skills and have lasting benefits for achievement (Anderson et al. 2001; Fisch, Truglio, & Cole 1999). But many young children regularly watch entertainment programs instead, and most of these shows overflow with aggressive content. Televised violence increases children's verbally and physically aggressive behavior, with lasting negative consequences into adulthood (Anderson et al. 2003). In addition, the more that children watch television, the less time they spend playing, reading, and interacting with parents and peers, and the poorer their school performance (Huston et al. 1999; Wright et al. 2001).

Preschool preparation

Nearly half of all 3- and 4-year-olds attend organized early childhood programs (U.S. Department of Labor 2002). When those experiences are of high quality—that is, consist of a developmentally appropriate curriculum, college-educated teachers, a small group size, and a high adult-child ratio—children of all socioeconomic and ethnic backgrounds benefit in cognitive, language, and social development. These positive effects persist at least into the early school years, with low-income children gaining the most (Burchinal &

Laura E. Berk

Cryer 2003; Burchinal et al. 2000; NICHD Early Child Care Research Network 2002). Preschool enrollment, however, varies across ethnic groups. While about 60 percent of white and black 4-year-olds attend preschool, only 50 percent of Hispanic 4-year-olds do (U.S. Department of Labor 2002).

Unfortunately, many early childhood programs serving American children are substandard. At worst, they are staffed by underpaid adults lacking specialized educational preparation and are overcrowded with children. The more time young children spend in poor-quality settings, the lower they score on measures of cognitive and social skills (Hausfather 1997; NICHD Early Child Care Research Network 2000, 2003). Kindergartners from low-income families are especially likely to have had inadequate preschool experiences (Sachs 2000). By the time children enter kindergarten, the cognitive, language, and literacy skills of low-income children trail their middle-class peers', and the gap often widens over the first few years of schooling (Entwisle, Alexander, & Olson 1997).

Although high-quality early education cannot entirely overcome the damaging effects of early, persistent disadvantage, model demonstration programs show that preschool has significant benefits. It considerably reduces the socioeconomic gap in grade-school achievement, prevents many children from being retained in grade or assigned to special education, and—in the long term—increases high school graduation and college enrollment rates, resulting in higher earnings and other indicators of life success in adulthood (Campbell et al. 2002; Lazar & Darlington 1982; Schweinhart et al. 2004).

The power of the kindergarten environment

Kindergarten children are undergoing profound transformations—in their capacity to think rationally, persist in the face of challenge, use language adeptly, suppress impulse, regulate emotion, respond sympathetically to others' distress, and cooperate with peers. These developing capacities, along with a buoyant belief in their own ability to master new skills, prepare kindergartners for a new "Age of Reason and Responsibility"—one in which they will spend many years acquiring the cognitive and social skills essential for becoming productive members of their society. A history of positive experiences—warm, patient adult support, developmentally appropriate educational activities, and positive interactions with peers—greatly eases adaptation to kindergarten (Birch & Ladd 1997).

The kindergarten setting, in turn, contributes profoundly to children's motivation and competencies. The kindergarten child is still within the age range during which the brain is highly sensitive to educational intervention (Nelson 2000). The vast differences in Sammy's and Jasmine's early experiences make it unlikely that the two children will ever perform equivalently in school—but not impossible. Development contains surprises. A strong bond with an encouraging adult (perhaps a teacher) and community resources (such as excellent schools) are sources of resilience. They fortify at-risk children such as Jasmine with inner strengths that enable them to bounce back from negative experiences (Masten & Reed 2002).

David's kindergarten classroom, with its class size of 20, richly equipped activity centers, multiple opportunities for small-group and independent work, and engaging teaching strategies, is responsive to children's collective and individual learning needs. At the end of the school year, David reports on the children's progress:

Sammy is reading at a second grade level, writing stories that are several sentences in length, and adding and subtracting two-digit numbers in the model recycling center that I, several parents, and the children assembled. Sammy also displays greater concern for others. He listens patiently as his classmates contribute to discussions, even when their comments are not as "right" as his own.

David met with Jasmine's parents regularly and explained the importance of their reading to her. He also held a special parent-child reading night, in which he demonstrated how to read to and talk about book content with kindergartners (see Whitehurst & Lonigan 1998). David reflects on her progress:

> As summer recess approaches, Jasmine has mastered many letter-sound correspondences, has acquired a handful of sight vocabulary words, and often chooses books as a way to enjoy Free Time in the classroom. She also draws more elaborate pictures, which she enthusiastically describes in detail to me, and participates confidently in group projects. She hasn't attained the standards for her grade, but she's made great strides. Best of all, she likes school, and that sets her up for continued growth.

Kindergarten plays a powerful role in children's successful introduction to formal schooling. Children need challenging learning experiences that help them move forward. But when classroom experiences are not attuned to children's developmental needs and individual characteristics, they undermine rather than foster children's learning. For example, when kindergartners spend much time in drill-oriented instruction, they display stress behaviors, express less confidence in their abilities, and are less advanced in motor, academic, language, and social skills at the end of the school year. These outcomes, moreover, are strongest for low-income children. Follow-ups reveal lasting effects through elementary school in poorer study habits and achievement (Burts et al. 1992; Hart, Newell, & Olsen 2003; Hart et al. 1998; Stipek et al. 1995).

To ensure optimum learning, the kindergarten year should be part of a coordinated approach to early childhood education—extending from preschool through the early school grades—that is grounded in the knowledge of developmental characteristics of young children.

References

Anderson, C.A., L. Berkowitz, E. Donnerstein, R. Huesmann, J.D. Johnson, D. Linz, N.M. Malamuth, & E. Wartella. 2003. The influence of media violence on youth. *Psychological Science in the Public Interest* 4 (3): 81–106.

Anderson, D.M., A.C. Huston, K.L. Schmitt, D.L. Linebarger, & J.C. Wright. 2001. *Early childhood television viewing and adolescent behavior.* Monographs of the Society for Research in Child Development, vol. 66, no. 1, serial no. 264. Chicago: University of Chicago Press.

Anglin, J.M. 1993. *Vocabulary development: A morphological analysis.* Monographs of the Society for Research in Child Development, vol. 58, no. 10, serial no. 238. Chicago: University of Chicago Press.

Bagwell, C.L., M.E. Schmidt, A.F. Newcomb, & W.M. Bukowski. 2001. Friendship and peer rejection as predictors of adult adjustment. In *The role of friendship in psychological adjustment,* eds. D.W. Nangle & C.A. Erdley, 25–49. San Francisco: Jossey-Bass.

Baumrind, D, 1997. Necessary distinctions. *Psychological Inquiry* 8: 176–82.

Beals, D.E. 2001. Eating and reading: Links between family conversations with preschoolers and later language and literacy. In *Beginning literacy with language: Young children's learning at home and school,* eds. D.K. Dickinson & P.O. Tabors, 75–92. Baltimore: Brookes.

Berk, L.E. 2001. *Awakening children's minds: How parents and teachers can make a difference.* New York: Oxford University Press.

Berk, L.E. 2005. Why parenting matters. In *Childhood lost: How American culture is failing our kids,* ed. S. Olfman, 19–53. New York: Guilford.

Birch, S.H., & G.W. Ladd. 1997. The teacher-child relationship and children's early school adjustment. *Journal of School Psychology* 35: 61–79.

Bloom, L. 1998. Language acquisition in its developmental context. In *Handbook of child psychology, Vol. 2: Cognition, perception, and language,* 5th ed., eds. D. Kuhn & R.S. Siegler, 309–70. New York: Wiley.

Bornstein, M.H., & M.E. Arteberry. 1999. Perceptual development. In *Developmental psychology: An advanced textbook,* eds. M.H. Bornstein & M.E. Lamb, 231–74. Mahwah, NJ: Erlbaum.

Bradford, K., B.K. Barber, J.A. Olsen, S.L. Maughan, L.D. Erickson, D. Ward, & H.E. Stolz. 2003. A multi-national study of interparental conflict, parenting, and adolescent functioning: South Africa, Bangladesh, China, India, Bosnia, Germany, Palestine, Colombia, and the United States. *Marriage and Family Review* 35: 107–37.

Bradley, R.H., R.F. Corwyn, H.P. McAdoo, & C. Garica Coll. 2001. The home environments of children in the United States. Part I: Variations by age, ethnicity, and poverty status. *Child Development* 72: 1844–67.

Brame, B., D.S. Nagin, & R.E. Tremblay. 2001. Developmental trajectories of physical aggression from school entry to late adolescence. *Journal of Child Psychology and Psychiatry* 42: 503–12.

Broidy, L.M., D.S. Nagin, R.E. Tremblay, J.E. Bates, B. Brame, K.A. Dodge, D. Fergusson, J.L. Horwood, R. Loeber, R. Laird, D.R. Lynam, T.E. Moffitt, G.S. Pettit, & F. Vitaro. 2003. Developmental trajectories of childhood disruptive behaviors and adolescent delinquency: A six-site, cross-national study. *Developmental Psychology* 39: 222–45.

Brooks-Gunn, J. 2003. Do you believe in magic? What can we expect from early childhood intervention programs? *SRCD Social Policy Report* 17 (1).

Brooks-Gunn, J., & L.B. Markman. 2005. The contribution of parenting to ethnic and racial gaps in school readiness. *Future of Children* 15: 139–68.

Laura E. Berk

Bruer, J.T. 1999. *The myth of the first three years*. New York: Free Press.

Bukowski, W.M. 2001. Friendship and the worlds of childhood. In *The role of friendship in psychological adjustment*, eds. D.W. Nangle & C.A. Erdley, 93–105. San Francisco: Jossey-Bass.

Burchinal, M.R., & D. Cryer. 2003. Diversity, child care quality, and developmental outcomes. *Early Childhood Research Quarterly* 18: 401–26.

Burchinal, M.R., E. Peisner-Feinberg, D.M. Bryant, & R. Clifford. 2000. Children's social and cognitive development and child-care quality: Testing for differential associations related to poverty, gender, or ethnicity. *Applied Developmental Psychology* 4: 149–65.

Burhans, K.K., & C.S. Dweck. 1995. Helplessness in early childhood: The role of contingent worth. *Child Development* 66: 1719–38.

Burts, D.C., C.H. Hart, R. Charlesworth, P.O. Fleege, J. Mosley, & R.H. Thomasson. 1992. Observed activities and stress behaviors of children in developmentally appropriate and inappropriate kindergarten classrooms. *Early Childhood Research Quarterly* 7: 297–318.

Campbell, F.A., C.T. Ramey, E.P. Pungello, J. Sparling, & S. Miller-Johnson. 2002. Early childhood education: Young adult outcomes from the Abecedarian Project. *Applied Developmental Science* 6: 42–57.

Case, R. 1992. *The mind's staircase*. Hillsdale, NJ: Erlbaum.

Case, R. 1998. The development of central conceptual structures. In *Handbook of child psychology, Vol. 2: Cognition, perception, and language*, 5th ed., eds. D. Kuhn & R.S. Siegler, 745–800. New York: Wiley.

Case, R., & Y. Okamoto, eds. 1996. *The role of central conceptual structures in the development of children's thought*. Monographs of the Society for Research in Child Development, vol. 61, nos. 1–2, serial no. 246. Chicago: University of Chicago Press.

Casellanos, F.X., W.S. Sharp, R.F. Gottesman, D.K. Greenstein, J.N. Giedd, & J.L. Rapoport. 2003. Anatomic brain abnormalities in monozygotic twins discordant for attention-deficit hyperactivity disorder. *American Journal of Psychiatry* 160: 1693–95.

Coplan, R.J., K. Prakash, K. O'Neil, & M. Armer. 2004. Do you "want" to play? Distinguishing between conflicted shyness and social disinterest in early childhood. *Developmental Psychology* 40: 244–58.

Cowan, N., L.D. Nugent, E.M. Elliott, I. Ponomarev, & J.S. Saults. 1999. The role of attention in the development of short-term memory: Age differences in the verbal span of apprehension. *Child Development* 70: 1082–97.

Cratty, B.J. 1986. *Perceptual and motor development in infants and children*, 3d ed. Englewood Cliffs, NJ: Prentice Hall.

Denham, S.A., & A.T. Kochanoff. 2002. Parental contributions to preschoolers' understanding of emotion. *Marriage and Family Review* 34: 311–43.

Deutsch, W., & T. Pechman. 1982. Social interaction and the development of definite descriptions. *Cognition* 11: 159–84.

Dunn, J., J.R. Brown, & M. Maguire. 1995. The development of children's moral sensibility: Individual differences and emotion understanding. *Developmental Psychology* 31: 649–59.

Eder, R.A., & S.C. Mangelsdorf. 1997. The emotional basis of early personality development: Implications for the emergent self-concept. In *Handbook of personality psychology*, eds. R. Hogan, J. Johnson, & S. Briggs, 209–40. San Diego, CA: Academic Press.

Education Commission of the States. 2004. *Access to kindergarten: Age issues in state statutes*. Denver, CO: Author. Online: www.ecs.org.

Eisenberg, N. 2003. Prosocial behavior, empathy, and sympathy. In *Well-being: Positive development across the life course*, eds. M.H. Bornstein & L. Davidson, 253–65. Mahwah, NJ: Erlbaum.

Eisenberg, N., & R.A. Fabes. 1998. Prosocial development. In *Handbook of child psychology, Vol. 3: Social, emotional, and personality development*, 5th ed., ed. N. Eisenberg, 701–78. New York: Wiley.

Eisenberg, N., & T.L. Spinrad. 2004. Emotion-related regulation: Sharpening the definition. *Child Development* 75: 334–39.

Ellison, C.G., & D.A. Powers. 1994. The contact hypothesis and racial attitudes among black Americans. *Social Science Quarterly* 75: 385–400.

Ely, R. 2005. Language and literacy in the school years. In *The development of language*, 6th ed., ed. J.B. Gleason, 395–443. Boston: Allyn & Bacon.

Entwisle, D.R., K.L. Alexander, & L.S. Olson. 1997. *Children, schools, and inequality*. Boulder, CO: Westview.

Fabes, R.A., N. Eisenberg, L.D. Hanish, & T.L. Spinrad. 2001. Preschoolers' spontaneous emotion vocabulary: Relations to likability. *Early Education and Development* 12: 1127.

Farrant, K., & E. Reese. 2000. Maternal style and children's participation in reminiscing: Stepping stones in children's autobiographical memory development. *Journal of Cognition and Development* 1: 193–255.

Fisch, S.M., R.T. Truglio, & C. Cole. 1999. The impact of Sesame Street on preschool children: A review and synthesis of 30 years' research. *Media Psychology* 1: 165–90.

Foy, J.G., & V. Mann. 2003. Home literacy environment and phonological awareness in preschool children: Differential effects for rhyme and phoneme awareness. *Applied Psycholinguistics* 24: 59–88.

Greenough, W.T., & J.E. Black. 1992. Induction of brain structure by experience: Substrates for cognitive development. In *Minnesota Symposia on Child Psychology*, Vol. 24, eds. M.R. Gunnar & C.A. Nelson, 155–200. Hillsdale, NJ: Erlbaum.

Greer, T., & J.J. Lockman. 1998. Using writing instruments: Invariances in young children and adults. *Child Development* 69: 888–902.

Hart, B., & T.R. Risley. 1995. *Meaningful differences in the everyday experience of young American children*. Baltimore: Brookes.

Hart, B., & T.R. Risley. 2003, Spring. The early catastrophe: The 30 million word gap. *American Educator* 27 (1): 4, 6–9.

Hart, C.H., D.C. Burts, M.A. Durland, R. Charlesworth, M. DeWorlf, & P.O. Fleege. 1998. Stress behaviors and activity type participation of preschoolers in more and less developmentally appropriate classrooms: SES and sex differences. *Journal of Research in Childhood Education* 13: 176–96.

Hart, C.H., L.D. Newell, & S.F. Olsen. 2003. Parenting skills and social/communicative competence in childhood. In *Handbook of communication and social interaction skills*, eds. J.O. Greene & B.R. Burleson, 753–97. Mahwah, NJ: Erlbaum.

Harter, S. 1996. Developmental changes in self-understanding across the 5 to 7 shift. In *The five to seven year shift*, eds. A.J. Sameroff & M.M. Haith, 207–36. Chicago: University of Chicago Press.

Harter, S. 2003. The development of self-representations during childhood and adolescence. In *Handbook of self and identity*, eds. M.R. Leary & J.P. Tangney, 610–42. New York: Guilford.

Hartup, W.W. 1996. The company they keep: Friendships and their developmental significance. *Child Development* 67: 1–13.

Hausfather, A., A. Toharia, C. LaRoche, & F. Engelsmann. 1997. Effects of age of entry, day-care quality, and family characteristics on preschool behavior. *Journal of Child Psychology and Psychiatry* 38: 441–48.

Hines, M. 2004. *Brain gender*. New York: Oxford University Press.

Hirsh-Pasek, K., & R.M. Golinkoff. 2003. *Einstein never used flash cards*. Emmaus, PA: Rodale.

Hofferth, S., & J. Sandberg. 2000. *Changes in American children's time, 1981–1997*. Online: http://ceel.psc.isr.umich.edu/pubs/papers/ceel013-00.pdf.

Howes, C., & C.C. Matheson. 1992. Sequences in the development of competent play with peers: Social and social pretend play. *Developmental Psychology* 28: 961–74.

Huston, A.C., J.C. Wright, J. Marquis, & S.B. Green. 1999. How young children spend their time: Television and other activities. *Developmental Psychology* 35: 912–25.

Huttenlocher, P.R. 2002. *Neural plasticity: The effects of environment on the development of the cerebral cortex.* Cambridge, MA: Harvard University Press.

Jacob, R.B., K.D. O'Leary, & C. Rosenblad. 1978. Formal and informal classroom settings: Effects on hyperactivity. *Journal of Abnormal Child Psychology* 6: 47–59.

Karmiloff-Smith, A., J. Grant, K. Sims, M. Jones, & P. Cuckle. 1996. Rethinking metalinguistic awareness: Representing and accessing knowledge about what counts as a word. *Cognition* 58: 197–219.

Kochanska, G., & A. Knaack. 2003. Effortful control as a personality characteristic of young children: Antecedents, correlates, and consequences. *Journal of Personality* 71: 1087–112.

Koestner, R., C. Franz, & J. Weinberger. 1990. The family origins of empathic concern: A 26-year longitudinal study. *Journal of Personality and Social Psychology* 58: 709–16.

Ladd, G.W. 1999. Peer relationships and social competence during early and middle childhood. *Annual Review of Psychology* 50: 333–59.

Ladd, G.W., E.S. Buhs, & M. Seid. 2000. Children's initial sentiments about kindergarten: Is school liking an antecedent of early classroom participation and achievement? *Merrill-Palmer Quarterly* 46: 255–79.

Ladd, G.W., S.H. Birch, & E.S. Buhs. 1999. Children's social and scholastic lives in kindergarten: Related spheres of influence? *Child Development* 70: 1373–1400.

Laible, D.J., & R.A. Thompson. 1998. Attachment and emotional understanding in preschool children. *Developmental Psychology* 34: 1038–45.

Laible, D.J., & R.A. Thompson. 2002. Mother-child conflict in the toddler years: Lessons in emotion, morality, and relationships. *Child Development* 73: 1187–1203.

Lazar, I., & R. Darlington. 1982. *Lasting effects of early education: A report from the Consortium for Longitudinal Studies.* Monographs of the Society for Research in Child Development, vol. 47, nos. 2–3, serial no. 195. Chicago: University of Chicago Press.

Lee, V.E., & D.T. Burkam. 2002. *Inequality at the starting gate: Social background differences in achievement as children begin school.* Washington, DC: Economic Policy Institute.

Maccoby, E.E., & C.N. Jacklin. 1987. Gender segregation in childhood. In *Advances in child development and behavior,* Vol. 20, ed. E.H. Reese, 239–87. New York: Academic Press.

Martin, C.L., & C.A. Fabes. 2001. The stability and consequences of young children's same-sex peer interactions. *Developmental Psychology* 37: 431–46.

Masten, A.S. 2001. Ordinary magic: Resilience processes in development. *American Psychologist* 56: 227–38.

Masten, A.S., & M.J. Reed. 2002. Resilience in development. In *Handbook of positive psychology,* eds. C.R. Snyder & S.J. Lopez, 74–88. New York: Oxford University Press.

McCabe, A. 1997. Developmental and cross-cultural aspects of children's narration. In *Narrative development: Six approaches,* ed. M. Bamberg, 137–74. Mahwah, NJ: Erlbaum.

McCall, R.B., M.I. Appelbaum, & P.S. Hogarty. 1973. *Developmental changes in mental performance.* Monographs of the Society for Research in Child Development, vol. 38, no. 3, serial no. 150. Chicago: University of Chicago Press.

Nelson, C.A. 2000. Neural plasticity and human development: The role of early experience in sculpting memory systems. *Developmental Science* 3: 115–30.

Nelson, C.A. 2002. Neural development and lifelong plasticity. In *Handbook of applied developmental science,* Vol. 1, eds. R.M. Lerner, F. Jacobs, & D. Wertlieb, 31–60. Thousand Oaks, CA: Sage.

Neuman, S.B. 2003. From rhetoric to reality: The case for high-quality compensatory prekindergarten programs. *Phi Delta Kappan* 85 (4): 286–91.

NICHD (National Institute of Child Health and Human Development) Early Child Care Research Network. 2000. The relation of child care to cognitive and language development. *Child Development* 71: 960–80.

NICHD Early Child Care Research Network. 2002. Child-care structure > process > outcome: Direct and indirect effects of child-care quality on young children's development. *Psychological Science* 13: 199–206.

NICHD Early Child Care Research Network. 2003. Does quality of child care affect child outcomes at age 4½? *Developmental Psychology* 39: 451–69.

Pettit, G.S. 2004. Violent children in developmental perspective. *Current Directions in Psychological Science* 13: 194–97.

Pons, F., J. Lawson, P.L. Harris, & M. de Rosnay. 2003. Individual differences in children's emotion understanding: Effects of age and language. *Scandinavian Journal of Psychology: Applied* 7: 27–50.

Quillian, L., & M.E. Campbell. 2003. Beyond black and white: The present and future of multiracial friendship segregation. *American Sociological Review* 68: 540–66.

Roberton, M.A. 1984. Changing motor patterns during childhood. In *Motor development during childhood and adolescence,* ed. J.R. Thomas, 48–90. Minneapolis: Burgess.

Roberts, J.E., M.R. Burchinal, & M. Durham. 1999. Parents' report of vocabulary and grammatical development of American preschoolers: Child and environment associations. *Child Development* 70: 92–106.

Rogoff, B. 1996. Developmental transitions in children's participation in sociocultural activities. In *The five to seven year shift: The age of reason and responsibility,* eds. A.J. Sameroff & M.M. Haith, 273–94. Chicago: University of Chicago Press.

Rubin, K.H., G.G. Fein, & B. Vandenberg. 1983. Play. In *Handbook of child psychology, Vol. 4: Socialization, personality, and social development,* 4th ed., ed. E.M. Hetherington, 693–744. New York: Wiley.

Rubin, K.H., K.B. Burgess, & P.D. Hastings. 2002. Stability and social-behavioral consequences of toddlers' inhibited temperament and parenting behaviors. *Child Development* 73: 483–95.

Sachs, J. 2000. Inequities in early care and education: What is America buying? *Journal of Education for Students Placed at Risk* 5: 383–95.

Scharrer, E., & G. Comstock. 2003. Entertainment televisual media: Content patterns and themes. In *The faces of televisual media: Teaching, violence, selling to children,* eds. E.L. Palmer & B.M. Young, 161–93. Mahwah, NJ: Erlbaum.

Schneider, W. 2002. Memory development in childhood. In *Blackwell handbook of childhood cognitive development,* ed. U. Goswami, 236–56. Malden, MA: Blackwell.

Schweinhart, L.J., J. Montie, Z. Xiang, W.S. Barnett, & C.R. Belfield. 2004. *Lifetime effects: The High/Scope Perry Preschool Study through age 40.* Boston: Strategies for Children. Online: www.highscope.org/Research/PerryProject/perrymain.htm.

Shonkoff, J.P., & D.A. Phillips, eds. 2000. *Neurons to neighborhoods: The science of early childhood development.* Washington, DC: National Academies Press.

Smith, J., G.J. Duncan, & K. Lee. 2003. The black-white test score gap in young children: Contributions of test and family characteristics. *Applied Developmental Science* 7: 239–52.

Sternberg, R.J. 2002. Intelligence is not just inside the head: The theory of successful intelligence. In *Improving academic achievement,* ed. J. Aronson, 227–44. San Diego: Academic Press.

Sternberg, R.J., & E.L. Grikorenko. 2004. Why we need to explore development in its cultural context. *Merrill-Palmer Quarterly* 50: 369–86.

Laura E. Berk

Stipek, D., R. Feiler, D. Daniels, & S. Milburn. 1995. Effects of different instructional approaches on young children's achievement motivation. *Child Development* 66: 209–33.

Strayer, J., & W. Roberts. 2004. Children's anger, emotional expressiveness, and parenting practices. *Social Development* 13: 229–54.

Tager-Flusberg, H. 2005. Putting words together: Morphology and syntax in the preschool years. In *The development of language,* 5th ed., ed. J.B. Gleason, 148–90. Boston: Allyn & Bacon.

Thatcher, R.W., G.R. Lyon, J. Rumsey, & J. Krasnegor. 1996. *Developmental neuroimaging.* San Diego: Academic Press.

Thelen, E., & L.B. Smith. 1998. Dynamic systems theories. In *Handbook of child psychology, Vol. 1: Theoretical models of human development,* 5th ed., ed. R.M. Lerner, 563–634. New York: Wiley.

Tremblay, R.E. 2000. The development of aggressive behaviour during childhood: What have we learned in the past century? *International Journal of Behavioural Development* 24: 129–41.

U.S. Department of Labor, Bureau of Labor Statistics. 2002. Preschool enrollment of 4-year-olds by race and ethnicity, 1968-2000. Online: www.bls.gov.

Vaughn, B.E., T.N. Colvin, M.R. Azria, L. Caya, & L. Krzysik. 2001. Dyadic analyses of friendship in a sample of preschool-age children attending Head Start: Correspondence between measures and implications for social competence. *Child Development* 72: 862–78.

Wellman, H.M., D. Cross, & J. Watson. 2001. Meta-analysis of theory-of-mind development: The truth about false belief. *Child Development* 72: 655–84.

West, J., K. Denton, & E. Germino-Hausken. 2000. *America's kindergartners* (NCES 2000-070). Washington, DC: National Center for Education Statistics, U.S. Department of Education.

White, S.H. 1996. The child's entry into the "Age of Reason." In *The five to seven year shift: The age of reason and responsibility,* eds. A.J. Sameroff & M.M. Haith, 17–30. Chicago: University of Chicago Press.

Whitehurst, G.J., & C.I. Lonigan. 1998. Child development and emergent literacy. *Child Development* 69: 848–82.

Wright, J.C., A.C. Huston, K.C. Murphy, M. St. Peters, M. Pinon, R. Scantlin, & J. Kotler. 2001. The relations of early television viewing to school readiness and vocabulary of children from low-income families: The Early Window Project. *Child Development* 72: 1347–66.

Youngblade, L.M., & J. Dunn. 1995. Individual differences in young children's pretend play with mother and sibling: Links to relationships and understanding of other people's feelings and beliefs. *Child Development* 66: 1472–92.

Zelazo, P.D., D. Frye, & T. Rapus. 1996. An age-related dissociation between knowing rules and using them. *Cognitive Development* 11: 37–63.

Considering Kindergarten Families

3

Douglas R. Powell & Hope K. Gerde

Beginning kindergarten is a major event for families as well as children. Many parents worry about whether they have done an adequate job of preparing their child to begin school and to manage relationships with a new set of peers. They wonder if the teacher will do well by their child, approve of their parenting, and respect their family's culture and traditions. Consider this set of nagging questions:

> Can the teacher really take care of my child? Will the teacher like her? Will [my child] humiliate me or enhance me in the eyes of the teacher? Will he reveal things about our family that are private? What will happen if my child gets hurt in school? Can I really trust this caregiver with her? (Balaban 2006, 8)

At the same time, teachers have their own set of questions about families:

> Will parents trust me to do a good job with their children? What types of learning experiences do children have with their families? How much time do parents actually spend with their children? What else is going on in parents' lives and does this interfere with parenting? How can I get parents to support at home what their children are learning at school?

Douglas R. Powell is a Distinguished Professor and Hope K. Gerde is a doctoral candidate, both in the child development and family studies department at Purdue University.

Kindergarten teachers have a unique opportunity to help families launch their children's school years. They can help build a solid foundation that will provide long-term benefits for children, families, and schools. For many parents, the kindergarten teacher is the first person at the school to have ongoing, personal contact with their family. The quality of this relationship helps set the stage for parents' connections with school.

This chapter offers suggestions on how teachers and school administrators can foster supportive relations with families during the kindergarten year. It begins with a description of the families of today's kindergarten children, including characteristics and consequences of family learning environments. For teachers, a general familiarity with families is a good starting point for developing productive relations with children and parents. The chapter also describes professional guidelines and promising practices to promote supportive school-family connections, with an emphasis on the roles of teachers and schools.

Family characteristics and their consequences

Today's kindergarten children come from increasingly diverse family backgrounds, with mothers who are likely to be employed outside the home, and parents who are frequently also doing something else when they spend time with their children. The number of books available to children at home, how often children are read and sung to, how much television they watch, and whether they have significant developmental delays at kindergarten entry are linked to powerful family factors. These factors include parent education and family income levels, racial and ethnic background, and living in a single- versus two-parent household.

Family characteristics

Useful information on the demographic characteristics of families with children in kindergarten is available from the Early Childhood Longitudinal Study–Kindergarten Cohort (ECLS-K). This nationally representative sample of 22,000 kindergarten children in 1,000 public and private schools showed that in 1998:

• 18 percent of kindergarten children were living in poverty

• 23 percent lived in single-parent households

• 9 percent were English-language learners

• 58 percent of the children were European American, 19 percent were of Hispanic origin, 15 percent were African American, 3 percent were Asian American, and 5 percent represented other racial/ethnic identities (West, Denton, & Germino-Hausken 2000)

The study results remind us that poverty is not evenly distributed across families in the United States. Nearly half of kindergarten children living in poverty resided in single-parent households (48 percent) and a substantial percentage of English-language learners (39 percent) lived in low-income households in 1998 (Lee & Burkam 2002).

The increase in working mothers represents one of the most significant developments in this country in recent decades. Information on mothers of kindergarten children only is not available, but in the year 2000, nearly 62 percent of mothers with children under the age of 6 were in the labor force (U.S. Census Bureau 2000), compared with about 45 percent in 1980 (U.S. Census Bureau 1983).

It is common for parents to experience major time binds as they try to work as much as possible to financially support their families and also spend as much time as possible with their children (Jacobs & Gerson 2004). Although there are concerns that working parents do not spend enough time with their children, studies point to a growth in the amount of time parents engage in child-rearing activities. From 1965 to 1998, the amount of time mothers spent on child-rearing increased from 87 to 104 minutes per day; fathers' time increased from 21 to 57 minutes per day. However, a large percentage of time that parents spend with their children includes doing something else as well ("multitasking"). In 1998, mothers spent about 70 percent of their time and fathers spent 63 percent of their time with children while they were engaged in other activities. These figures had increased from 30–40 percent in 1975 (Sayer 2001, as cited in Jacobs & Gerson 2004).

Learning experiences

What types of learning experiences do families provide kindergarten children? The ECLS-K found that, overall, children in kindergarten in the United States had an average of 73 children's books available to them at home. They were read to by an adult in their household more than three times per week (West, Denton, & Germino-Hausken 2000). They watched an average of 14 hours of television each week at home (Lee & Burkam 2002). Parents reported engaging in learning activities such as playing games, building things, and doing art projects three to six times per week (West, Denton, & Germino-Hausken 2000).

The frequency and quality of learning experiences at home vary across different types of families. For example, children whose mothers had less than a high school diploma were likely to have fewer than 26 children's books at home, while children whose mothers had completed college were likely to have between 51 and 100 books. A mother's education level was also related to how often she read with her children. For instance, 36 percent of mothers who had graduated from high school reported reading to their kindergarten child every day, while nearly twice as many mothers (59 percent) who had graduated from college reported reading to their children every day (West, Denton, & Germino-Hausken 2000).

Other factors make a difference, too: Children in single-mother households, families who use welfare services, and African American families were all less likely to be read to every day than were children in two-parent households, families not receiving welfare support, and European American, Hispanic, and Asian American families. A different pattern exists for the family practice of singing songs with children. Children in single-mother households, families with a history of using welfare services, and African American families were more likely to be sung to every day than were children in two-parent households, families who had never used welfare services, and European American, Hispanic, and Asian American families (Nord et al. 1999).

Family characteristics also are related to kindergarten entry decisions. A national study found that parents with higher levels of education were more likely to delay sending their children to kindergarten than parents with lower levels of education were. Also, European American parents were more likely than other parents to delay kindergarten entry, although parents who were not European American were significantly more likely to report concerns about their children's readiness for kindergarten. In general, parents placed more emphasis on their children's academic abilities than on social or emotional skills in decisions about delaying kindergarten entry (Diamond, Reagan, & Bandyk 2000).

Children's outcomes

There are major differences in children's abilities at kindergarten entry that carry on into later grades (Rathburn, West, & Germino-Hausken

2004; Stipek & Ryan 1997). Third-graders who lag behind their peers in literacy skills tend to be largely the same children who had arrived at kindergarten with gaps in their literacy skills (Rathburn, West, & Germino-Hausken 2004). Four family factors have consistently been identified as strong predictors of children's achievement at kindergarten entry and beyond: (1) living at or below the poverty level, (2) a single-parent household, (3) a low level of parent education, and (4) a parent(s) who speaks a language other than English in the home. For example, at school entry, children from lower-income families score lower than do children from higher-income families in verbal fluency and word knowledge (Stipek & Ryan 1997) and in reading and math skills (Lee & Burkam 2002; West, Denton, & Reaney 2001).

Fifty-six (56) percent (2.2 million) of the 3.9 million kindergarten children in 1998–1999 had a delay in physical health, cognitive achievement, or social and emotional development. Fifteen (15) percent of children had delays in two of these three areas, and 5 percent had delays in all three areas. Of the children who lagged behind in all three areas at the end of kindergarten, 55 percent resided in families living at or below the poverty level, 33 percent were living with a single parent, and 63 percent of the parents had a high school diploma or less (Wertheimer et al. 2003).

Today, obesity is a significant health problem with medical and psychological consequences for children (Hammer et al. 1991). Both kindergarten boys and girls whose mothers have less than a bachelor's degree are more likely to be overweight than children whose mothers have a four-year degree or higher. Hispanic boys are more likely than their European American and African American counterparts to be overweight. Children whose families have never used public assistance are more likely to be in excellent general health than children whose families have used public assistance (West, Denton, & Germino-Hausken 2000).

Family economic background does not seem to influence children's motivation at the beginning of the school year. Most children enter school enthusiastic, self-confident, and willing to take on

> Compared with parents of preschoolers, parents of kindergartners have less frequent, more formal contact with their children's teachers and school administrators.

Douglas R. Powell and Hope K. Gerde

learning challenges. However, in one study, children from low-income families who had relatively poor cognitive skills developed a more negative view of their competencies and more negative attitudes toward school than did children from higher-income families. Motivation may become a problem in later grades for children from low-income backgrounds who exhibit cognitive delays (Stipek & Ryan 1997).

Family-school relationships

Children gain from mutually supportive connections between home and school. Goals for children are best achieved when teachers and parents make complementary rather than disconnected or competing contributions to children's learning and development. This concept is central to developmentally appropriate practice, which calls for teachers to "ensure that learning experiences are meaningful, relevant, and respectful for the participating children and their families" (Bredekamp & Copple 1997, 9). Partnerships between teachers and parents (or primary caregivers) are vital to schools and families coordinating and building on each other's efforts (Powell 2001). Current thinking about family-school relationships emphasizes the joint or shared responsibilities of parents and teachers, rather than schools and families having separate influences on the child (Epstein & Sanders 2002).

Guidelines and realities

Professional practice guidelines place reciprocal parent-teacher relationships at the heart of family-school connections. The National Association for the Education of Young Children (NAEYC) statement on developmentally appropriate practice identifies "establishing reciprocal relationships with families" as one of five interrelated dimensions of good early childhood program practice. This includes regular and frequent two-way communication, parent participation in child and program decisions such as child assessment and program planning, and assistance to families in connecting with community resources (Bredekamp & Copple 1997). Family-centered

approaches to early childhood education are also emphasized in the NAEYC statement on linguistic and cultural diversity, which calls for teachers to become familiar with the child's community (NAEYC 1996a), for example; and in the NAEYC code of ethical conduct, which emphasizes principles of mutual trust in parent-teacher relations as well as teacher respect for family child-rearing values and decision-making rights (NAEYC 1996b). Practice recommendations of the Division for Early Childhood of the Council for Exceptional Children also emphasize this theme of collaboration (Sandall, McLean, & Smith 2000).

In 1997 the National Parent-Teacher Association established six national standards for parent/family involvement programs: (1) communication between home and school is regular, two-way, and meaningful; (2) parenting skills are promoted and supported; (3) parents play an integral role in assisting student learning; (4) parents are welcome in the school, and their support and assistance are sought; (5) parents are full partners in the decisions that affect children and families; and (6) community resources are used to strengthen schools, families, and student learning (National PTA 1997).

Existing practices fall short of these standards. National survey information indicates that about 35 percent of children in kindergarten have parents who exhibit a high level of parent involvement in school activities (such as attending school meetings or events); 32 percent have moderately involved parents; and 33 percent have parents who demonstrate a low level of involvement (Zill 1999). Compared with parents of preschoolers, parents of kindergartners have less frequent, more formal contact with their children's teachers and school administrators (there is a greater use of notes, for example) and a more frequent exchange of negative news with teachers (Rimm Kauffman & Pianta 1999).

In general, teachers in schools enrolling a large percentage of children from low-income or minority backgrounds have less personal contact with parents. In one study, kindergarten teachers in schools serving urban and higher percentages of minority and/or poor students reported they had less personal contact with families and used generic methods of contact with parents (such as flyers, brochures, open houses) more often than did teachers in non-urban schools serving lower percentages of minority and/or poor children (Pianta et al. 1999). Also, a survey of a nationally representative sample of 900 public elementary schools enrolling kindergarten through eighth grade students found that 28 percent of schools with a high poverty concentration reported that "most or all" parents attended the school open house, compared with 72 percent of schools with a low concentration of poverty, and 48 percent of schools with a moderate poverty concentration. There was a similar pattern for schools regarding the percentage of minority students (Carey, Lewis, & Farris 1998).

The benefits of parent-teacher partnerships are clear, however. There is a positive association between success in kindergarten and parent involvement in their children's education. For example, a study of some 300 ethnic minority kindergarten children (95 percent African American) and their primary caregivers from a large urban school district in the Northeast found links between parent participation in school and children's outcomes. A pattern among parents of low levels of involvement in school-based activities and of high levels of barriers to involvement in their children's education (such as time constraints and competing responsibilities) was associated with children's problem behaviors at school and hyperactive behavior at home. Also, children of parents with a high level of barriers to involvement in their children's education received lower ratings from teachers on overall academic performance and reading achievement. In contrast, kindergarten children of parents who provided rich learning environments at home demonstrated positive engagement with their peers, adults, and learning (McWayne et al. 2004).

The teacher's roles

Teachers foster positive family-school relationships by focusing on learning and sharing information and on creating ways to respectfully include family knowledge and contributions in the classroom.

Learning and sharing

Teachers often share information with parents through classroom-based newsletters, parent-teacher conferences, notes and phone calls, and handouts on how to extend curriculum activities at home. These useful communication methods contribute to two-way exchanges of information between parents and teachers. However, developing reciprocal relationships with families requires teachers to move beyond a view of parent involvement as a series of isolated events or activities. In order to form partnerships, teachers need to learn information about families through personal exchanges. They can then appropriately act on pertinent information through classroom activities and opportunities for parents to make meaningful contributions to their children's education.

In order to understand and appropriately respond to children's behavior in the classroom, teachers must learn how cultural background affects how families approach their children's education. Educational beliefs, values, and practices vary significantly across cultural groups. For example, most traditional Hispanic families view education as the school's responsibility, with parents feeling they do not have the right or authority to question a teacher's practices. In contrast, mothers in traditional Asian cultures are commonly held responsible for their children's education, with children's school performance reflecting directly on the family (Diffily 2004; Lynch & Hanson 2004). This type of information is helpful to teachers in anticipating which parents are likely to need special appeals and supports for school participation activities such as volunteering in the classroom.

But teachers also need to learn about *particular* families, because there are profound individual differences across families in any cultural group (Lynch & Hanson 2004). Teachers should not act on assumptions about families based on generalizations or stereotypes. There are major differences between African American families living in suburban versus inner-city neighborhoods, for

Douglas R. Powell and Hope K. Gerde

example. it is also difficult to identify characteristics typical of Native American family life (Diffily 2004).

Many teachers find that personal contact with parents or extended family members in an informal setting is a good way to connect with families. A Hispanic teacher working with Hispanic families notes, for example, that she had to develop relationships with families before asking them to do anything related to school. She capitalized on the pattern of mothers walking to school to retrieve their children at the end of the school day. "I always went outside where the mothers were waiting. I'd play with the baby, tell a quick story about something their child had done or said, ask about other members of the family. That was the way I pulled them into the classroom" (Diffily 2004, 117).

In addition to learning about a family's beliefs and practices, it is useful for kindergarten teachers to have a basic grasp of the family's living circumstances. Families who recently immigrated to the United States, for instance, may be striving to simply survive in a new country. Struggles to find employment and money to meet basic family needs are likely to be combined with limited English-language skills and crowded living arrangements with other relatives. Parents' focus on daily support of the family leaves little or no time to help their children adjust to kindergarten or to learn how schools work in the United States (Diffily 2004). Providing a predictable, supportive classroom for children in this situation is a valuable contribution toward a family's adjustment and a child's sense of secure membership in the school. Families also may benefit from referrals to community resources or to a school staff member responsible for helping families find health and human services.

Information about family experiences can help teachers understand and ease children's adjustment to kindergarten. Teachers may learn that, for some families, having a child in kindergarten requires a significant change in family routines—such as a five-day-a-week school schedule and the limited availability of the kindergarten child as a playmate for a younger sibling(s) at

home (Pianta & Kraft-Sayre 1999). More generally, teachers are likely to learn that some of the family risk factors linked to children's academic gaps in kindergarten are also associated with parent involvement in their children's education. In a study of families of more than 380 kindergarten and first grade children from high-risk neighborhoods, for example, parent education, maternal depression, and single-parent status were linked to dimensions of parent involvement in school (Kohl, Lengua, & McMahon 2000). It is tempting to interpret an absence from a school event as an indication of limited parental interest in their children's education ("They don't care about their kids"), but other powerful factors such as conflicting job schedules or mental health issues may be at work.

Teachers also need to learn about *particular* families, because there are profound individual differences across families in any cultural group.

Respectfully including

One way that teachers can help bridge family and classroom learning environments is to responsively incorporate family information and contributions into the classroom. There are many inexpensive ways to develop this continuity between home and school that do not impose expectations of classroom volunteering on parents with competing job, school, or family responsibilities.

Family albums are a creative and substantive way to tap the "funds of knowledge" held by families. Teachers can provide parents and children with materials to create a book about the family (such as its members, favorite activities, a recent event) or to organize the child's drawings, writing attempts, and other memorabilia into a portfolio that includes simple captions and descriptions written by the parent (and perhaps dictated by the child). Homemade books, which often reflect the unique traditions and activities of their authors, can become an ongoing part of classroom life through joint reading time, discussions of the books led by the child-authors, and their prominent placement in the classroom library (Neuman 1999; Neuman & Roskos 1994). Similarly, audiotapes of books read by a parent or other family member can become a permanent part of a classroom's books-on-tape collection for independent use by children.

When communicating with parents, teachers may find it helpful to emphasize the importance of parents in a child's educational achievements and the opportunities they have to help shape their child's education through close connections with the classroom. A study of former Head Start parents with children in kindergarten found that parents who believed they had some control over their children's education reported being more actively involved in their child's school than those who felt they had less control (Seefeldt et al. 1998).

The school's roles

Teachers' parent-involvement practices go a long way in promoting a family's participation in their children's education. School practices can also facilitate strong partnerships between parents and teachers. In addition to embracing productive family-school relations across all grade levels, it is beneficial for schools to support activities aimed at helping families and their children make a successful transition to kindergarten.

For example, one preschool-to-kindergarten transition project involving high-risk children and families enlisted the help of family workers employed by the school system. These family workers organized transition activities such as parent orientations, newsletters, and interactions with kindergarten teachers. Families were paired with a family worker. Most of the activities were new to the schools and therefore not standard practice. A vast majority of families participated in the transi-

Effective teachers share classrooms with families by encouraging parents to become integral parts of their children's education at home and at school.

tion activities, and most chose to have their children visit a kindergarten classroom (typically with a preschool teacher). The least popular transition activity was the parent attending a kindergarten orientation meeting (La Paro, Kraft-Sayre, & Pianta 2003).

Kindergarten teachers reported that they found the transition activities in which they participated helpful. However, there were significant limits on the range of activities in which teachers participated. A majority of kindergarten teachers reported involvement in the visits of preschool children and their teachers to kindergarten classrooms, but few teachers (19 percent) reported visiting preschool classrooms. A majority of kindergarten teachers took part in a spring orientation for parents, but fewer than 25 percent of them held a conference with parents of a preschool child. Kindergarten teachers generally did not participate in school-to-school transition activities such as sharing records or meeting about curriculum, although about half met with a preschool teacher about a specific child. Barriers to the participation of kindergarten teachers in preschool-to-school transition activities included unpaid summer work and delays in the availability of class lists (La Paro et al. 2003).

Schools seeking to offer transition activities could build on some of the lessons of this project. One guideline is to accommodate work schedules by offering meetings during evening hours. Nearly three-quarters of the parents reported that their work schedule interfered with participation in transition activities for their child (La Paro et al. 2003). Another lesson is to support kindergarten teachers in visiting preschool classrooms, conducting individual meetings with parents, and, more generally, connecting with families in a range of settings that include but are not limited to the school building (La Paro et al. 2003). Further, involving preschool teachers in transition activities seems beneficial. Some 90 percent reported that they visited kindergarten classrooms, and mothers rated their children's preschool teacher as more helpful than other sources of support in the kindergarten transition, with ratings of helpfulness increasing from fall to spring (Pianta et al. 2001).

Douglas R. Powell and Hope K. Gerde

Classes or groups that provide information on good parenting practices are another promising way to support families and their children during the transition to kindergarten. One research-based example is a couples group program in which meetings began before children started kindergarten. Groups of four to five couples met weekly with a staff couple (mental health professionals) for 16 weeks. The format was semi-structured and focused on parenting and couple relationships. (For example, group participants may have been asked to consider how their stress as individuals or a couple affected their reactions to their children.) Participating couples represented a range of socioeconomic backgrounds.

Results indicate that the couples groups contributed to positive change in family relationships and in children's adaptation to elementary school. Compared with control families, children of couples participating in the couples groups had higher academic achievement scores and more positive self-reports of adaptation in kindergarten. In first grade, these children were seen by their teachers as exhibiting fewer behavior problems (Cowan, Cowan, & Heming 2005).

The persistence of kindergarten memories speaks to the importance of early school experiences. We typically remember details of our kindergarten year well into adulthood. Parents can long recall their child's first days at school. Many families record the event with photographs and samples of children's schoolwork that occupy prominent places in family albums. Kindergarten is a benchmark in parenting and in childhood.

Kindergarten teachers play a significant role in helping children and their families make the most of the kindergarten year. Effective teachers share classrooms with families by encouraging parents to become integral parts of their children's education at home and at school. Significant forces well beyond the school walls contribute to the nature of children's learning experiences at home and family perspectives on school. Teachers and school administrators face important challenges and special opportunities for understanding and working with the family contexts of their students' lives. To ignore children's lives outside of school is to forego a rare chance to marshal the resources of a powerful set of relationships for learning in kindergarten and beyond.

References

Balaban, N. 2006. *Everyday goodbyes: Starting school and early care—A guide to the separation process*. New York: Teachers College Press.

Bredekamp, S., & C. Copple, eds. 1997. *Developmentally appropriate practice in early childhood programs*. Rev. ed. Washington, DC: NAEYC.

Carey, N., L. Lewis, & E. Farris. 1998. *Parent involvement in children's education: Efforts by public elementary schools* (NCES 98-032). Washington, DC: National Center for Education Statistics, U.S. Department of Education.

Cowan, C.P., P.A. Cowan, & G. Heming. 2005. Two variations of a preventive intervention for couples: Effects on parents and children during the transition to school. In *The family context of parenting in children's adaptation to school,* eds. P.A. Cowan, C.P. Cowan, J.C. Ablow, V.K. Johnson, & J.R. Measelle, 277–312. Mahwah, NJ: Erlbaum.

Diamond, K.E., A.J. Reagan, & J.E. Bandyk. 2000. Parents' conceptions of kindergarten readiness: Relationships with race, ethnicity, and development. *Journal of Educational Research* 94: 93–101.

Diffily, D. 2004. *Teachers and families working together*. Boston: Allyn & Bacon.

Epstein, J.L., & M.G. Sanders. 2002. Family, school, and community partnerships. In *Handbook of parenting, Vol. 5: Practical issues in parenting*, 2d ed., ed. M.H. Bornstein, 407–37. Mahwah, NJ: Erlbaum.

Hammer, L.D., H.C. Kraemer, D.M. Wilson, P.L. Ritter, & S.M. Dornbusch. 1991. Standardized percentile curves of body-mass index for children and adolescents. *American Journal of Diseases of Children* 145: 259–63.

Jacobs, J.A., & K. Gerson. 2004. *The time divide: Work, family, and gender inequality*. Cambridge, MA: Harvard University Press.

Kohl, G.O., L.J. Lengua, & R.J. McMahon. 2000. Parent involvement in school conceptualizing multiple dimensions and their relations with family and demographic risk factors. *Journal of School Psychology* 38: 501–23.

La Paro, K.M., M. Kraft-Sayre, & R.C. Pianta. 2003. Preschool to kindergarten transition activities: Involvement and satisfaction of families and teachers. *Journal of Research in Childhood Education* 17: 147–58.

Lee, V.E., & D.T. Burkam. 2002. *Inequality at the starting gate: Social background differences in achievement as children begin school.* Washington, DC: Economic Policy Institute.

Lynch, E.W., & M.J. Hanson, eds. 2004. *Developing cross-cultural competence: A guide for working with children and their families.* 3d ed. Baltimore: Brookes.

McWayne, C., V. Hampton, J. Fantuzzo, H.L. Cohen, & Y. Sekino. 2004. A multivariate examination of parent involvement and the social and academic competencies of urban kindergarten children. *Psychology in the Schools* 41: 363–77.

NAEYC. 1996a. *Responding to linguistic and cultural diversity—Recommendations for effective early childhood education.* Position statement. Online: www. naeyc.org/about/positions/linguistic_and_cultural _diversity.asp.

NAEYC. 1996b. *NAEYC's code of ethical conduct and statement of commitment.* Position statement. Online: www.naeyc.org/about/positions/ethical_conduct.asp.

National PTA (Parent-Teacher Association). 1997. *National standards for parent/family involvement programs.* Chicago: Author.

Neuman, S.B. 1999. Creating continuity in early literacy: Linking home and school with a culturally responsive approach. In *Best practices in literacy instruction,* eds. L.B. Gambrell, L.M. Morrow, S.B. Neuman, & M. Pressley, 258–70. New York: Guilford.

Neuman, S.B., & K. Roskos. 1994. Bridging home and school with a culturally responsive approach. *Childhood Education* 70: 210–14.

Nord, C.W., J. Lennon, B. Liu, & K. Chandler. 1999. *Home literacy activities and signs of children's emerging literacy, 1993 and 1999* (NCES 2000-026). Washington, DC: National Center for Education Statistics, U.S. Department of Education.

Pianta, R.C., M.J. Cox, L. Taylor, & D. Early. 1999. Kindergarten teachers' practices related to the transition to school: Results of a national survey. *The Elementary School Journal* 100: 71–86.

Pianta, R.C., & M. Kraft-Sayre. 1999. Parents' observations about their children's transitions to kindergarten. *Young Children* 54 (3): 47–52.

Pianta, R.C., M. Kraft-Sayre, S. Rimm-Kaufman, N. Gercke, & T. Higgins. 2001. Collaboration in building partnerships between families and schools: The National Center for Early Development and Learning's kindergarten transition intervention. *Early Childhood Research Quarterly* 16: 117–32.

Powell, D.R. 2001. Visions and realities of achieving partnership: Parent-school relationships at the turn of the century. In *Children in play, story, and school,* eds. A. Göncü & E.L. Klein, 333–57. New York: Guilford.

Rathbun, A., J. West, & E. Germino-Hausken. 2004. *From kindergarten through third grade: Children's beginning school experiences* (NCES 2004-007). Washington, DC: National Center for Education Statistics, U.S. Department of Education.

Rimm-Kaufman, S.E., & R.C. Pianta. 1999. Patterns of family-school contact in preschool and kindergarten. *School Psychology Review* 28: 426–38.

Sandall, S., M.E. McLean, & B.J. Smith, eds. 2000. *DEC recommended practices in early intervention/early childhood special education.* Denver, CO: Division for Early Childhood of the Council for Exceptional Children.

Seefeldt, C., K. Denton, A. Galper, & T. Younoszai. 1998. Former Head Start parents' characteristics, perceptions of school climate, and involvement in their children's education. *The Elementary School Journal* 98: 339–49.

Stipek, D.J., & R.H. Ryan. 1997. Economically disadvantaged preschoolers: Ready to learn but further to go. *Developmental Psychology* 33: 771–23.

U.S. Census Bureau. 1983. *General social and economic characteristics.* 1980 Census of Population. Washington, DC: Author.

U.S. Census Bureau. 2000. *Employment status and work status in 1999 of family members: 2000.* Census 2000 Summary File 3. Washington, DC: Author.

Wertheimer, R., T. Croan, K.A. Moore, & E.C. Hair. 2003, December. *Attending kindergarten and already behind: A statistical portrait of vulnerable young children* (Publication No. 2003-20). Washington, DC: Child Trends.

West, J., K. Denton, & E. Germino-Hausken. 2000. *America's kindergarteners* (NCES 2000-070). Washington, DC: National Center for Education Statistics, U.S. Department of Education.

West, J., K. Denton, & L. Reaney. 2001. *The kindergarten year* (NCES 2001-023). Washington, DC: National Center for Education Statistics, U.S. Department of Education.

Zill, N. 1999. Promoting educational equity and excellence in kindergarten. In *The transition to kindergarten,* eds. R.C. Pianta & M.J. Cox, 67–105. Baltimore: Brookes.

Douglas R. Powell and Hope K. Gerde

Part II

Developing
Foundations in
the Kindergarten Year

Developing Key Cognitive Skills

Susan L. Golbeck

"I think, therefore I am." Or, in Latin, *cogito ergo sum*. These words were written in the 17th century by Rene Descartes, French mathematician and philosopher. Descartes was interested in the meanings of "understanding" and "knowing." Descartes tells us that our understanding of the world depends on more than just our perceptions and experiences (Lerner 2002). Our understanding comes from our ability *to think about* what we experience. And this ability to think makes us human.

The English word *cognition* comes from the Latin word for thinking or thought processes. According to the dictionary, cognition is "an act or process of knowing in the broadest sense; an intellectual process by which knowledge is gained about perceptions or ideas." So, cognitive skills are skills for thinking.

We can apply our thinking skills to everything we do, learn, and feel. Seeing, hearing, feeling, and problem solving are all experiences that we can think about. And when we think, we understand in new ways and see the world with new eyes.

Six-year-old Margaret sees the sky become gray and cloudy. She hears the sound of thunder. And then she feels the rain falling on her head. She thinks about all

these sensations and realizes they all go together. She connects these experiences with the word *rain.* And she compares these sensations and experiences with other similar sensations and experiences: water pouring on her hands from the faucet, the spray of water from the lawn sprinkler. She notices that there is no thunder or gray sky when the wetness comes from the faucet or the sprinkler. But she is told that water from the sprinkler and rain both help the flowers grow.

Margaret picks up the garden hose, and water comes spurting out. She is surprised, she laughs. She pretends to spray her sister. Now pointing the hose at a patch of bare earth, she announces that she is "watering her garden." Her sister laughs too, understanding that Margaret is playing. Aunt Susan smiles at the two of them and says, "Maybe we should plant a little garden!"

It seems hard to imagine not knowing what water is. But such events, perceptions and sensations, experiences, insights, and connections with past experiences occur continuously in life. Sometimes these connections occur so quickly that we are barely aware of them. These insights can also lead to entirely new ideas, such as a very young child like Margaret might have:

What if I tried pouring some water though the funnel on the side of the water table? Where will the water go? Will the water go into the bucket near the funnel? Maybe the water will just disappear? . . . Is there a way I could grow plants right in the water table? Or could I

Susan L. Golbeck is a professor in the educational psychology department in the Graduate School of Education at Rutgers, The State University of New Jersey.

use the water in it to water the plants in flower pots? . . . Could I put the water table outside and catch the rain when it falls?

Cognitive skills encompass a rich and diverse range of mental processes. Our natural human inclination to wonder about the world and to look for answers is at the core of all our cognitive functioning. *Reflecting, observing, applying strategies for comprehending, problem solving, imagining, problem posing, visualizing, evaluating*—all these terms describe cognitive skills. Cognitive skills are used in our interactions with family, friends, and the community; they are important in both work and play. We use our cognitive skills every day as we solve problems, comprehend conversations and written materials, and create and reflect.

Young children use cognitive skills in social interactions as they play board games with friends (thinking about the rules, remembering that each player must wait for a turn, determining the number of moves to take, challenging a player who "cheats" by moving too far). Children use their cognitive skills as they negotiate movement in the physical world (figuring out the best way to bicycle home to avoid the big hill). We also see cognitive skills in action as we watch a child decide how to create a structure with blocks.

> Cognitive skills are used in our interactions with family, friends, and the community; they are important in both work and play.

Cognitive skills are included in the standards and guidelines developed by professional organizations concerned with children's learning, including the National Council of Teachers of Mathematics, the National Council of Teachers of English, the International Reading Association, the National Association for the Education of Young Children, and the National Research Council (which generated the National Science Education Standards). Other closely related skills include processes such as *critical thinking, planning,* and *thinking ahead.* There are also a variety of skills specific to content areas—mathematical reasoning (such as *estimating*), scientific thinking (such as

observing), and reading (such as *decoding*), to name a few. Teachers and curriculum developers use these guidelines and standards—along with state standards—to plan and organize instructional experiences. While few, if any, states identify cognitive skills as a "stand alone" set of learning goals independent of content (Neuman & Roskos 2005), they are embedded within each of the academic discipline areas mentioned above.

Are cognitive skills really just another name for academic skills? Cognitive and cultural psychologists tell us that cognitive skills are needed to acquire academic skills such as reading, writing, and formal mathematics, but that the two are not the same. Cognitive skills such as reasoning, planning, and critical thinking occur in humans whether or not they have attended school. However, while all humans possess cognitive skills, going to school does broaden and change those thinking skills. School influences both *what* children know (they can read and write) and *how* they think. Research from parts of the world where schools are not widely available shows that "schooling" (participation in formal instruction) leads to distinctive styles of thinking, problem solving, and remembering.

People who have been schooled are more likely to look for *abstract* relationships among objects in the world, while people who have learned through everyday life experience rather than formal schooling focus on everyday, *experiential* relationships. In one study (Cole, Cole, & Lightfoot 2005), for example, schooled people were more likely to group items by category (hammers, shovels, spoons, pots); the unschooled were more likely to group items as they would be found in a home (four groups, each containing a hammer, shovel, spoon, and pot).

Schooling also leads to the acquisition of particular styles of remembering. For example, when asked to remember a list of unrelated words, such as items on a shopping list, older children with school experience are more likely to mentally rearrange or reorganize the words into categories so that the words that share a category can be chunked together (Flavell, Miller, & Miller 2002). This mental "rearranging" of the words makes it

Susan L. Golbeck

easier to remember the complete list of items. Children were probably not directly taught such mental actions, or "memory strategies," at school. But by the age of 10 or so, children in school are likely to discover this memory strategy in the course of working on school-like tasks; children who have never been to school are unlikely to do so.

For young children, the term *cognitive skills* refers to thinking and problem-solving skills as they are applied in a wide range of settings. These skills support children's academic learning, communication skills, and social interactions in many different intellectual endeavors. We would hope children's cognitive skills are nourished and nurtured well before they enter kindergarten. But it is when children enter kindergarten, or in some cases prekindergarten, that the responsibility for developing cognitive skills officially extends beyond the family.

By kindergarten, all children should be participating in a curriculum that systematically incorporates the key cognitive skills identified by the leading education organizations. (Some children may have begun participating at a younger age.) Kindergarten teachers should plan for the foundational cognitive skills associated with thinking. They should also plan for problem solving, reflection, and written representations. Unfortunately, all too often kindergarten teachers think they must focus all their attention on specific academic knowledge, such as the letter and number knowledge associated with reading and writing, or the math knowledge tied to number recognition, counting, and calculation. This specific knowledge is important, but a narrow focus on this alone can lead teachers to neglect the cognitive skills that support learning across all settings and situations.

The 5- to 7-year shift: A key transition in cognitive skills

Children's minds are typically changing in important ways at about age 5 or 6, around the time they enter kindergarten. Similar changes in children's thinking and in their schooling have been described in cultures around the world (Case & Okamoto 1996; Tobin, Wu, & Davidson 1989). Developmental researchers have identified distinctive thought patterns that characterize this age period. An awareness of these general patterns can help teachers as they make decisions about curriculum and instruction. It is important, however, to note that these are only general patterns. In the real world of real children, there is a great deal of variability. While broad patterns are useful for a broad understanding, any single situation should be interpreted with caution.

Preschool thinking

By the time they are 5, children's thinking is quite accomplished. They have started to develop abilities to represent thoughts and ideas in a variety of ways, although these representations are not always interpretable to adults. Children organize and express their ideas through oral language, play, writing and drawing, and construction with materials such as blocks (Flavell, Miller, & Miller 2002).

Children can generate simple causal explanations of the events in the world. Their explanations draw upon the knowledge they have acquired and constructed in their everyday experience. Certain domains of knowledge are especially important for young children. Even preschool children have a basic understanding of the *physical world,* the *world of feelings, social knowledge* (such as when someone might know something), and rudimentary knowledge about *biological change.*

Although this basic causal knowledge allows young children to make many simple predictions, their explanations are often logically flawed. In one study, researchers analyzed the talk of children from the time they were 2 years old until they were 5, especially the talk that focused on causal explanations of events in everyday life (Hickling & Wellman 2001). For each of the four domains above, they identified corresponding types of explanations typical of preschoolers: (1) *physical* explanations, typically applied to objects and used to explain things in terms of mechanical force where one object came into contact with another ("The doll's arm fell off because you twisted it too far"); (2) *psychological* explanations, in which events are explained in terms of actors' mental states such as beliefs, intentions, and desires ("I talking very quiet because I don't want somebody to wake me up"); (3) *social* explanations, referring to interpersonal rules or cultural conventions and traditions ("I got this candy because it is a prize"); and (4) *biological* explanations, referring to phenomena such as growth, nutrition, reproduction, and illness ("He needs more meat because he growing long arms").

Preschool children often leave problems poorly analyzed, and they treat things globally rather than recognizing the ways in which parts fit together to form a whole (as, for example, in the way several blocks can fit together to form a structure). Preschoolers miss patterns and regularities that are immediately obvious to older children. This can be seen in children's drawings. Young children usually begin drawing people as blob-like shapes with four lines that radiate outward. After drawing the circle-like blob, they usually add eyes and a mouth. These "tadpole" people preserve the holistic notion of a body with arms and legs, yet the body and head are fused together in a very unusual way that is neither a head nor a body. Difficulty integrating all the parts into the whole is characteristic of young children's thinking.

Preschoolers are also limited in their ability to combine simple ideas into more complex ones. For example, young children have difficulty drawing a scene that includes several objects. When asked to make a drawing of two brothers playing ball in the park, the preschooler might draw two figures as well as a ball, but it is unlikely that the figures will be placed on a ground line and be oriented toward each other, or that any park-like context will be included. Instead, two people and a ball will probably be free-floating in space.

Kindergarten thinking

By the age of 6 or 7, children's thought becomes more systematic and organized within each of the four domains (physical, psychological, social, and biological). This is evident in the way children explore new situations, respond to direc-tions, play games, and carry out everyday activi-ties. By the end of kindergarten, children are more aware of patterns and regularities. They also begin to redefine confusing problems and combine concepts they previously used only alone. Kinder-gartners begin to recognize event sequences in many ways—as they appear in stories, in the physical world, in biological cycles within the physical world, in daily routines within the class-room, and in larger societal routines.

Kindergarten children also demonstrate an emerging awareness of part-whole relationships. This development becomes more evident in the next few years as children's awareness of stories and the complex connections between plot lines and characters' emotions as motivating factors grows. Newly emerging understandings of part-whole relations are also evident in mathematics and science, in spontaneous comments such as "I see two blue fish and three yellow fish."

At about age 5 or 6, children's thinking typi-cally becomes less rigidly fixed and egocentric; it better accounts for multiple perspectives, it is more flexible, and it is beginning to be able to transform ideas and representations. In the physi-cal domain, children can now grasp that the same object or set of objects can look very different depending on the observer's vantage point. In the psychological domain, children can make simple inferences about what another person knows or feels. For example, if a child sees someone "try to trick" someone else, the child might infer that the child being tricked is unaware of the situation. In a variety of situations, children begin to see mul-tiple sides of an issue. Unlike preschoolers, who assume that other people see things as they do, 5-year-olds begin to recognize that their own per-spective on a situation may differ from someone else's. Five-year-olds struggle to predict precisely what it is that someone else sees, but they are not surprised that the other's view is different from their own. For example, a child may turn a book or picture around so her friend can see it better. She begins to recognize that what her father would like for a present is not what she would like. This awareness reflects an emerging ability to consider more information at one time. This expanding

Susan L. Golbeck

information-processing capacity will have wide-ranging implications for thought and "the power of the mind."

An increase in flexible thinking is evident in other ways, as well. Children can mentally rearrange or transform information—they are less bound by the first thing they see. For example, a kindergartner can figure out a couple of ways to combine blocks to create a building of a particular shape. Or sometimes children can temporarily ignore their own feelings and be sensitive to the needs of another (especially if they are close to that person). This flexibility of thinking is apparent in geometric, spatial, and mathematical thinking. Children discover principles of number as they count actions and objects. Children begin to apply spatial visual strategies and mental images to solve problems in the everyday world. Children understand that they can divide things, such as a big piece of candy so that everyone can have some—*one* thing becomes *many*. Or children understand that a puzzle with five or six separate pieces can be returned to its original appearance by putting the pieces together again—*many* things become *one*.

This idea applies to stable objects, such as puzzles and their parts, and to things that move through space. With a bit of exploring, for example, the child may be able to predict the expected pathway of a cone-shaped object rolling down an incline. Or he will understand that shadows are influenced by the orientation of the light source. A child's skill in using these mental transformations will expand and improve throughout the course of middle childhood, but significant changes begin to appear in the early primary school years.

In comparison with preschoolers, 5- and 6-year-olds are more likely to look for conceptual categories rather than just simple associations. For example, they understand that when they are in the grocery store to buy cereal, they probably will not find it in the dairy aisle. They also have a greater ability to think about their own thinking—that is, to engage in *metacognition*. For example, the child is able to recognize that he knows something that someone else does not know.

This transition—from preschool thought to the style of thinking more typical of middle childhood—has been dubbed the "5- to 7-year shift" by psychologists (Flavell, Miller, & Miller 2001; Newcombe 2005).

Changes in the brain

Cognitive psychologists have long debated the causes of these changes in young children's thinking. Some have argued that changes in thinking patterns result from differing societal expectations for children as they move from home to the larger social world (Bijou & Baer 1970; Vygotsky 1983). Others have attributed the shift to maturation and underlying cognitive changes (Gesell 1940; Piaget & Inhelder 1969). The nature of biological changes has not been known until recently.

New research in cognitive neuroscience sheds light on the cognitive changes of early childhood, and shows that the neurological system grows dramatically during the early childhood years (Halfon, Shulman, & Hochstein 2001). We now know that there is rapid brain growth during this time, including mylenization in the nerve cells (a thickening of their white coating) in the brain's cerebral cortex and "pruning" of neural networks. Pruning is a process by which brain and nerve cells are recombined so that the cells that are not being used are redirected to areas in which rapid learning is occurring. This pruning enables active portions of the brain and neurological system to become more powerful, as the areas that are not used atrophy. Such changes enable the child to better meet the particular demands of the environment.

> This transition—from preschool thought to the style of thinking more typical of middle childhood—has been dubbed the "5- to 7-year shift."

These changes in the brain and nerve system seem to accompany significant and widely observed cognitive changes (Nelson & Luciana 2001). One of these changes is the amount of information children can think about at one time. Children become able to hold more information in their working memory, which is an important factor for problem solving. This improvement in information processing permits the child to learn more efficiently and flexibly. When a child encounters a problem, he can identify a possible course of action and evaluate how well a solution is working. If the first strategy he tries does not work, he can modify his approach, or start again with a new approach. These neurological changes, observed at about age 5 or 6, greatly increase the effectiveness of children's thinking.

New research also shows that children's mental self-regulatory skills develop during the late preschool and early school years. Compared with younger preschoolers, children are better at focusing their attention. They are less easily distracted and less impulsive. They are better at defining their goals and planning, as well as recognizing relevant information in a problem situation (Gauvain 2001). Increased memory capacity then makes it easier for them to combine simple routines into more complex strategies.

Clearly, the changes that characterize the 5- to 7-year shift are extensive. These changes lay the groundwork for children's ability to appreciate new kinds of experiences beyond the immediate family. As children's thinking becomes more systematic and self-regulated, they are ready to learn traditional academic skills such as reading, writing, and mathematical computation. At the same time, children continue to need support from their teachers and parents as they master the self-regulatory skills they are working on at this time. Recent research shows that emotional support and mastery of cognitive skills are closely related (Keating & Miller 1999; Pianta 1999).

Promoting kindergartners' cognitive skills

Questions to encourage making connections between people, places, things, and events

Comparing—*finding similarities and differences; finding ways things "go together"; putting things in categories*

- How are these alike? Is there anything that doesn't belong in this group? What would be a good way of organizing things so we can tell what's here?

- What name could you give this group?

- This bottle holds almost eight scoops of rice. How many scoops do you think this jar will hold?

Quantifying—*finding out about how much and how many; breaking apart and recombining*

- How many of you have families with one child? two children? etc. . . . How many of you come from families with a grandma and five children? [Engage children in keeping track with tally marks or a bar graph.] So how many have more than one child?

- Can you show me another way to make . . . ?

- [Compare quantities of unit blocks with different shapes or triangles, prisms, cylinders, etc.] Do we have the same number of each shape? Which one has the most? Which has the least? What would be a good way to remember how many we have?

- When I cover some of the eight bears, look and see how many you can still see. How many do you think are hidden?

Sequences—*finding temporal and spatial order*

- Let's arrange our towers of cubes from shortest to tallest.

- Let's make a "timeline" that shows what happened first, last, and in-between.

- Let's lay out these pictures of food from hottest to coldest.

Spatial relationships—*finding positions*

- Suppose we want to put the chairs in two lines, like seats on a bus. How would we do that?

- Can you tell me how to get to the cafeteria from here?

- How many Big Blocks will it take to cover this rug?

- Do you think this shape would roll?

Susan L. Golbeck

Cognitive skills in kindergarten: A system undergoing change

What is happening in a child's mind to enable the extensive changes that characterize the 5- to 7-year shift? The mind's system of cognitive activities and skills is helping the child adapt to the demands of the world. One way the child adapts is through active problem solving. Initially the mind helps the child solve the real problems of daily life. By kindergarten, these problems also include the real and not so real problems presented to the child at school.

As a cognitive system, the mind is made up of several distinct components—somewhat like a computer. One set of components consists of *cognitive schemes*, or thought patterns. These schemes are used by the child during active problem solving, a bit like a computer runs software programs. *Memory* is the second component of the cognitive system. Memory is important in two ways: it stores information (acting as a "work space") during active problem solving, and it "runs the mental programs" of problem solving itself. Finally, the cognitive system is directed by a special set of *overarching schemes* (mental processes or thinking activities), which function like a computer's operating system to regulate the mind's activity. Some psychologists call these overarching schemes the "executive function" (Isquith, Gioia, & Espy 2004). Others refer to them as "metacognitive" processes, because they involve thinking about or monitoring memory, problem solving, or other mental activity.

Activities to prompt thinking about thinking (metacognition)

Describing the present

• *Using connections*: Children plant a window box garden. The class talks about gardening, farming, and agriculture. They read books about gardening and visit a county experimentation farm. They plant their classroom gardens.

• *With words*: Each child starts a science journal and describes what is happening in the classroom garden. Dictations supplement drawings and children's writing.

• *In space*: Children make a chart showing the progress of plant growth, adding information three times a week.

• *By movement:* Children use their bodies to demonstrate how a plant grows.

Remembering the past

• *Using connections:* Ask: "Do you remember how you felt when we went into the jungle exhibit at the zoo? Did it remind you of anything you had done before?"

• *With words:* Ask children to describe something they saw at the zoo. Invite them to make a page for the memory album.

• *In space:* Have children build a model of the zoo with clay and other materials. Provide children with landscape and aerial photographs [but probably not maps] as memory supports.

• *By movement:* Ask: "Do you remember how the waves in the ocean tank moved? Let's pretend we are the waves."

Planning and predicting

• *Using connections:* Ask: "What do you think would happen if we put our plants in the closet?" "How many times will we need to fill the watering can to water each plant?"

• *With words:* Have children write/dictate directions for Mrs. Smith, who will take care of the plants while school is closed for vacation.

• *In space:* Engage children in making an illustrated chart that shows the steps in the sequence of how to take care of the plants.

• *By movement:* Ask: "What would a plant do if it didn't get water all week? Can you be the plant and show us?"

This description of the mind is useful for understanding how learning occurs over the short term. But how does the child begin to think more flexibly, hold more information in mind, and think more effectively about the future? What changes occur in the mind during the 5- to 7-year shift?

During a child's early years, important changes occur in his or her thought patterns. Changes also occur in the child's memory capabilities. These changes are triggered by *internal* forces within the child (such as physical growth within the neuromotor system) and by *external* conditions and events in the child's environment (such as adequate nutrition and social interactions). The changes we see in children occur through the dynamic interaction of both factors. A child's engagement with the world through active problem solving and thinking initiates changes in his cognitive system. These changes include more efficient coordination of cognitive schemes and memory. The mind becomes better adapted to the demands of the world, and the child is able to solve problems that are more and more complex. Finally, active involvement with other people can extend and support cognitive skills. Taken together, all these factors lead to "upgrades" in the child's developing cognitive system.

This upgrade in the cognitive system is mobilized by two factors that teachers can influence significantly. First, all children possess the internal motivation, or "power source," for cognitive problem solving. But this power source does not always function optimally. The teacher and the learning environment need to regulate or support and direct it. An environment of trusting relationships with other people is key to a smooth operation. Second, the child needs good "input data"—new knowledge and interesting problems—to grapple with. In order for the environment to be supportive of children's learning, it must be continually refreshed and adapted to each child's intellectual needs. All these aspects of the kindergarten classroom are the responsibility of the teacher.

The teacher's role in supporting children's cognitive skills

Teachers promote children's cognitive skills in a number of ways. When teachers offer inviting, well-organized classrooms and establish warm and trusting relationships with children, they create the conditions for fostering children's thinking abilities. Emotional security frees children to devote energy to the cognitive tasks they encounter in the classroom.

Much of the description here has emphasized similarities in cognitive skills across areas of learning. But it would be a mistake not to recognize the importance of learning within particular domains of understanding. Earlier we noted the importance of children's knowledge in particular domains for understanding cause and effect. Children continue to build on these early knowledge areas, creating systems of understanding—or *mental models*—about the world. Children's knowledge is more advanced in some conceptual domains than in others.

Teachers need to be sensitive to children's mental models and help them elaborate on those models. Often, these ideas can be linked to specific curriculum content. For example, learning in science can be linked to children's pre-existing ideas about the physical world (Gelman & Brenneman 2004). It is clearly important to understand how children make sense of the world for this to work.

Beyond these essentials, teachers can promote and support kindergartners' cognitive development in a number of ways. One way is by asking questions and making comments that provoke or encourage children to think and reflect. The box on pages 42–43 gives examples of the kind of questions that teachers can ask during an ongoing classroom project or other learning experience. The questions are divided into two broad categories. The first focuses on descriptions of events and changes in the physical and social world. The second concerns thought processes themselves and encourages "thinking about thinking," directing children's attention to how they know something and how they might remember or solve a problem.

Susan L. Golbeck

Promoting children's planning and reflection

Teachers can promote the development of children's planning and reflecting skills by using teaching strategies such as these:

1. Make planning and reflection a regular part of the program day. When children get accustomed to such a time, they begin (without prompting) to think ahead to what they want to do and how to carry it out and, afterwards, to think back over what they have just done.

2. Make sure children can see the areas and materials in the room when they are planning. Seeing everything enhances planning and leads children to incorporate a wider variety of materials into their activities.

3. Ask open-ended questions. A question such as "What will your book have in it?" generally elicits more detail than "Will you have pictures in your book?"

4. Listen attentively to children's plans. By paying attention to children's words and gestures, you learn about each child's ability to anticipate and think about the details of a plan. Then you can choose the most appropriate support strategies to help children elaborate their ideas and consider options for implementing them.

5. Interpret and expand what children do and say. Add words to children's gestures or limited verbalizations, checking with the child to ensure that you have understood correctly.

6. Support, accept, and extend all the ways children express their plan. Take care not to criticize a child's plan or pose an alternative to what he has in mind. This can undermine children's thinking about and expressing of their own intentions.

7. Encourage children to describe their plans and their reflections on what they have done. As the child gives details of her planned or completed work, the materials used, the sequence of her activities, and the outcomes she expects or achieves, she often engages in more elaborated thinking.

8. Document children's plans. Documentation—including writing, drawing, and photography at all stages of their work—helps children become more conscious of the process and value of planning. They are more likely to think through and elaborate on their ideas as they record them concretely. Children can also review their documented plans as they reflect on their experiences and compare their intentions with the actual outcomes.

9. Encourage children to carry over their activities to the next day. As children reflect on their experiences, they may recall problems they encountered or spin-offs they did not anticipate. As they consider these things, children can think about different solutions or ways to build on newly discovered interests the following day.

The mental representations that children draw on and clarify in planning and reviewing their activities are important in themselves. As Ann Epstein points out, planning and reflection have additional long-term value for children:

> [Planning and reflection] encourage children to take the initiative in pursuing their interests, engendering a sense of control over the environment and one's ability to transform it. As children make plans and review their experiences, they enhance their predictive and analytical abilities, harness self-regulatory mechanisms, and develop a sense of responsibility for themselves and the choices they make. By encouraging these twin processes—expressing intentions and evaluating actions—we can equip young children with the thinking skills they need for later schooling and adult life.

Source: Adapted from A. Epstein, How planning and reflection develop young children's thinking skills (2003), *Young Children* 58: 5, 28–36. **Ann Epstein** is the early childhood director of the High/Scope Educational Research Foundation.

Teachers also promote cognitive development when they encourage children to record and document their knowledge by using various representational methods, such as words and gestures, writing, and drawing, and by making diagrams, graphs, and models. A child is most highly motivated when she is sharing a message that is important to her. She will notice, for example, whether her message is getting across, or if it needs to be modified. An important focus in the kindergarten year is enhancing children's understanding of the many ways that we use representations to communicate and share knowledge.

Children learn from their interactions not only with adults but also with peers. Sometimes the child's peers understand him and respond positively to his ideas—sometimes they do not. Children frequently test their ideas with peers, and learn a lot from the reactions they receive. Teachers greatly promote kindergartners' cognitive development by recognizing the value of peer interactions for children's cognitive growth, and by designing learning environments that encourage children to interact and collaborate.

Finally, children need to be able to make choices. Choices empower children to be active

thinkers who challenge themselves. Teachers who offer children choices do not give up control. Nor are they passive. Rather, teachers must constantly look for ways to be active participants in children's learning processes while ensuring that the children are also active and engaged. The box on page 45 illustrates the kinds of strategies that teachers can use to create this kind of learning environment.

In summary, effective kindergarten teachers promote children's cognitive skills across a wide array of activities. They establish an emotionally safe learning environment and work to create learning experiences that are attuned to children's cognitive capabilities—challenging, but within reach. To ensure that there are many such experiences for each child, teachers observe and assess children regularly and use the information gained to design and adapt instruction and curriculum. Teachers also make a point of allowing children to make choices to increase the likelihood of a good match between their interests and abilities and the activities in which they are engaged.

References

Bijou, S.W., & D.M. Baer. 1975. *Child development: A systematic and empirical inquiry,* Vol. 1. New York: Appleton-Century-Crofts.

Case, R., & Y. Okamoto, eds. 1996. *The role of central conceptual structures in the development of children's thought.* Monographs of the Society for Research in Child Development, vol. 61, nos. 1–2, serial no. 246. Chicago: University of Chicago Press.

Cole, M., S. Cole, & C. Lightfoot. 2005. *The development of children.* 5th ed. New York: Worth.

Flavell, J., P. Miller, & S. Miller. 2002. *Cognitive development.* 4th ed. Upper Saddle River, NJ: Prentice Hall.

Gauvain, M. 2001. *The social context of cognitive development.* New York: Guilford.

Gelman, R., & K. Brenneman. 2004. Science learning pathways for young children. *Early Childhood Research Quarterly* 19: 150–58.

Gesell, A. 1940. *The first five years of life.* New York: Harper & Row.

Golbeck, S. 2001. Instructional models for early childhood: In search of a child-regulated/teacher guided pedagogy. In *Psychological perspectives on early childhood education: Reframing dilemmas in research and practice,* ed. S. Golbeck, 3–34. Mahwah, NJ: Erlbaum.

Halfon, N., E. Shulman, & M. Hochstein. 2001. Brain development in early childhood. *Policy Briefs,* no. 13, pp. 1–4. Los Angeles: UCLA Center for Healthier Children, Family and Communities, California Policy Research Center.

Hickling, A.K., & H.M. Wellman. 2001. The emergence of children's causal explanations and theories: Evidence from everyday conversation. *Developmental Psychology* 37 (5): 668–83.

Isquith, P., G. Gioia, & K.A. Espy. 2004. Executive function in preschool children: Examination through everyday behavior. *Developmental Neuropsychology* 26 (1): 403–22.

Keating, D.P., & F.K. Miller. 1999. Individual pathways in competence and coping: From regulatory systems to habits of mind. In *Developmental health and wealth of nations: Social, biological and educational dynamics,* eds. D.P Keating & C. Hertzman, 220–33. New York: Guilford.

Lerner, R.M. 2002. *Concepts and theories of human development.* 3d ed. Mahwah, NJ: Erlbaum.

Nelson, C.A., & M. Luciana, eds. 2001. *Handbook of developmental cognitive neuroscience.* Cambridge, MA: MIT Press.

Neuman, S.B., & K. Roskos. 2005. The state of state pre-kindergarten standards. *Early Childhood Research Quarterly* 20: 125–45.

Newcombe, N.S. 2005. What do we mean when we say modularity? Master lecture presented at the biennial meeting of the Society for Research in Child Development, Atlanta, April 7–10.

Piaget, J., & B. Inhelder. 1969. *The psychology of the child.* New York: Basic.

Pianta, R. 1999. *Enhancing relationships between children and teachers.* Washington, DC: American Psychological Association.

Tobin, J.J., D.Y. Wu, & D.D. Davidson. 1989. *Preschool in three cultures.* New Haven, CT: Yale University Press.

Vygotsky, L. 1983. The history of higher mental functions. In *Collected Works,* Vol. 3. Moscow: Pedagogika. [in Russian, written in 1931]

Susan L. Golbeck

Developing Social and Emotional Competence

5

Martha B. Bronson

Supporting the growth of social and emotional competence has always been a primary goal for kindergarten. The first part of this chapter describes our current understanding of the components of social and emotional competence. The second part describes how parents and teachers can support the development of competence in the kindergarten year.

What is social and emotional competence?

Definitions of competence and an understanding of what practices are likely to nurture it have evolved over the years, as knowledge about child development has grown and public expectations of school programs for young children have changed. Until the mid 20th century, the primary focus of most early childhood and kindergarten programs was "socialization"—the process through which a young child adopts and internalizes the values and behaviors of society. Schools and families generally agreed that children needed to learn to get along well with others, to obey the rules, and to control their emotions and aggression toward others.

During the 1950s and 1960s, the United States became increasingly concerned about falling behind other countries in academic achievement. This led to a new focus on helping children who were not meeting expectations for success in school. These "disadvantaged" children, often from poor and less educated segments of the population, not only were academically under-prepared but also demonstrated social difficulties. The terms *social competence* and *social and emotional competence* began to be used to describe the skills these children lacked (Anderson & Messick 1974). Definitions of competence varied from the 1960s through the 1990s.

Over the last decade, an increasing emphasis on standards and accountability has led to a greater tendency in kindergarten to teach academic subject matter such as literacy and mathematics, to assess children's progress, and to focus on the types of social and emotional skills that allow young children to benefit from instruction, such as self-control, curiosity, self-direction, and persistence. At the same time, school populations have become increasingly diverse. Children today need the types of social and emotional skills that allow them to value and get along well with peers from a wide variety of backgrounds. These competencies include *prosocial* skills such as the ability to cooperate, demonstrate caring, and resolve conflicts with peers (Shonkoff & Philips 2000).

Martha B. Bronson is retired from Boston College, where she was a professor of developmental and educational psychology.

Developmental tasks for kindergartners

As kindergartners, children are expected to regulate their emotions and behavior appropriately under most circumstances. They are expected to be able to delay, defer, and accept substitutions for their preferred goals without becoming aggressive or disorganized by frustration. They are also expected to cope well with high levels of arousal, whether due to challenges in the environment or to novel events (Sroufe 1995).

Kindergarten children are intensely interested in interacting with their peers.

Compared with younger children, kindergartners are typically more able to control their behavior and the way in which they express emotions as they interact with other people (Eisenberg, Fabes, & Losoya 1997). They are now capable of true internal control that uses rules, strategies, and plans to guide behavior (Kopp 1982). They internalize standards and are beginning to monitor their own actions (Schunk 1994). Kindergarten children are also starting to develop a conscience and may feel guilt when they violate internal standards (Hoffman 1982). As they approach age 6, they are more likely to act responsibly and to hold themselves accountable for their behavior (Whiting & Edwards 1988).

Kindergarten children are intensely interested in interacting with their peers. Success in establishing relationships with peers is a central issue during kindergarten, and children need to regulate their emotions and control their behavior in order to have age-appropriate interactions (Howes 1990; Maszk, Eisenberg, & Guthrie 1999). Children at 5 to 6 years old are developing a greater understanding of others' minds and emotions (Perner, Lang, & Kloo 2002) and are more able to interact cooperatively. They can use negotiation and reciprocity to settle disputes.

In addition to being more skilled at dealing with potential conflicts by sharing and taking turns, kindergarten children can use proactive strategies to organize, direct, and sustain interactions with others (Bronson 1994). These include making initial suggestions about what to do ("Let's pretend the baby has to go to the hospital"), continuing suggestions about how to proceed ("Now let's say the baby is all better and we take her home"), assigning roles or resources to the participants ("You take the thermometer and I'll use the stethoscope"), and laying out the rules or constraints of a proposed activity ("The doctor has to say it's okay for the baby to go home"). These proactive strategies allow children to have more complex interactions with fewer conflicts.

Impacts of diversity

As an increasingly diverse population of children enters kindergarten today, it is important for the development of social and emotional competence that all children be valued and treated with equal respect and consideration. By communicating often with parents, teachers can understand the values and expectations that parents and children bring with them to school. Teachers need to be especially careful to avoid stereotypes in language and behavior, and to intervene if children tease or reject others. Proactively, they can provide activities and discussions for children that help develop positive self-identity and teach them to value differences. It is also helpful to provide children with models, visual images, and play materials related to differing abilities and ethnic or cultural backgrounds.

The development of social and emotional competence

To understand the most effective ways to nurture social and emotional competence, it is necessary to understand how it develops. This section briefly describes major theoretical perspectives and related research on the development of this competence and its implications for teaching.

Biological roots of behavior

Some aspects of social behavior are universal across cultures and appear to be biologically based, pervasive, and long lasting (Kagan 1998). Examples in young children include a strong attachment to the mother or other primary

Martha B. Bronson

caregiver, a protest against separation from that caregiver, a fear of strangers, and a general sociability that is characteristic of humans as a species.

Environment affects young children's biology, too. Early socialization experiences can produce neurohormonal changes in the developing brain (Schore 1994). A variety of negative circumstances early in life—such as trauma, neglect, institutionalization, maternal depression, or poverty—have negative effects on brain development and behavior (Shore 1997). A young child's secure attachment to the primary caregiver seems necessary for the development of independence, self-regulation, successful interaction with peers, and positive prosocial behavior patterns (Eisenberg & Fabes 1992). A lack of responsive care or a separation from adult attachment figures seems to reduce brain development and lead to long-lasting cognitive and social problems, including a tendency toward violence (Perry 1996).

To some extent, *temperament* (personality characteristics that are consistent across situations and relatively stable over time) also appears to have biological roots and effects on social and emotional competence (Rothbart & Bates 1998). Temperament categories that are at least partially based in biology include *extraversion* (a tendency to approach others or display emotion), *fearfulness* (inhibited behavior or anxiety), *sociability/ adaptability* (affiliative behavior or agreeableness), *irritability* (showing negative emotion or distress), and *effortful control* (length of attention span or persistence). All have a bearing on the development of emotional and social competence.

Characteristics that are attributed to temperament, however, develop through interactions with the environment, and so are somewhat modifiable. The warmth, sensitivity, and socialization methods of a child's family make a significant difference in how that child's biological temperament is expressed in behavior (Rothbart & Bates 1998). Temperamental differences in emotionality and attention regulation contribute to the development of prosocial behavior and empathy in children but are not thought to be the major determinants of those positive behaviors (Eisenberg & Fabes 1998).

In the human species, there is a major shift in brain development between the ages of 5 and 7 (Barkley 1997)—a period that begins in the kindergarten year. During this time, children develop better self-control and are able to behave in more reliable and responsible ways. While they are not as independent of adults and ready for external demands as older primary school children are, they are generally cooperative and ready for social and cognitive challenges within their range of capabilities.

Psychoanalytic theory

The primary goals of psychoanalytic theory are to describe emotional development and the conditions that lead to emotional health or problems. From the psychoanalytic perspective, competence, control of emotional impulses, and positive relationships with others are enhanced as a child develops *ego strength*. "Ego" is the name Sigmund Freud (1920, 1923) gave to a part of the mind that he believed channeled basic biological drives into socially acceptable goals and behaviors. In more recent portrayals, the ego is described as more proactive and independent, and less driven by biology (Erikson 1963; White 1959, 1960). A strong ego is considered necessary for developing social and emotional competence.

Psychoanalytic theory tells us that the ego is strengthened when a child is successful in coping with the social and physical world and feels competent and accepted by others (Block & Block 1980). A strong ego is also associated with warm and responsive relationships with caregivers, including teachers (Sroufe 1995). From this perspective, it is important to have warm and responsive teachers who provide children with opportunities to be successful in the classroom setting.

Theorists in the psychoanalytic tradition have also suggested that fantasy or pretend play can help children "work through" difficult emotions (Breger 1973). They suggest that this form of play can help children develop self-regulation (Sroufe, Cooper, & Dehart 1996), and that adults can help by arranging social and physical environments so that children are rarely in situations beyond their control.

Behavioral theory

Behaviorists such as B.F. Skinner (1974) focus on ways in which the social and physical environments shape behavior through rewards and punishments. Behaviorists break down social competence into specific strategies and behaviors that promote successful social interaction and that can be taught. For behaviorists, a child's goal is to obtain social or material rewards. He learns to use certain strategies that are likely to obtain those rewards, and to avoid other strategies that have negative consequences.

For instance, children learn to assess the value of different rewards ("If I grab Jim's truck, I'll have the truck [immediate reward]; if I don't grab the truck, Jim will stay and play with me [long-term reward]"). They learn to choose goals that are appropriate to the setting and to their individual level of skill. Children also learn to give themselves previously learned instructions ("I'm not supposed to run inside") or follow instructions given by others, and to monitor their own performance, noticing both their successes and mistakes.

Social learning theory

Social learning theory focuses on the power of learning from observing others. Even young children can acquire positive behaviors from seeing others rewarded for those behaviors. They can learn what *not* to do by observing others perform actions that have negative or punishing consequences. Peers, parents, and other adults who are significant in children's lives are powerful models for them.

Social learning theorists also argue that as children grow older, they are more able to praise and blame themselves. These *self-evaluations* become more powerful for children than external rewards and punishments are. From this theoretical perspective, self-evaluation is the basis for self-regulated behavior (Bandura 1977, 1997). During early childhood, children gradually develop internal *performance standards* from their own experiences of being rewarded or punished and from observing others. These standards become the basis of their self-evaluation. Kindergar-

ten children can monitor their own behavior and are beginning to make judgments about their activities and products.

From the social learning theory perspective, it is vital that kindergarten children have good models in important areas of competence to observe and learn from, and that children develop accurate and appropriate performance standards by seeing competence rewarded in themselves and in others. Performance standards must also be relevant to a child's age and skills. If the standards are too high, the child will not be able to meet them and may feel bad about herself; if they are too low, the child may not be sufficiently challenged.

Cognitive developmental theory

Cognitive developmental theorists Jean Piaget (Piaget & Inhelder 1969) and Lev Vygotsky (1978) draw attention to the relationship between cognitive development and social and emotional competence. Both assume that children have an innate interest in understanding and influencing the world around them, and propose that children *construct* an understanding of aspects of their social and physical surroundings. Both also assume that children construct such understandings through active interaction with others and with their physical environment. While Piaget focuses more on the individual child's active experimentation, Vygotsky emphasizes the role of the social environment and culture.

Piaget, Vygotsky, and other cognitive developmentalists consider that children's interactions with peers are significant in both social and cognitive development. Piaget suggests that conflicts and negotiations with peers help children recognize that others have different perspectives from their own, challenge them to rethink their own positions, and may enable them to reach a higher level of understanding. When children work together to solve problems they are more likely to reach a higher level of knowledge than when they are working alone (Azmitia 1988). Moreover, interactions with friends are more likely to promote social-emotional and cognitive growth, because friends tend to talk freely and challenge

Martha B. Bronson

each other's thoughts and actions more than non-friends do (Azmitia & Montgomery 1993).

Vygotsky sees interactions with others as essential for the development of social skills, cognitive skills, and self-regulation. Interactions with adults and more experienced peers help children "co-construct" and internalize the mental tools that allow them to develop higher levels of functioning. Interactions with peers allow them to engage in joint regulation with others. Interactive dramatic play (*sociodramatic* play) is especially helpful, because children can practice both regulating and being regulated by peers (Vygotsky 1977). The roles and rules of sociodramatic play are particularly effective in supporting self-regulation. Within a pretend role, children can often regulate their activities in a more advanced way than they could without those constraints. The role supports, or *scaffolds,* self-regulation at a level higher than the child can reach without the role. High levels of sociodramatic play are connected to self-regulatory behaviors (Elias & Berk 2002).

Vygotsky also emphasizes the role of language. A child internalizes the instructions given by others and begins to give herself directions ("I have to wash my hands"). Such self-guiding speech is seen in children by the time they are 3 to 5 years old (Berk 1994). Children usually say these *self-directions* aloud in kindergarten. However, by the age of 6 or 7, they learn to think the directions as "private speech" without speaking them aloud. This self-direction supports an increased delay of gratification (Mischel, Shoda, & Rodriguez 1989) and self-control (Kopp 1982).

Supporting the development of competence in kindergarten

Now let us consider how the important adults in children's lives can support their social and emotional development. We will look at the three basic areas in that development: the ability (1) to form and sustain social relationships, (2) to regulate emotions and behavior, and (3) to cooperate in a prosocial manner with others and with the rules of school and society.

Development of social interaction skills

Children learn how to interact with others from their early close relationships. A child's attachment to a caregiver and the caregiver's loving interest and involvement with the child influence the child's sense of self and interactions with others (Bronfenbrenner 1990). Adults also provide models and verbal guidelines that greatly influence children's social interest and understanding, their social involvement, and their interaction patterns and styles.

> Children's interactions with peers are significant in both social and cognitive development.

Socially competent, popular children tend to have parents who believe that social skills are important and actively try to foster those skills. These parents are warm, interested in feelings, and more likely to use reasoning and explanations to encourage their children's compliance (Hart, Ladd, & Burleson 1990). When a child makes social mistakes or is aggressive, these parents tend to attribute such behaviors to changeable factors such as fatigue or stress rather than to the child's innate disposition (Rubin, Mills, & Rose-Krasnor 1989). Poorly regulated and aggressive children are more likely to have parents who use power-assertive or inconsistent discipline strategies. These parents are also more likely to be either rejecting or permissive and indulgent, and to fail to supervise their children adequately (Rubin, Stewart, & Chen 1995).

Peers play an important role in the development of social competence, but mere exposure to peers is not enough (Clarke-Stewart, Gruber, & Fitzgerald 1994). Socially competent children are more likely to have parents who provide opportunities for them to interact with peers and who coach them in how to interact successfully (Pettit & Mize 1993). Children who participate in positive social interactions with peers develop more advanced social skills and effective strategies for communicating with peers (Strayer 1989). Too much peer dependence may be a cause for concern, however, because adults are better sources of guidance for children than peers are (Katz & McClellan 1997).

What the kindergarten teacher can do. Children who have warm, positive attachments to their kindergarten teachers are more likely to do well in school (Birch & Ladd 1997). When a teacher is warm, caring, and responsive to children's interests and feelings, he creates an atmosphere that fosters social development. Children are more likely to use such a teacher as their model, and the teacher is more likely to elicit their compliance and cooperation. When children can rely on the teacher to care about them as individuals, validate their interests and feelings, and support their efforts to regulate themselves, they are more likely to develop trust and to feel secure and ready to interact confidently with the social and physical environment.

Teachers must be careful to show a positive attitude toward *all* children, though, because kindergartners notice when an adult likes or dislikes particular children. Children may also model a teacher's attitudes and interaction styles, so it is important that the teacher exhibit values and behaviors that are desirable for them to imitate, such as a belief in the importance of social interaction; interest in others; and respect for their ideas, points of view, and emotions.

Because interactions with peers are critical for social learning, teachers must make sure to provide children ample time and opportunities for those interactions, such as space, materials, and encouragement for sociodramatic play, cooperative work and problem-solving activities, conversations, and group discussions. They should also help children who need social assistance to find play partners and should teach children proactive strategies for entering and participating in social activities. Part of a teacher's role is to monitor children's social activities and provide positive ways of solving problems, settling disputes, and keeping interactions fair and inclusive, without interfering unnecessarily. He also models and teaches the use of language to communicate ideas and emotions and to negotiate differences.

> Kindergarten children are mature enough to participate in discussions about classroom problems, and they can help generate ideas about possible solutions.

Development of emotional and behavioral control

The development of emotional and behavioral control is part of the development of *self-regulation*—the ability to control and direct emotions, behavior, attention, and thinking (Bronson 2000). A child with a secure attachment to her mother or other primary caregiver is better able to regulate emotions (Saarni 1999). Parents help a child develop emotional and behavioral control by modeling appropriate control, helping the child understand and cope with emotions, and fostering the development of independent self-regulated action (Bronson 2000).

Guidance methods are important. A balance of warmth and firm, consistent guidance that is appropriate to a child's age and understanding supports the development of the child's self-control. A collaborative approach that considers the goals of all parties concerned also supports self-regulation (Crockenberg, Jackson, & Langrock 1996). When a child's compliance is coerced by means of external rewards, punishments, or physical force, it undermines the development of her internal control (Lepper 1983). Giving reasons for directions and rules helps children understand and internalize the constraints.

Adults can also help children develop emotional control by talking to them about feelings (Dunn & Brown 1991). Words help children label what they are feeling, and discussions help them understand and cope with emotions. Words can help children understand, for instance, the difference between the feeling of anger and what they do about that feeling. Adults can also help children think about what others might be feeling.

The ways in which adults organize the environment affect children's ability to exercise control. Children are more likely to learn to control their own behaviors and to be effective problem solvers in social or cognitive situations if they are

Martha B. Bronson

given a considerable amount of choice and control over their own activities (Deci & Ryan 1985). Choices should be appropriate for the child's age and skills. It is also important to minimize sources of frustration, overstimulation, and stress in the environment that might be more than children can handle.

What the kindergarten teacher can do. Children who have warm, secure relationships with their teachers exhibit fewer behavior problems (Howes & Ritchie 1998). A teacher provides basic support for children's control over emotions and behavior by creating a safe, warm, and supportive atmosphere that enables them to feel secure and capable of emotional control. When necessary, a teacher can help children maintain self-control, and provide language that children can internalize and use for self-guidance in the future. She also can help children understand the relationship between their goals and the behavior strategies they use to reach those goals.

When a child's control fails, the teacher's reactions should focus on problem solving and on appropriate alternative behaviors—not on punishment. Children then become aware of making choices and using more effective strategies another time, rather than just curbing their behaviors when they might get caught and punished.

Guidelines for children's behavior should be simple, clear, and consistent and include rationales so they can understand that rules are designed to help and protect them. Kindergarten children are mature enough to participate in discussions about classroom problems, and they can help generate ideas about possible solutions. Such discussions help children understand why guidelines are necessary and give them a sense of control and responsibility.

Kindergarten teachers can also discuss emotions with children. Children can learn to talk about what they and others are feeling, possible causes for the feelings, and what might be done about them ("How do you think he felt when you wouldn't let him be in the game? How could you make him feel better?"). Talking about emotions separates emotions from action and allows children to reflect and to exercise more self-control.

Given the importance of sociodramatic play in developing self-regulation, teachers should arrange the classroom schedule and environment so there is time and material support for such play. Guidelines for the use of the environment should clarify what is expected of the children and not require the teacher to mediate disputes. For instance, guidelines might specify how many children are permitted in a specific area and how they are to take turns with materials. Self-control and self-direction are supported when children understand that they are expected to regulate many of their activities independently.

Development of prosocial behavior and attitudes

Relating to others provides a social context that supports children's internalization of the rules and values in their world (Sroufe 1995). A warm and responsive relationship between parents and children may be the most important promoter of prosocial behavior (Zahn-Waxler et al. 1992). When important people in children's lives model prosocial attitudes and behaviors, it is a powerful way of teaching them. With young children, altruistic actions may be more effective than words (Zahn-Waxler et al. 1992).

Adults are more likely to foster prosocial behavior if they provide clear and explicit rules of social behavior ("You don't kick people") with clearly described consequences ("If you kick Mary it will hurt her"). Young children are not likely to internalize simple prohibitions ("No!" "Stop it!") as guidelines. Adults should express strong feeling about rules related to behavior that affects others, so children appreciate the rules' importance (Hoffman 1983).

It is also important that adults attribute prosocial qualities to the child. When children are frequently told that they are "helpful," "generous," or "kind," they internalize these attributions and try to exhibit them in the future (Zahn-Waxler et al. 1992). Positive attributions also help children understand that motivation and control of social behavior come from inside themselves, and that they are responsible for their actions.

What the kindergarten teacher can do. Children who have warm and supportive teachers demonstrate greater prosocial behavior, empathy, self-regulation, and social competence (Eisenberg & Fabes 1998). Teachers strengthen children's prosocial tendencies when they model prosocial behaviors; call attention to prosocial statements made by children; give explicit instructions about helping, sharing, and like behaviors; and reward these behaviors when they occur (Eisenberg & Mussen 1989). It is also important that teachers monitor children's interactions in the classroom, because peers can model both negative and positive behaviors. Indirect methods of supervising peer interaction, such as *stage setting* (providing time, space, materials, and arrangements of materials for positive and appropriate interactions) and *coaching* (suggesting positive social interaction and problem-solving strategies as needed in the context of ongoing interactions between children) are useful (Hoffman 1983).

In addition to creating a warm, responsive emotional climate, teachers can model prosocial attitudes by interpreting social situations in ways that show sympathy and caring. For example, when a teacher responds to an accident by saying, "Oh, Jane's paint spilled; let's help her clean it up," children learn to be sympathetic and helpful to others. Modeling caring behaviors accompanied by a general prosocial lesson ("We must help people who are hurt") promotes these attitudes in children.

As with all other aspects of social competence, guidance strategies are important. Kindergarten children are beginning to understand the feelings of others, and they are more likely to develop prosocial dispositions when their teacher connects behaviors with consequences ("He is sad because you wouldn't let him play the game with you") and rules with reasons ("We don't push others on the steps because somebody might fall"). Teachers can also encourage cooperative interactions by suggesting sharing, taking turns, or other ways of negotiating disputes.

Encouraging children to take responsibility for tasks that serve the classroom community also helps to promote prosocial attitudes. When teachers expect children to contribute to the common good, the children internalize these expectations.

The lasting importance of social and emotional competence

Social and emotional competence matters a great deal in school and in life. A lack of adequate skill in any of the three areas that are basic to overall competence has pervasive and long-lasting consequences. These skill areas are:

The ability to form and sustain relationships with others. This skill is central to a child's social development and preparedness for school. Positive social interactions with peers are also related to positive attitudes toward school and learning (Ladd & Price 1987). Conversely, a lack of social skills is associated with aggressive or withdrawn behaviors (Rubin, Stewart, & Chen 1995) and with isolation from or rejection by peers (Dodge et al. 1986).

Many children make significant gains in social competence during the preschool period. But children who are rejected by their peers in kindergarten and the early elementary school years are more likely to have long-term problems. A lack of peer interaction skills and peer acceptance during kindergarten and primary school is related to difficulties in establishing peer relationships in the middle childhood years, which in turn predicts adjustment in adulthood (Achenback & Edelbrock 1991). Rejected children are more likely to do poorly at school (Wentzel & Asher 1995), to have problems with the law as early as adolescence (Kupersmidt & Coie 1990), and to experience psychological problems as adults (Cowen et al. 1973).

The ability to regulate the expression of emotions and inhibit negative behaviors. This skill is highly valued in the school setting (Alexander & Entwisle 1988). With age and experience, children become more able to control their emotions and behavior, and a large body of research relates emotional self-regulation to social acceptance (Eisenberg & Fabes 1992). Social competence is also associated with behavior control and low levels of problem behavior (Caspi 1998).

Martha B. Bronson

Early control is related to later control, and, as is the case with peer acceptance, emotional control in childhood predicts emotional control in adulthood (Sroufe, Carlson, & Shulman 1993).

The ability to cooperate with others and with the rules of school and society. This skill is highly valued by parents and teachers. Teachers of young children have always valued positive and cooperative behavior (Pallas et al. 1987) and the ability to follow classroom rules and adult requests (Reynolds 1991). Recently there has been a surge of interest in fostering prosocial skills in order to cope with the growing number of serious conduct problems in schools (Gartrell 2004). Research relates prosocial behaviors such as cooperation to both social competence (Katz & McClellan 1997) and peer acceptance (Howes 1988). Preschool, kindergarten, and elementary school children with strong prosocial dispositions also are more likely to be well adjusted, good at coping, and self-controlled (Eisenberg & Mussen 1989).

Clearly, fostering social and emotional competence is and should be a primary goal in the kindergarten classroom. Teachers need to understand the various aspects of social and emotional competence, and what nourishes their development. They need developmentally appropriate goals and standards for such competence, which should be taken as seriously as the goals and standards for academic competence. Teachers must have appropriate ways of evaluating social and emotional competence that focus on observing children's behaviors in social interactions in the natural settings of the classroom and playground. Given the enormous importance of social and emotional competence for success in school and in life, there is no aspect of the teacher's role in the kindergarten year more important than promoting this competence.

References

Achenback, T.M., & C. Edelbrock. 1991. *National survey of the problems and competencies among four- to sixteen-year-olds.* Monographs of the Society for Research in Child Development, vol. 56, no. 3, serial no. 225. Chicago: University of Chicago Press.

Alexander, K.L., & D.R. Entwisle. 1988. *Achievement in the first two years of school: patterns and processes.* Monographs of the Society for Research in Child Development, vol. 53, no. 2, serial no. 218. Chicago: University of Chicago Press.

Anderson, S., & S. Messick. 1974. Social competence in young children. *Developmental Psychology* 10: 282–93.

Azmitia, M. 1988. Peer interaction and problem solving: When are two heads better than one? *Child Development* 59: 87–96.

Azmitia, M., & R. Montgomery. 1993. Friendship, transitive dialogues, and the development of scientific reasoning. *Social Development* 2: 202–21.

Bandura, A. 1977. *Social learning theory.* Englewood Cliffs, NJ: Prentice Hall.

Bandura, A. 1997. *Self-efficacy: The exercise of control.* New York: W.H. Freeman.

Barkley, R.A. 1997. *ADHD and the nature of self control.* New York: Guilford.

Berk, L.E. 1994. Why children talk to themselves. *Scientific American* 271: 78–83.

Birch, S.H., & G.W. Ladd. 1997. The teacher-child relationship and children's early school adjustment. *Journal of School Psychology* 35: 61–79.

Block, J.H., & J. Block. 1980. The role of ego-control and ego-resiliency in the organization of behavior. In *Minnesota Symposia on Child Psychology, Vol. 13: Development of cognition, affect, and social relations,* ed. W.A. Collins, 39–101. Minneapolis: University of Minnesota Press.

Breger, L. 1973. *From instinct to identity.* Englewood Cliffs, NJ: Prentice Hall.

Bronfenbrenner, U. 1990. Who cares for children? *Research and Clinical Center for Child Development* 12: 27–40.

Bronson, M.B. 1994. The usefulness of an observational measure of children's social and mastery behaviors in early childhood classrooms. *Early Childhood Research Quarterly* 9: 19–43.

Bronson, M.B. 2000. *Self-regulation in early childhood.* New York: Guilford.

Caspi, A. 1998. Personality development across the life span. In *Handbook of child psychology, Vol. 3: Social, emotional, and personality development,* 5th ed., ed. N. Eisenberg, 311–88). New York: Wiley.

Clark-Stewart, A., C.P. Gruber, & L.M. Fitzgerald. 1994. *Children at home in day care.* Hillsdale, NJ: Erlbaum.

Cowen, E.L., A. Pedersen, H. Babigian, L.D. Izzo, & M.A. Trost. 1973. Long-term follow-up of early detected vulnerable children. *Journal of Consulting and Clinical Psychology* 41: 438–46.

Crockenberg, S., S. Jackson, & A.M. Langrock. 1996. Autonomy and goal attainment: Parenting, gender, and children's social competence. In *Children's autonomy, social competence, and interactions with adults and other children: Exploring connections and consequences,* ed. M. Killen, 41–55. New Directions for Child Development, no. 73. San Francisco: Jossey-Bass.

Deci, E.L., & R.M. Ryan. 1985. *Intrinsic motivation and self-determination in human behavior.* New York: Plenum.

Dodge, K.A., G.S. Pettit, C.L. McClasky, & M.M. Brown. 1986. *Social competence in children.* Monographs of the Society for Research in Child Development, vol. 51, no. 2, serial no. 213. Chicago: University of Chicago Press.

Dunn, J., & J. Brown. 1991. Relationships, talk about feelings, and the development of affect regulation in early childhood. In *The development of emotion regulation and dysregulation,* eds. J. Garber & K.A. Dodge, 89–109. New York: Cambridge University Press.

Eisenberg, N., & P.H. Mussen. 1989. *The roots of prosocial behavior in children.* Cambridge, UK: Cambridge University Press.

Eisenberg, N., & R.A. Fabes. 1992. Emotion, regulation, and the development of social competence. In *Review of personality and social psychology, Vol. 14: Emotion and social behavior,* ed. M.S. Clark. Newbury Park, CA: Sage.

Eisenberg, N., & R.A. Fabes. 1998. Prosocial development. In *Handbook of child psychology, Vol. 3: Social, emotional, and personality development,* 5th ed., ed. N. Eisenberg, 701–78. New York: Wiley.

Eisenberg, N., R.A. Fabes, & S. Losoya. 1997. Emotional responding: Regulation, social correlates, and socialization. In *Emotional development and emotional intelligence: Educational implications,* eds. P. Salovey & D. Sluyter, 129–63. New York: Basic.

Elias, C.L., & L.E. Berk. 2002. Self-regulation in young children: Is there a role for sociodramatic play? *Early Childhood Research Quarterly* 17 (2): 216–38.

Erikson, E.H. 1963. *Childhood and society.* New York: Norton.

Freud, S. 1920. *General introduction to psychoanalysis.* New York: Washington Square.

Freud, S. 1923. *The ego and the id.* London: Hogarth.

Gartrell, D. 2004. *The power of guidance: Teaching social-emotional skills in early childhood classrooms.* Clifton Park, NY: Delmar Learning.

Hart, C.H., G.W. Ladd, & B.R. Burleson. 1990. Children's expectations of the outcomes of social strategies: Relations with sociometric status and maternal disciplinary styles. *Child Development* 61: 127–37.

Hoffman, M.L. 1982. Development of prosocial motivation: Empathy and guilt. In *Development of prosocial behavior,* ed. N. Eisenberg, 281–313. New York: Academic Press.

Hoffman, M.L. 1983. Affective and cognitive processes in moral internalization. In *Social cognition and social development: A sociocultural perspective,* eds. E.T. Higgins, D.N. Ridale, & W.W. Hartup, 236–74. Cambridge, UK: Cambridge University Press.

Howes, C. 1988. *Peer interaction of young children.* Monographs of the Society for Research in Child Development, vol. 53, no. 1, serial no. 217. Chicago: University of Chicago Press.

Howes, C. 1990. Social status and friendship from kindergarten to third grade. *Journal of Applied Developmental Psychology* 11: 321–30.

Howes, C., & S. Ritchie. 1998. Changes in teacher-child relationships in a therapeutic preschool. *Early Education and Development* 4: 411–22.

Kagan, J. 1998. Biology and the child. In *Handbook of child psychology, Vol. 3: Social, emotional, and personality development,* 5th ed., ed. N. Eisenberg, 177–235. New York: Wiley.

Katz, L.G., & D.E. McClellan. 1997. *Fostering children's social competence: The teacher's role.* Washington, DC: NAEYC.

Kopp, C.B. 1982. Antecedents of self-regulation: A developmental perspective. *Developmental Psychology* 18: 119–214.

Kupersmidt, J., & J.D. Coie. 1990. Preadolescent peer status, aggression, and school adjustment as predictors of externalizing problems in adolescence. *Child Development* 61: 1350–62.

Ladd, G.W., & J.M. Price. 1987. Predicting children's social and school adjustment following the transition from preschool to kindergarten. *Child Development* 58: 1168–89.

Lepper, M.R. 1983. Social control processes and the internalization of social values: An attributional perspective. In *Social cognition and social development: A sociocultural perspective,* eds. E.T. Higgins, D.N. Ruble, & W.W. Hartup, 294–330. Cambridge, UK: Cambridge University Press.

Maszk, P., N. Eisenberg, & I.K. Guthrie. 1999. Relations of children's social status to their emotionality and regulation: A short-term longitudinal study. *Merrill-Palmer Quarterly* 45 (3): 468–92.

Mischel, W., Y. Shoda, & M.L. Rodriguez. 1989. Delay of gratification in children. *Science* 244: 933–38.

Pallas, A.M., D.R. Entwisle, K.C. Alexander, & D. Cadigan. 1987. Children who do exceptionally well in first grade. *Sociology of Education* 60: 256–71.

Perner, J., B. Lang, & D. Kloo. 2002. Theory of mind and self-control: More than a common problem of inhibition. *Child Development* 73 (3): 752–67.

Perry, B.D. 1996. Incubated in terror: Neurodevelopmental factors in the "cycle of violence." In *Children in a violent society,* ed. J.D. Osofsky, 124–49. New York: Guilford.

Pettit, G.S., & J. Mize. 1993. Substance and style: Understanding the ways in which parents teach about social relationships. In *Learning about relationships,* ed. S. Duck, 118–51. Newbury Park, CA: Sage.

Piaget, J., & B. Inhelder. 1969. *The psychology of the child.* New York: Basic.

Reynolds, A.J. 1991. Early schooling of children at risk. *American Educational Research Journal* 28: 392–422.

Rothbart, M.K., & J.E. Bates. 1998. Temperament. In *Handbook of child psychology, Vol. 3: Social, emotional, and personality development,* 5th ed., ed. N. Eisenberg, 105–76. New York: Wiley.

Rubin, K.H., R.S. Mills, & L.R. Rose-Krasnor. 1989. Maternal beliefs and children's social competence. In *Social competence in developmental perspective,* eds. B. Schneider, G. Attili, J. Nadel, & R. Weissberg, 313–31. Boston: Klewer Academic.

Rubin, K.H., S. Stewart, & X. Chen. 1995. Parents of aggressive and withdrawn children. In *Handbook of Parenting,* Vol. 1, ed. M.H. Bornstein, 255–23. New York: Plenum.

Saarni, C. 1999. *The development of emotional competence.* New York: Guilford.

Schore, A.N. 1994. *Affect regulation and the origin of the self: The neurobiology of emotional development.* Hillsdale, NJ: Erlbaum.

Schunk, D.H. 1994. Self-regulation of self-efficacy and attributions in academic settings. In *Self-regulation of learning and performance: Issues and educational implications,* eds. D.H. Schunk & B.J. Zimmerman, 75–100. Hillsdale, NJ: Erlbaum.

Shonkoff, J.P., & D.A. Phillips, eds. 2000. *From neurons to neighborhoods: The science of early childhood development.* Washington, DC: National Academies Press.

Shore, R. 1997. *Rethinking the brain: New insights into early development.* New York: Families and Work Institute.

Skinner, B.F. 1974. *About behaviorism.* New York: Knopf.

Sroufe, L.A. 1995. *Emotional development: The organization of emotional life in the early years.* Cambridge, UK: Cambridge University Press.

Sroufe, L.A., E. Carlson, & S. Schulman. 1993. Individuals in relationships: Development from infancy through adolescence. In *Studying lives through time: Personality and development,* eds. D.C. Funder, R.D. Parke, C. Tomlinson-Keasey, & K. Widaman, 315–42. Washington, DC: American Psychological Association.

Sroufe, L.A., R. Cooper, & G. DeHart. 1996. *Child development: Its nature and course,* 3d ed. New York: McGraw-Hill.

Strayer, F.F. 1989. Co-adaptation within the early peer group: A psychobiological study of competence. In *Social competence in developmental perspective,* eds. B. Schneider, G. Attili, J. Nadel, & R. Weissberg, 145–74. Boston: Klewer Academic.

Vygotsky, L.S. 1977. Play and its role in the mental development of the child. In *Soviet developmental psychology,* ed. M. Cold. White Plains, NY: M.E. Sharp.

Vygotsky, L.S. 1978. *Mind in society: The development of higher psychological processes.* Cambridge, MA: Harvard University Press.

Wentzel, K.R., & S.R. Asher. 1995. The academic lives of neglected, rejected, popular and controversial children. *Child Development* 66: 754–63.

White, R.W. 1959. Motivation reconsidered: The concept of competence. *Psychological Bulletin* 104: 36–52.

White, R.W. 1960. Competence and the psychosexual stages of development. In *Nebraska Symposium on Motivation,* Vol. 8, ed. M.R. Jones, 97–141. Lincoln: University of Nebraska Press.

Whiting, B.B., & C.P. Edwards. 1988. *Children of different worlds: The formation of social behavior.* Cambridge, MA: Harvard University Press.

Zahn-Waxler, C., M. Radke-Yarrow, E. Wagner, & M. Chapman. 1992. Development of concern for others. *Developmental Psychology* 28: 126–37.

Martha B. Bronson

Part III

Teaching, Curriculum, and Assessment in Kindergarten

Teaching in the Kindergarten Year

6

Cate Heroman & Carol Copple

Kindergarten has the potential to be a wonderful year in a child's life. For some children, it is their first experience in "school"; for others, it is the bridge between preschool and "big" school. Kindergarten teachers have a unique opportunity. The decisions they make about their program will convey positive messages about school to the children and their families and will help children lay a solid foundation for future learning—or they will not. In the following vignette, consider how the teacher in this kindergarten classroom supports children's success:

> Walking into the classroom, you see children engaged in different tasks and projects, working purposefully with a variety of materials and cooperating with other children. Individuals and small groups are seated throughout the room, at tables, in centers, and on the rug in the meeting area. The teacher interacts with children individually and in groups, commenting on what she observes and asking occasional questions. As she finds out more about what the children think and know, she is able to build on and help them extend their ideas and language. You see evidence of learning as you watch and listen to children and see the interesting work they do, examples of which are

Cate Heroman is director of preschool and kindergarten initiatives at Teaching Strategies, Inc. Carol Copple is in the professional development division of the National Association for the Education of Young Children (NAEYC).

respectfully displayed. Images familiar to the children's culture and community can be seen throughout the room.

> The class schedule, posted at children's eye level, includes time for music and movement, outdoor play, snack, and lunch—all important opportunities for children to develop physically and learn healthy habits. Posted by the door is a schedule for family conferences, a place to sign up to volunteer in the classroom, and a copy of the most recent newsletter to families. A parent volunteer is reading with some children on the rug in the meeting area. You can see that families play a pivotal role in supporting their children's development and learning at school. Children's comments let you know that they look forward to coming to school each day.

This is a high-quality program because this teacher is an effective decision maker. At the core of her decision making are three essential domains in which she has substantial knowledge and deep understanding: child development, content and standards, and instructional strategies. She understands child development—who children are and how they learn—and uses this knowledge to ensure reasonable expectations for children. She uses observation and other assessment strategies to learn about children as individuals—their interests, abilities, backgrounds, needs, language, and culture—so that she can individualize the program in ways that allow each child to be successful.

She is also familiar with all areas of the curriculum, that is, the key skills, concepts, and knowledge important for kindergarten children to acquire. In part, what children need to know and be able to do is identified in state standards and in the standards published by professional organizations in the various disciplines. These standards provide her with targets or learning goals so that she knows what she needs to accomplish with the children. In addition to the relevant standards and learning goals, this teacher knows the learning paths that children typically follow to reach these goals.

And finally, in her teaching repertoire she has effective instructional strategies that weave the knowledge base about child development with kindergarten standards and content knowledge in ways that are engaging, meaningful, and relevant to those children.

This chapter introduces curriculum and teaching in the kindergarten year at a general level (later chapters in this section address the major subject areas). It features six dimensions of teaching that serve as a framework for decision making for a high-quality kindergarten program.

Implementing curriculum in the kindergarten year

The *curriculum* consists of the knowledge and skills to be taught in the educational program and the plans for experiences through which learning will take place. The curriculum should reflect standards defining what children should know and be able to do in particular subject areas and grade levels. Kindergarten teachers today often are given a specified curriculum, which has been selected by their school, district, or state.

But kindergarten curricula can vary in numerous ways. They might be: locally developed or commercially published; comprehensive (including all subject areas and developmental areas) or focused on a single subject area (such as literacy); highly scripted (telling teachers exactly what to say and do) or flexible (allowing teachers to design or adapt activities and experiences); or com-

plete packages (including all books and materials), curriculum guides (requiring teachers to gather materials), or something between the two.

Fundamental to the teacher's work is having a curriculum that is clear, and then actually using it as a blueprint for classroom decision making. Implementing curriculum effectively means developing well-articulated, standards-based learning goals as well as plans for learning experiences through which these goals will be realized. Teachers also need to account for children's needs, interests, abilities, prior knowledge, and background (Bransford, Brown, & Cocking 2000).

To change, develop, or adapt a kindergarten curriculum to help children achieve the standards, a teacher's first step is to become familiar with that curriculum. Next, he looks at all of the experiences he provides or might provide during the course of a day through the lens of those standards. He asks himself, "What standards am I addressing? How does the curriculum address the standards? What adaptations do I need to make?" Later, this chapter will discuss ways to integrate standards from multiple subject areas.

Kindergarten teachers apply their core understandings of child development, content standards, and teaching strategies to the myriad decisions they make all day, every day, as they do their work. Effective teachers are thoughtful decision makers. This chapter describes six dimensions of teaching an effective kindergarten program (Jablon et al., in press; Bredekamp & Copple 1997). They cut across all areas of the curriculum to help ensure that curriculum is implemented in ways that foster children's success as learners:

(1) Knowing kindergartners in general, and the children of the specific classroom in particular

(2) Building a classroom community in the kindergarten

(3) Establishing a structure for the kindergarten classroom

(4) Guiding kindergarten children's learning

(5) Assessing children's learning in kindergarten

(6) Building a partnership with kindergarten families

Cate Heroman and Carol Copple

Knowing the children

Good teaching begins with knowing the learners— what they are like developmentally, individually, and culturally. When teachers know what kindergarten children are like *developmentally,* it means they are familiar with the typical social and emotional, physical, cognitive, and language characteristics of children at this age. This knowledge enables teachers to have reasonable expectations of what children in a class are likely capable of. To know children *individually* means to recognize that each child comes with unique needs, interests, abilities, language, temperament, prior experiences, and background knowledge. Teachers who know children *culturally* are sensitive to multiple perspectives and consider those perspectives as they make decisions about children's development and learning (Bredekamp & Copple 1997). To know children, effective teachers:

- Establish positive, personal relationships with each child
- Learn the developmental characteristics of kindergarten children and consider ways to be responsive in setting up the environment, structuring the day, and guiding and assessing children's learning
- Are flexible in adapting the curriculum to meet the needs of each child and the group as a whole
- Learn about the values, traditions, and expectations for behavior of the cultural groups represented in the classroom

For children of kindergarten age, the most important strategy for teachers is to form relationships with them. Because it is through relationships that teachers of young children can guide their learning and behavior.

Building a classroom community

People in a *community* share common interests and activities. Children in kindergarten come to the classroom from many different backgrounds and with a wide range of experiences. By creating a community of learners in the classroom, teachers establish common ground among all the children—ways in which the group can function successfully together. In building community, a teacher bases her decisions on the knowledge that young children learn best in the context of social relationships, and that they need to feel accepted, respected, and confident that their individuality is encouraged. Strategies that promote a sense of community include:

- Welcoming children into the room by labeling cubbies and hooks with their names
- Using class meetings to encourage group discussions, social problem solving, and sharing of ideas and information
- Bringing each child's home culture and language into the shared culture of the classroom
- Developing classroom rules with children
- Planning ways for children to work and play together collaboratively

Creating a community of learners in the classroom has a significant impact on how children work together, how they feel about school, and the relationships that are built with them as individuals and as a group.

Establishing a structure for the classroom

Establishing a *structure* includes creating the physical learning environment and organizing the day to be responsive to children's needs and to make the best use of time. The structure of the classroom has a powerful impact on how children learn.

Kindergarten straddles the worlds of preschool and elementary school. The children are not the same developmentally as first-graders, but they are more "grown up" than preschoolers. Teachers struggle with creating classrooms that are responsive to the developmental needs and potentials of kindergarten children and that support the learning outcomes that prepare children for the curriculum and accountability systems of the upper grades. Kindergarten classrooms look different from preschool or first grade classrooms in their complexity, the levels of responsibility that children assume, their use of symbolic representations, and their reflection of children's growing skills and abilities (Barbour & Seefeldt 1993).

Elements of an effective physical environment

Each kindergarten classroom will be different, first as teachers consider the space, furnishings, and materials available. Later the classroom will be shaped and reshaped as children's new interests and needs emerge. But all classrooms must have certain elements, regardless of their individual resources:

• A space for children to store their work and personal belongings—This space can be cubbies, storage bins, or baskets.

• A place for group meetings—The space should be large enough so children can sit comfortably, either on the floor or on benches, and see one another during conversations.

• A variety of spaces for working—This might mean carefully planned learning centers, a large table, and an open area on the floor. Spaces can be defined with dividers, storage units, and bookshelves. Moveable furnishings allow teachers to create big spaces for larger projects and cozier spaces for a few children to work, as needed.

• Quiet places—Young children need nooks and seating areas where they can get away or work quietly together with a friend or in a small group.

• Places to store materials—Organizing materials logically enables children to find them when needed and return them to their proper place afterward. Creating picture-word labels with the children helps them not only care for the classroom environment but also learn print concepts.

• Places to display children's work respectfully—When children's art and other work are displayed attractively, it conveys the message that what they do is important. Display also invites them to reflect on their work and expand their ideas.

Setting up learning centers

Kindergarten children thrive when they can work independently and cooperatively with a small group of peers. They are eager to practice and apply the skills they are learning, engage in conversations, and make choices about what they can do. Using centers to organize and manage the learning environment is a strategy attuned to who kindergarten children are and how they learn.

Learning centers offer children a powerful opportunity to develop independence, risk taking, perseverance, initiative, creativity, reasoning, and problem solving—the "learning to learn" skills.

Learning centers, when set up and used effectively, allow children to develop skills in multiple domains. In this vignette, notice the wide range of skills children are practicing and applying:

During center time three children decide they want to create their own board game. They go to various learning centers in the room to find the materials they need, and bring them back to a table. Their teacher observes, strategically posing questions to help them with their planning but careful not to interrupt their progress. They use Lego pieces for markers, create their own dice by drawing dots on small empty boxes, and design their game board on poster board. They write the words *Go, Stop here, Bonus,* and *You win,* as well as draw shapes and numbers, in the various spaces. When they do not know how to write a word or number, they refer to a chart or word wall in the room or ask a peer or the teacher. They create a rule book. For a timer, the teacher suggests they use a small empty water bottle and sand. Using a drawing program on the computer, they create play money and print it out. The children persist and return to the task for days until it is complete. When the game is ready, they play again and again and teach others how to play.

This example illustrates how a variety of skills and concepts in multiple learning domains were practiced and applied during purposeful play. (See the box on the next page for more examples of how children practice and use skills and concepts in play.) The three children were allowed to make their own choices. They used the learning centers to locate necessary resources but did not actually work in a particular center. The teacher played an important role in guiding their planning and learning. The activity included skills and concepts in all curriculum areas and enhanced the children's social, emotional, physical, cognitive, and language development. Moreover, problem solving, initiative, persistence, resourcefulness, and creativity had a role.

Learning centers can be used in various ways. During a designated choice time, children might choose their center and what they will do there.

Cate Heroman and Carol Copple

How a child practices and uses skills and concepts in play

Literacy
- Writes for a purpose
- Uses language to communicate
- Understands print concepts
- Writes letters and words
- Reads simple words

Mathematics
- Uses number concepts
- Develops mathematical language
- Makes predictions
- Creates two- and three-dimensional geometric shapes
- Measures time, money

Science
- Uses recycled materials
- Explores physical properties of materials

Social studies
- Develops rules with others and follows them
- Uses geographic thinking and mapping skills to move marker forward, backward
- Learns about money and its use

The arts
- Draws and creates

Technology
- Uses basic computer skills
- Navigates through software program

Some teachers include a "must do" or a required activity in the centers before opening them up for choice. In planning for learning centers, effective teachers:

- Consider space constraints in determining whether all centers will be used on a given day
- Are creative in thinking about new possibilities for locations of centers (for example, a rarely used teacher's desk might be converted into a learning center, using the drawers for storage, the sides for magnetic boards and flannel boards, and the cozy space underneath as an ideal place for children to work or read alone)
- Rotate or change the materials in the area if children are no longer interested or challenged and as the specific learning focus changes
- Make a popular area larger to accommodate more children, and reduce its size as interest wanes

Most kindergarten teachers have some basic learning centers that remain throughout the year. The box on the next page presents a basic list of centers and the types of materials they might include to support children's learning. Not all will be full-fledged centers set off from the rest of the room; some might be "materials hubs" or resource areas, where children go to find a game or set of materials then take these to a work space at a table or on the floor. For example, there might be an art resource area, but art experiences take place throughout the room.

Other learning centers are not so basic and might be set up depending on the available space, materials, and children's interests. Some of these might include centers for cooking, sensory experiences, sand/water play, games, investigating how things work (a "take-apart" center), and project-related activities.

Organizing the day

The daily schedule provides the framework for what teachers will do each day to help children develop and learn. Planning and organizing the day in a thoughtful, intentional way help teachers achieve their goals for children.

Young children feel secure when they know what happens next. They also gain a sense of time and sequence as they move from event to event. A predictable daily schedule helps kindergartners develop independence, responsibility, and a sense of order. Some of the predictable events likely to be a part of any daily schedule include whole-

Centers and the materials they might include

Learning center	Examples of materials
Books	Books of all genres (predictable, informational, poetry, narrative, wordless, decodable), listening center with books on tape or CDs, storytelling and retelling props (flannel boards, puppets, story clothesline)
Writing	Writing paper, envelopes, blank booklets, journals, pencils, pens, markers, word banks, letter stamps, alphabet cards
Mathematics and games	Collections of objects (buttons, stickers, erasers, bottle caps), number cards, interlocking cubes, parquetry blocks, attribute games, graphing mats, sorting trays, deck of cards, board games, dice
Science/discovery	Plants, class pets, nature objects, collections (shells, rocks, leaves, balls, shiny things), tools for investigating (magnifying glasses, magnets, funnels, lenses), science journals, clipboards
Music and movement	Collection of CDs, musical instruments, keyboard with headphones, picture songbooks, song cards (color-coded to correspond with colored instruments), props for movement (scarves, flags, streamers)
Art	Materials to paint and draw on (newsprint, butcher paper, finger paint paper, foil), painting and drawing implements (markers, crayons, paints, pens, pencils, charcoal, chalk), materials for molding and sculpting (clay, playdough, tools), cutting and pasting materials (scissors, paste, glue, collage materials) and materials for constructing (foam pieces, wood scraps, wire, pipe cleaners, recyclable materials), art books, photographs, posters
Dramatic play	Props and dress-up clothes, homelike materials reflecting children's culture (kitchen furniture, dolls, phone, message board, empty food containers), open-ended materials (large pieces of fabric, plastic tubing, cardboard boxes), literacy materials (magazines, books, pads of paper, cookbooks, junk mail), mathematics and science materials (calculators, kitchen and bathroom scales, calendars, cash registers, measuring cups and spoons, store coupons)
Blocks	Unit blocks, hollow blocks, props (people figures, vehicles, hats, animal figures), open-ended materials (cardboard tubes, cardboard panels, PVC pipes, vinyl rain gutters), literacy materials (writing tools and paper, signs, books about bridges and buildings)
Technology	Computers, printers, optional technology (Web cam, digital camera, scanners, computer microscopes)

Cate Heroman and Carol Copple

group times, small-group times, learning center time, and outdoor play. Routine events such as arrival, departure, rest, transitions between activities, and meals or snacks must also be included in the schedule. When developing a schedule, a teacher often must work around factors outside of her control. Besides beginning and ending times, these factors might include lunch; scheduled time for resource teachers; and special events such as field trips, visiting experts, school-wide events, and unexpected happenings.

Although a daily schedule helps children make sense of their day, it is not intended to be rigidly followed. If children are highly engaged in an activity, extending it for a while is a reasonable decision. Effective teachers also take cues from the children to gauge whether an activity is not working, and they make adjustments accordingly. In some districts and schools, teachers are required to adhere to a schedule specifying the times for each part of the curriculum. Sometimes activities and even what the teachers are to say are tightly scripted.

When is not the only question teachers must address in organizing the day. They must also do important planning for *what* will happen in their classrooms. Effective kindergarten teachers reflect on what they know about the children and make thoughtful decisions about the activities and experiences they will offer to help these children progress. Teachers make plans for meeting the needs of individual children, small groups of children, and the class as a whole. They also consider how they are going to address the numerous learning outcomes in the short time they have with children. An efficient and meaningful way of doing this is through integrating curriculum in projects/studies and units/themes, as discussed later in this chapter.

Guiding children's learning

Guiding children's learning takes place all day, every day, across all six dimensions of a teacher's work. While having a well-stocked, thoughtfully organized, and attractive classroom environment enhances the kindergarten program, it is only the beginning. The effective teacher motivates children, builds on their prior knowledge and strengths, and supports their learning using a variety of strategies to increase their skills, knowledge, and understandings.

In order to guide children's learning effectively, kindergarten teachers must be knowledgeable in three specific areas. First, they must understand the content of the various curriculum domains and the learning paths kindergartners typically follow in developing the relevant knowledge, skills, and understanding. Second, kindergarten teachers must know their specific children—what they are like as a group, as well as their individual needs, interests, learning styles, and cultures. And third, teachers must understand which methods work best given the characteristics of kindergarten children and the content to be learned. Knowledge in these three areas provides teachers with a mental roadmap to guide their planning, teacher-child interactions, and assessing.

Teacher-child interactions

Teacher-child conversations play an important role in shaping what children learn. It is through these conversations that the teacher *scaffolds* learning. This concept of effective teaching comes from the work of Lev Vygotsky (1978). Just as a carpenter uses a physical scaffold to work on a part of a building that is otherwise out of reach, the teacher provides varying levels of support to help children stretch to learn new concepts, skills, and understandings that are challenging but achievable (Copple and Bredekamp 2006). As children work to master a new skill or acquire a new understanding, the teacher gradually pulls back on the level of support (scaffolding) she offers. The box on the next page describes the varying levels of support one teacher offers after the classroom hamster goes missing.

This example incorporates several aspects of effective scaffolding of children's learning: The teacher motivates the children by seizing an opportunity to write for a purpose; she sets the context for learning and offers children multiple ways to learn, practice, and apply skills. She taps

Scaffolding in action

At their morning meeting, Ms. Ankersen tells the children that their hamster, Sparky, has escaped overnight. She asks, "What can we do to find Sparky?"

High level of teacher support	← Scaffolding →		Low level of teacher support
I do . . . you watch	**I do . . . you help**	**You do . . . I help**	**You do . . . I watch**
In morning meeting, the children and Ms. Ankersen discuss the problem and make plans for how to solve it. As she writes the children's ideas on a chart, she mentions using periods to let people know when to stop reading. She also talks about using capital letters to start a new sentence. She says that names are very special, so Sparky's name will begin with a capital letter, too.	The next day, the children dictate a "Missing Hamster" story to be read by the principal over the intercom during morning messages. Ms. Ankersen reminds the children that the periods and capital letters will help the principal know when one sentence ends and a new one begins. As she records their thoughts, she calls on various children to use the marker to make the period or the capital letter.	For the day's entry into their journals, the children write about the missing hamster. The children are at varying stages in their writing development. Ms. Ankersen makes occasional comments on their use of periods and capital letters and offers suggestions as she talks to them about their entries. To help them in spelling words, she draws their attention to the word walls, their own personal word banks, and other resources.	The children create signs at the writing center to post around the school about the missing hamster, one solution to the problem suggested at the morning meeting. Knowing that their messages will be read by others, they seek to write in a way that will be understood. They refer to the sign on Sparky's cage to make sure their spelling is correct and read their messages to Ms. Ankersen for affirmation.

into children's prior knowledge; all the children in the class are familiar with Sparky and help take care of him. These children also have participated in dictating stories, morning messages, group meetings, and journal writing as part of their daily activities. She demonstrates her knowledge of these kindergarten children; she knows where various children are in their writing development and the kind of support each is likely to need. She understands the content to be taught; she knows the developmental stages of writing and the conventions of print. Keeping her learning goals in mind, the teacher is intentional in guiding children's learning about print and in choosing which instructional strategies—conversations, discussions, modeling, or specific feedback—to use at what point. She observes children as they write and helps them reflect on their writing. She offers a safe, supportive environment to take risks.

As noted in earlier chapters, today's kindergartners come from a range of backgrounds, have differing needs, and because of age-eligibility differences, range in age from 4½ to 6 years old or more. Kindergarten teachers are most successful in supporting children's development and learning when they use a range of approaches to address the unique needs of each child in the classroom. No one approach works for all children and all occasions.

Using a variety of instructional strategies

In building a table or repairing a roof, no carpenter tries to do each part of the work with a single tool. Like competent carpenters, good teachers have many tools, or *instructional strategies,* in their tool belts. The best strategy to use at any given moment depends on the learning goal, the specific situation, and the individual child.

Cate Heroman and Carol Copple

The teacher chooses the strategy that will be most useful in the particular situation. Often she tries one strategy, sees that it does not work, and tries something else. What is important is to have a variety of strategies ready and to remain flexible and observant. Here are several of the many strategies teachers need to have at their disposal to do their jobs well (Copple & Bredekamp 2006):

Encourage. Offer comments or nonverbal actions that promote children's persistence and effort ("That wasn't easy, but you kept trying different things") rather than giving evaluative praise ("Good job").

Give specific feedback. Offer specific rather than general comment on the child's performance ("That's a *d*, Lily, not a *b*—it looks a lot like a *b* but it's turned the other way, see?").

Model. Display for children a skill or desirable way of behaving (whispering when you want the children to lower their own voices; modeling cooperation and problem solving by saying, "You both want to use the computer, so let's think about how you could use it together").

Create or add challenge. Generate a problem or add difficulty to a task so that it is just beyond what children already have mastered (once a child counts up to five items accurately, begin engaging him in counting sets of six to eight).

Give a cue, hint, or other assistance. Help children to work "on the edge" of their current competence (such as initially labeling cubbies with both picture and print labels, with the pictures to be removed later).

Provide information. Directly give children facts ("Birds make nests like this one to live in"), verbal labels ("This is a cylinder"), and other information.

Give directions. Provide specific instructions for children's action or behavior ("Move the mouse to this icon and click on it"; "Pour very slowly so we don't lose any of the liquid").

Teachers can and do use these strategies in any context. For instance, when children are engaging in an open-ended activity such as investigating at the water table, the teacher might choose to model a technique, provide information, or create challenges. Likewise, in a planned small or large group, the teacher might engage the children in open-ended thinking and use any of the instructional strategies in her repertoire.

Using a variety of learning contexts

Each part of the day offers opportunities to guide children's learning. Key learning contexts are whole group, small group, learning centers, and daily routines.

Whole group. Also called large group, group meeting, or circle time, whole group is ideal for class discussions, making plans, and sharing work. At whole-group gatherings during the day, opportunities are provided for children to learn and practice a variety of social and academic skills, such as speaking to a group about their experiences, listening to their classmates and responding appropriately with questions or comments, working cooperatively, and using and processing new information.

Small group. In a small-group setting, teachers can give children more focused attention than in a whole group. Children also have the opportunity to engage in conversations with peers and solve problems collaboratively. Teachers often use this format for planned, focused experiences in which they might introduce a new skill or concept or reinforce skills and concepts the children have recently encountered. Small-group experiences tend to take place during learning center time. Some children work with one adult in a small group while the others work more or less independently with the other adult available to them. Small groups vary in size, usually ranging from four to six children and might be formed based on a common interest or on a need as determined by assessment information.

> What is important is to have a variety of strategies ready and to remain flexible and observant.

Learning centers. For each center, the teacher carefully selects materials to support educational goals. The teacher's role is to observe what children are doing and respond when he sees opportunities to extend their exploration,

It is especially difficult in a linear culture to communicate the power of play as a nonlinear, dynamic, powerful network of relationships to learning. It is much easier for some adults to check off a list of boxes on standardized tests.

Parents and policy makers need labels for playful-looking activities that they can understand as significant, in their terms. It may be politic to advertise continuously what children *are* learning when they play and to interpret children's play, without calling it play. Alternative language such as "integrated learning experiences," "learning activities," "active study projects," "science experiments," "center time," "activity periods," and "work periods" may help. Parents and policy makers may also need more information about the power of play and "active learning" in early childhood. Below are some suggested responses when communicating with parents about their children's learning.

Q. What is my child learning in school?

Your child is having important experiences with the sciences, the social sciences, mathematics, literacy, and the arts. Many of the activities look like play and feel like play because he is an active learner.

Q. If children play, then how will you cover the curriculum?

Play is one powerful way in which children learn. Research tells us that play helps youngsters to improve their thinking skills, social skills, language skills, and problem-solving skills. We plan events in school that integrate the full range

of school learning, and include play as well as other ways that children learn. For example, our curriculum emphasizes playful activities in the sciences and the social sciences. Each part of the program builds in literacy and number skills that make sense to the children because they need to draw, read, write, and measure in order to solve real problems that have meaning to them. We usually do much more than the minimal state curriculum expectations.

Q. How are you preparing my child for the rigors of the teacher next year?

Your child has educational choices that can both challenge her and offer her a chance to feel successful in school. When she feels successful, she tries harder. It is easier for her to learn more concepts when she feels confident. We work toward making this the richest year possible, knowing that this is the best way to prepare her for the future.

Q. How do you keep control of the class if the children have choices?

The choices are educationally important. Different children may be doing different things at different times and have equivalent experiences in which they can feel successful. When they make a choice, they feel more responsible for their activity and work harder in playful ways.

Source: Adapted from D.P. Fromberg, *Play and Meaning in Early Childhood Education* (Boston: Allyn & Bacon, 2002), 131–2. Copyright © 2002 Pearson Education. By permission of the publisher. **Doris Pronin Fromberg** is director of early childhood teacher education at Hofstra University.

play, and problem solving. The teacher also serves as a resource person to help children locate what they need to accomplish tasks. Sometimes he proactively engages children, and might even become a co-player with them to promote richer play and learning.

Daily routines. Other opportunities for learning occur throughout the day during daily routines

such as arrival, departure, meals and snacks, and transitions. Children learn skills and concepts at each of these times, as they sing a song focusing on phonemic awareness during a transition, make comparisons of the number of boys and girls present during circle time, or figure out how many crackers will be needed in order for each person to have three. When children practice and apply new skills during such routines, the skills become more meaningful to them.

Individualizing and differentiating for all learners

No two kindergartners are alike. Each child has unique needs, temperament, interests, abilities, background knowledge, and life experiences. Based on this understanding, teachers offer children multiple ways of taking in information and making sense of ideas. The three essential understandings presented earlier in this chapter—child development, content and standards, and instructional strategies—serve as a foundation for a teacher to guide children's learning.

To individualize for children, teachers need to observe what children are doing throughout the day. Then they ask themselves, "What does this mean? How does this relate to my learning goals and content standards? How can I use this experience to help this child progress?" Having considered these questions, a teacher is able to respond in ways that take into account each child's individual needs and help that child progress along the learning path. The box on the next page offers one example to consider.

Another aspect of meeting individual needs is *differentiated instruction* (Tomlinson & McTighe 2006). This type of instruction offers children multiple paths to the same learning goals. Teachers modify elements such as the materials used, the experiences offered to achieve desired outcomes, the ways in which children represent their ideas, and the physical learning environment. For example, to help children learn the concept of patterning, a teacher first considers how patterning skills develop and what the children as a group already know about patterns. To get a picture of each child's level of understanding, she offers multiple opportunities in different modalities for children to create patterns: using interlocking cubes, sponge painting a patterned border on a picture, repeating a clapping pattern. As the teacher observes children, she scaffolds their learning to enable them to take the next step in that learning. A child who is able to copy various

patterns might be next encouraged to extend a pattern created by the teacher. Another child might be challenged with a more complicated pattern or asked to describe the pattern he created. Differentiated learning gives children multiple paths to reach similar goals.

Approaches to content teaching and learning

Teachers use multiple strategies to help children learn, understand, and apply content knowledge. They make informed decisions regarding the most effective teaching method to use for a given learning goal. When teachers are skilled, they will always engage in quite a bit of on-the-spot teaching. Though not planned in advance, this teaching too is intentional. That is, such teaching is guided by the teacher's goals, her familiarity with what children need to know and be able to do, and her knowledge of the learning paths to enable them to achieve these goals. For example, on the playground a child spontaneously hands the teacher a dandelion; the teacher shows how to blow it and talks about how the seeds travel by the wind to faraway places where new dandelions will grow.

Knowing children—including their prior knowledge, abilities, interests, learning styles, and culture—serves as the foundation for all learning to take place. In some instances, it makes the most sense to teach a concept or skill directly. In other cases, higher levels of thinking and engagement can occur during an in-depth study of a topic. During the course of the year in kindergarten, teachers might use one or more of a broad spectrum of approaches (some of which are defined below). Helm and Katz (2001) point out that these approaches vary by the level of child involvement, initiation, participation, and decision making, as well as by the time devoted to the topic, the teacher's role, the timing of field trips, and the use of a variety of resources.

Single-concept or single-skill approach. Some skills and concepts need to be taught directly. For example, the kindergarten teacher writes the morning message on a chart about a field trip to the flower shop and models how to begin each sentence with a capital letter. He invites the chil-

Responding to children as individuals

Teacher observes	Teacher reflects	Teacher responds
Tyrone repeatedly rolls a truck down a block ramp. He tilts the ramp and says, "Wow! Look at this, Kelly! It's going faster!" Kelly picks up another ramp and tilts it at different angles. The two continue to experiment with different ways they can make their truck move faster.	Tyrone wondered "what will happen if" and tested out the possibility. He is *exploring cause and effect,* one of the program's learning goals. Tyrone was engaged in his task, collaborated with a friend, and continued to work even when he encountered difficulties. Here he *shows persistence in approaching tasks,* another key learning goal. When Tyrone experimented with how things move, he was meeting the learning goal of *exploring physical properties of objects.* What other materials can I offer to help him explore motion? What kinds of questions or comments from me will help him understand these concepts? What physical concepts involved in this situation are Tyrone and Kelly likely to be ready to explore?	Offer other materials to try rolling down the ramp, such as balls of various sizes or spools. Ask, "What do you think would happen if we used a longer ramp?" Show Tyrone how he might create different ramps in the block area. Let him leave his experiment up for several days. On a group outing, point out ramps to Tyrone and talk about how they make work easier. Talk about how the slide on the playground is a ramp or how the deliveryman rolls his cart down a ramp.

Source: Adapted from D.T. Dodge, L.J. Colker, & C. Heroman, *The Creative Curriculum for Preschool* (Washington, DC: Teaching Strategies, 2002), 170–72. Copyright © 2002 by Teaching Strategies, Inc. Adapted with permission.

dren to circle each capital letter used in the message. Later children will have the opportunity to practice using capital letters as they write in their flower journals, and the teacher will assess their understanding of the concept.

Unit/theme approach. In a unit approach, the teacher identifies key concepts for a topic and introduces the concepts over a designated period of time. The children take part in follow-up activities related to the unit topic. For example, in a unit on flowers, the teacher reviews the science standards and determines that children should learn that flowers are living things; that they are part of a plant; that they need water, air, and sunlight to live and grow; and that plants and animals depend on each other to live. She uses different methods

for teaching these concepts, such as informational books, experiments, field trips, and visits from experts.

In addition to the strategies used in planning a unit, the teacher can also examine other skills she must teach and find a way to link them to the topic, creating a theme for the class. These activities might help children develop skills, but not all are planned in order to help children gain a deeper understanding of the topic. For instance, in a thematic unit on flowers, not only will children learn about how flowers live and grow, but they also will engage in flower-related activities to learn skills in other content areas. They might count plastic flowers and place them in pots with numerals written on them. They might add flower words

Cate Heroman and Carol Copple

to the word wall and make a flower dictionary. They might practice scissor skills by cutting out construction paper flowers. One topic can open the door to countless new opportunities.

Project-based approach. Project-based learning takes many forms, such as the project approach (Helm & Katz 2001; Katz & Chard 1989), emergent curriculum (Jones & Nimmo 1994), Reggio Emilia's projects (Edwards, Gandini, & Forman 1998), and long-term studies (Bickart, Jablon, & Dodge 1999; Dodge, Colker, & Heroman 2002). It offers children rich opportunities to investigate, make decisions, and become deeply engaged in building content knowledge. The focus of project-based learning is to follow children's interests or potential interests and find answers to their questions. Much thought is devoted to selecting appropriate topics.

For the most part, children study topics that they can investigate firsthand. Before deciding whether a topic is worthy of investing valuable class time, the teacher might identify big ideas related to the topic in science, social studies, mathematics, and other areas by creating a *concept web*. Once a project begins, children investigate their questions using literacy, mathematics, science, and technology skills to gain a deeper understanding of the topic and to represent and communicate their learning. For example, in a study of flowers, children might wonder why birds and insects are attracted to some flowers and not others. They represent their ideas through discussions, drawings, and other art forms. To find out the answer, the children make predictions about which flowers birds and insects like best. They observe the flowers over time and record what they see by creating observational drawings and writing in journals. The teacher offers remarks or open-ended questions: "I wonder what color of flowers butterflies like best. How can we find out?"

The project or study duration is determined by children's engagement and usually is not predetermined. As the project culminates, children can share what they have learned with others outside of their classroom. In the study of flowers, they might set up a flower show with flowers they have grown and share the findings of their investigations with invited guests.

Assessing children's learning

Assessment and instruction go hand in hand. Teachers assess continually in order to make careful, intentional decisions about children's learning. In a joint position statement, NAEYC and the National Association of Early Childhood Specialists in State Departments of Education (NAECS/SDE) define assessment as "a systematic procedure for obtaining information from observations, interviews, portfolios, projects, tests, and other sources that can be used to make judgments about children's skills, dispositions, health, or other characteristics" (2003, 27).

In the kindergarten classroom, a major assessment tool is teachers' observing children to learn about them. *Observation* provides information they need to build relationships with individual children and enable those children to be successful learners (McAfee, Leong, & Bodrova 2004). With the information gained from observing, teachers can select materials to match children's style and level of learning; plan activities that respond to children's interests, experiences, and skills; and ask questions that extend children's thinking and learning (Jablon, Dombro, & Dichtelmiller 1999).

(The Gullo chapter in this volume offers a fuller description of assessing children's learning in kindergarten.)

Building a partnership with families

Finally, a crucial dimension of a kindergarten teacher's work is to welcome families into the "school" system. The relationship that the teacher forms with them during the kindergarten year sets the tone for their children's entire school career.

Entering kindergarten is a huge transition for most children. Families talk about going to school, meeting the new teacher, and making new friends. The more a teacher knows the children in her classroom and their families, the more she will be able to ease their transition into kindergarten and start off the year on a positive note. At the beginning of the school year, teachers can use these strategies to establish positive relationships with families:

• Contact children and families before the school year begins. This helps children feel more at ease on the first day and conveys a positive message to families. Initial contacts might include phone calls, letters to the children, letters to families, home visits, and an informal meet-the-teacher day.

• Gather information such as previous group experiences, number of siblings, parent occupations, and languages in the home. Find out critical health information such as allergies, disabilities, and medication. Ask family members to help supply this information.

• Invite families to share their goals for their children through informal conversations, initial contacts or conferences, and at parent orientation.

• In parent orientation, whether done individually or with all the families together, talk about goals for the year ahead, their approach to teaching, and other plans for the year.

Throughout the year, teachers must maintain open lines of communication with families. Families want to know that the teacher knows their children. Moreover, they want to share with that teacher and hear about their children's strengths, likes and dislikes, and social relationships. When a teacher has formed a positive relationship with a family, it's much easier to cooperate in solving problems that might arise.

(For more on families, see the Powell and Gerde chapter in this volume.)

The kindergarten teacher is vital to children's school success. Effective teachers use what they know about children's learning and development to create an exciting and dynamic learning experience for each child. They make time to build positive relationships with children and families. They take pleasure in children's successes. They bring passion to the classroom by sharing their interest in learning with them. Rather than being daunted by the myriad of expectations for teaching and learning in kindergarten, teachers can use the powerful tool of reflective decision making to steer by as they help children achieve.

References

Barbour, N.H., & C. Seefeldt. 1993. *Developmental continuity across preschool and primary grades: Implications for teachers.* Wheaton, MD: Association for Childhood Education International.

Bickart, T.S., J.R. Jablon, & D.T. Dodge. 1999. *Building the primary classroom: A complete guide to teaching and learning.* Washington, DC: Teaching Strategies.

Bransford, J.D., A.L. Brown, & R.R. Cocking, eds. 2000. *How people learn: Brain, mind, experience and school.* Report of the National Resource Council, Committee on Developments in the Science of Learning, Commission on Behavioral and Social Sciences and Education. Washington, DC: National Academies Press.

Bredekamp, S., & C. Copple, eds. 1997. *Developmentally appropriate practice in early childhood programs.* Rev. ed. Washington, DC: NAEYC.

Copple, C., & S. Bredekamp. 2006. *Basics of developmentally appropriate practice: An introduction for teachers of children 3 to 6.* Washington, DC: NAEYC.

Dodge, D.T., L.J. Colker, & C. Heroman. 2002. *The creative curriculum for preschool.* 4th ed. Washington, DC: Teaching Strategies.

Edwards, C., L. Gandini, & G. Forman. 1998. *The hundred languages of children: The Reggio Emilia approach.* Greenwich, CT: Ablex.

Helm, J.H., & L.G. Katz. 2001. *Young investigators: The project approach in the early years.* New York: Teachers College Press.

Jablon, J.R., A.L. Dombro, & M.L. Dichtelmiller. 1999. *The power of observation.* Washington, DC: Teaching Strategies.

Jablon, J.R., C. Heroman, D.T. Dodge, & T.S. Bickart. In press. *Building the kindergarten classroom.* Washington, DC: Teaching Strategies.

Jones, E., & J. Nimmo. 1994. *Emergent curriculum.* Washington, DC: NAEYC.

Katz, L.G., & S.C. Chard. 1989. *Engaging children's minds: The project approach.* Norwood, NJ: Ablex.

McAfee, O., D.J. Leong, & E. Bodrova. 2004. *Basics of assessment: A primer for early childhood educators.* Washington, DC: NAEYC.

NAEYC & NAECS/SDE (National Association of Early Childhood Specialists in State Departments of Education). 2003. *Early childhood curriculum, assessment, and program evaluation: Building an effective, accountable system in programs for children birth through age 8.* Joint position statement. Washington, DC: NAEYC. Online: www.naeyc.org/about/positions/pdf/pscape.pdf.

Tomlinson, C.A., & J. McTighe. 2006. *Integrating differentiated instruction and understanding by design: Connecting content and kids.* Alexandria, VA: Association for Supervision and Curriculum Development.

Vygotsky, L. 1978. *Mind in society.* Cambridge, MA: Harvard University Press.

Cate Heroman and Carol Copple

Language and Literacy in Kindergarten

Dorothy S. Strickland

Kindergarten teachers Janet Bell and Cheryl DeLisi exchange anxious looks as they discuss the curriculum standards recently issued by the Board of Education. Janet is a veteran of nearly 15 years; Cheryl has just started her second year. Yet they share similar concerns. Janet worries that with the increased emphasis on literacy, play could disappear from the curriculum. Cheryl is concerned that even with their full-day program, it will be difficult to fit all the new requirements into her schedule.

Janet and Cheryl have arranged to meet with Mae Dickson, the school principal, who is sympathetic to their concerns. The three have been working collaboratively and positively to address new standards in all areas of the curriculum in ways that are consistent with the age and developmental needs of kindergarten children. They are particularly concerned about standards and accountability for language and literacy. As Mrs. Dickson put it, "We must work together to preserve our developmentally appropriate curriculum and, at the same time, increase language and literacy expectations for ourselves and for our students."

The scene described above could have taken place in virtually any school in the nation. Educators have had to rethink their mission under increased expectations and demands for accountability at all levels of schooling. This is especially

true as it relates to language and literacy. Tension at the kindergarten level has been particularly apparent, given its traditional role as the year when children are "gently eased" into the more formal aspects of school. "Children form lifelong habits and impressions about school in kindergarten. We must keep the experience positive," Janet often reminds parents.

This chapter both describes the knowledge base and offers related practical suggestions for implementing a developmentally appropriate and intellectually stimulating language and literacy kindergarten program. It addresses three areas of concern—standards, curriculum, and assessment—and concludes with a discussion of critical issues and policy considerations that play a major role in fostering language and literacy.

Language and literacy development: Some key ideas

Teachers can foster language and literacy in children by engaging their physical, social, emotional, and cognitive selves at an early age; by building on children's knowledge of oral language; and by helping them read and understand what is read to them through shared reading and discussion about books.

Dorothy S. Strickland is the Samuel DeWitt Proctor Professor of Education at Rutgers, The State University of New Jersey.

All domains of development have important roles

In order to learn, children must be physically healthy and provided with an environment that supports the development of social competence and emotional well-being. Effective teachers draw on the work of a wide range of cognitive psychologists and theorists such as Jean Piaget (1926), B.F. Skinner (1974), and Lev Vygotsky (1962) as they plan language and literacy experiences for children.

A teacher draws on Piaget when she assists children in their use of cognitive strategies to link the known to the unknown. For example, when children read an informational book about bridges, the teacher might mention a well-known bridge in the area that they would be familiar with. A teacher draws on Skinnerian principles when she presents instructional tasks in small incremental steps that systematically reinforce children's behavior. For example, guiding children to move from recognizing their names with an accompanying picture, to recognizing them without pictures, to recognizing their names when listed in a group of names is a gradual move from easy to more difficult.

A teacher applies Vygotsky's "zone of proximal development" when she observes and assesses children's accomplishments in order to frame tasks that provide just the right amount of challenge. For example, children who can identify their own names within a list of names are probably ready to look at a list of names more closely to see which ones start the same, end the same, have letters in them that they know, and so on.

Oral language is the foundation for literacy development

Oral language provides children with a sense of words and sentences. It builds sensitivity to the sound system so that children can acquire phonological awareness and phonics. It is also the means by which children demonstrate their understanding of the meanings of words and written materials. From the moment of birth, humans begin learning language, learning about language, and learning through language (Halliday 1969).

Infants and toddlers listen as adults talk and read to them. They learn that listening and talking are pleasant activities. They learn how to take turns talking, how to use language to get what they want, and how to handle books that have been read to them. Before age 5 or 6 most children have mastered most of the conventions of oral language. They know the sounds in their language, its sentence structure, and the meanings of many words. They also are acquiring knowledge about language rules that govern different social situations. For instance, their use of language is different at the dinner table than on the playground. These remarkable accomplishments provide the foundation for language and literacy learning throughout life (IRA/NAEYC 1998; Neuman, Copple, & Bredekamp 2000).

Young children have little difficulty acquiring more than one language. When children learn a second language they follow a process similar to the one they used to acquire the first (Jimenez 2004). All the skills of the second language do not develop at an equal rate, however. For example, children learning English as a second language will develop their listening abilities much more quickly than their speaking abilities. It is also important to note that young children thrive best in an atmosphere where their home language is valued and respected (Strickland 2002).

Literacy learning starts early and persists throughout life

Learning to read and write is an ongoing process that begins in infancy. Contrary to popular belief, this process does not suddenly begin in kindergarten or first grade. From the earliest years, everything that adults do—or don't do—to support children's language and literacy really counts.

Though oral language provides a foundation for literacy development, the two develop hand-in-hand. What children learn from listening and talking contributes to their ability to read and write, and vice versa. For example, young children's *phonological awareness* (their ability to identify and make oral rhymes; to identify and work with syllables in spoken words; and to hear,

Dorothy S. Strickland

identify, and manipulate the individual sounds, called *phonemes,* in spoken words) is an important indicator of their potential success in learning to read (Adams et al. 1997). Phonological awareness begins early, with rhyming games and chants, often on a parent's knee.

Children's experiences influence their comprehension

True reading involves understanding. Children's experiences with the world and with books and print greatly influence their ability to comprehend what is read to them and what they read on their own. What children bring to a text, whether it's an oral or a written text, influences the understandings they take away. The more limited a child's experiences, the more likely he or she will have difficulty with reading (Snow, Burns, & Griffin 1998).

Two kinds of experiences are highly influential to language and literacy development: (1) background knowledge about the world and (2) background knowledge about print and books (RAND 2002). Shared book reading experiences, where child and adult read together, at home and at school, have a special role in fostering early literacy development (Burns, Griffin, & Snow 1999). It is not just the reading but also the talk that surrounds the reading that help children understand the book's content and how print works.

Language and literacy standards for today's kindergartners

The pressure on teachers to deliver standards-driven instruction can be overwhelming. It reflects a national effort to improve student achievement throughout the grades. Academic standards or expectations declare what every student should know and be able to do, and how they are to demonstrate their knowledge and skills in core academic content areas (Seefeldt 2005).

This attention to standards and the resulting link to student performance are relatively recent in early education, and attention is largely focused on language and literacy. The box opposite offers

Typical kindergarten language and literacy standards

1. **Listening.** Children will:
   1.a. Identify sounds in their environment
   1.b. Create sounds by singing and music making
   1.c. Listen and speak with attention
   1.d. Listen for pleasure
   1.e. Develop phonemic awareness
   1.f. Identify letter-sound relationships

2. **Speaking.** Children will:
   2.a. Develop conversation skills with peers and adults
   2.b. Speak in small groups and before the whole class
   2.c. Use vocabulary introduced through explicit experiences or book reading
   2.d. Ask and answer questions
   2.e. Use increasingly complex sentence structure

3. **Reading.** Children will:
   3.a. Recognize that written symbols and print convey meaning
   3.b. Increase receptive and expressive vocabulary
   3.c. Develop book familiarity
   3.d. Interact in read-alouds
   3.e. Develop an understanding of story structure
   3.f. Increase word-decoding skills

4. **Writing.** Children will:
   4.a. Recognize graphemes (the letters of the alphabet)
   4.b. Engage in pencil/paper/drawing/painting activities
   4.c. Incorporate print into drawings
   4.d. Express ideas through writing using emergent spelling, and progress to conventional spelling
   4.e. Gain meaning by reading their own writing and that of others

Source: Reprinted by permission of the publisher from C. Seefeldt, *How to Work with Standards in Early Childhood Classrooms* (New York: Teachers College Press, 2005), 79. Copyright © 2005 Teachers College, Columbia University. All rights reserved.

a list of language and literacy standards that are typical of those presented to teachers of young children. The standards are both declarative, in that they identify the content children are to learn, and procedural, describing what children will be able to do.

Here are three key points to keep in mind about language and literacy standards:

Language and literacy knowledge and skills are highly integrated. Standards tend to artificially separate them. It's hard to tease apart listening and speaking. Yet, the very nature of standards makes the related aspects of these two language arts appear to be discrete entities. For example, when children listen and respond to books read aloud, they bring their background knowledge to the text and use it to relate to the content, understand what they hear, and talk about it in meaningful ways. The same is true when they listen to a storyteller or view a videotape. In every case, they are both receiving and expressing information based on a text that has been shared with them. Teachers use children's responses to help judge the quality of their understanding. But they also realize that some children are better than others at expressing what they understand.

Thus, listening and speaking are both separate and interrelated. When a kindergarten teacher guides children in reading directions in order to plant seeds, then systematically guides them in observing and recording the growth of the seeds on a chart, that teacher is intentionally addressing a variety of language and literacy skills through a broad-based series of engaging activities. One of the most compelling challenges for teachers is to consistently plan for and assesses specific language and literacy outcomes within the frame of an integrated activity.

Opportunities to address standards occur incidentally throughout the entire day and are, at times, specified for activities designed to meet particular standards. Effective kindergarten teachers provide a balance between explicit instruction and opportunities for indirect, incidental learning to occur. Explicit instruction is generally linked closely to the standards outlined in a district's curriculum guide, such as those in the box on page 75. Often these standards are introduced to

children in a group setting. They might include a shared reading activity involving a Big Book (an oversized book with enlarged text) about farm animals. The class reads the names of the animals and discusses their characteristics. Center-based activities planned by the teacher, but not explicitly guided by the teacher, provide reinforcement. These activities might include a science center containing a replica of a farm with the farm animals labeled. Children engage in a word-matching activity with a set of word cards that have the same animal labels written on them. A nearby chart about farms, created by the group, provides opportunities for more independent reinforcement. In addition, small-group follow-up is provided for those who need extra or more specialized help and for advanced children who need to be stretched beyond the given curriculum. These cross-curricular activities are intentionally planned to reinforce literacy and language standards during social studies, science, and other activities throughout the day.

Kindergarten teachers should have intimate knowledge of their district's kindergarten standards and be well acquainted with those for prekindergarten and the primary grades. Today's kindergarten and primary grade teachers place a high premium on articulation across the grades. Shared professional development opportunities with prekindergarten and primary grade teachers that provide time to express ideas and concerns across grade levels is an important way to ensure curriculum continuity. Kindergarten teachers are likely to pass along portfolios that include such things as checklists and inventories about children's knowledge of print concepts and the alphabet as well as samples of children's drawing and attempts at writing.

In summary, although literacy standards such as those in the box on page 75 are listed in specific and discrete terms, teachers should address them within the context of broad-based activities centered on content that is meaningful and engaging to children. For example, when children follow along as their teacher writes what they dictate about a book they have shared, many literacy standards are addressed and the children learn many things: We can think and talk about ideas

Dorothy S. Strickland

that are important to us. Our ideas can be written down and read. Certain words might be repeated and look the same. Written words need spaces between them. Some words look and sound the same at the beginning. Some words are similar to our names and other words we know. We can ask and answer questions about what is written. We can draw and write about our ideas as a group and on our own.

Toward a balanced curriculum

Effective kindergarten language and literacy programs reflect a balanced approach in a number of ways. This balance is reflected when children are offered a wide variety of instructional opportunities, both formal and informal (direct or explicit instruction by the teacher as well as opportunities for incidental learning); when instruction is differentiated to accommodate individual needs and approaches to learning (small group and one-to-one); and when opportunities to learn language and literacy are offered in connection with meaningful content (integration of science, social studies, and mathematics with literacy).

Here are the key points to keep in mind about the language and literacy curriculum:

It is critically important to diversify instruction to meet individual needs. Plan for whole group, small group, and one-to-one opportunities to learn. Make use of visual, tactile, and auditory means for learning.

Keep instruction active and consistent with how young children learn. Children are not miniature adults. Young children learn best in certain ways, and these ways change as they develop and learn.

Instruction should go beyond the acquisition of isolated skills to help learners strategically apply what they have learned. For example, learning the sounds associated with letters is a skill. Learning to use that knowledge to read and write words is a strategy.

It is important to maintain a balance between explicit instruction and informal, incidental learning. Both have a role in the curriculum. Both require planning.

The prevailing method of instruction should be scaffolded instruction, in which teachers: model; engage children in collaborative literacy activities (shared reading and writing, for example); and provide opportunities for guided independent practice.

The box beginning on the next page lists typical curriculum components for language and literacy instruction, the strategies and activities teachers can use to implement them, and the key standards they address.

A word about scaffolded instruction

Virtually all of the curriculum components offered in the box on pages 78–79 can be taught through scaffolded instruction. *Scaffolding* refers to the process whereby a child's learning occurs in the context of full performance as adults gradually relinquish support (Cazden 1988). Think of the phrase "everybody needs a helping hand," and it will be easy to remember what scaffolding is. As adults we frequently help children accomplish things they want to do, such as work with a puzzle, write the first letter of their name, or ride a bike. First we show them how we do it. In fact, they might have been observing us for a while on their own, but we are largely in control. Then we invite them to try, and we help as they attempt to do it. At times we intervene, but only when our assistance is needed. When we think they are ready, we let them try on their own. The box on page 80 outlines the scaffolding process.

An example of scaffolding occurs when teachers use Big Books and charts to read aloud to children. When children see the print as teachers read aloud, they observe the reading process. Although the teacher is in control (she is the one reading the book), the children can follow along mentally as some words are pointed out and as they notice how the reader moves across and down the page, and from front to back. Very often, after one or two repeated readings of the same book, the teacher might pause occasionally and point to a particular word that has been repeated several times. The children share in the reading by "filling in" that word. If the book is left in the

(continued on p. 80)

Typical curriculum components and instructional strategies

Curriculum components	Examples of instructional strategies
Oral language development Speaking—oral language expression Listening—comprehension of spoken language; listening to distinguish between sounds in the language Vocabulary development—knowledge and use of words and related concepts *Curriculum goals*: Develops oral language directly and indirectly in rich contexts with meaningful practice.	Time is set aside for children to respond to literature, engage in dramatic play, and recall and share information of common interest to the group. Children are encouraged to use the vocabulary of books being shared and the topics and themes under study. Teachers make time for extended conversations with individual children. *Key standards addressed:* Listening, speaking
Reading aloud and writing aloud Demonstrations and modeling of reading and writing processes. Students observe, listen, and respond. *Curriculum goals*: Builds general background knowledge about the world and specific knowledge related to topics under study. Provides knowledge about various forms of print and literary genres (narratives, informational books, poetry, concept books) and opportunities to comprehend, reflect, and respond to various forms of print.	Reading aloud and opportunities for response to literature occur daily using a variety of literature and forms of response, such as discussion, drawing/writing, and drama. Material read aloud might be related to a theme under study, such as "transportation" or "how things grow." Discussion follows. Writing aloud occurs when children watch as the teacher thinks aloud while composing a sentence or two about what was learned from the books, then reads aloud what has been written. *Key standards addressed*: Reading, writing, listening, speaking
Shared reading and shared writing Involves student participation in teacher-led reading and writing activities. Goes beyond teacher modeling. Students are actively engaged in activities such as reading repetitive words or lines in Big Books, and participate in composing written language. *Curriculum goals*: Develops an understanding of how speech is transformed to print through writing and back to speech again through reading. Develops concepts about print, such as print carries a message, spaces between words, and directionality.	Teacher leads and involves children in interactive reading and writing activities. Often occurs after repeated readings of books, Big Books, and charts, with teacher tracking the print as children read. Group charts and lists might be constructed, with children helping to compose what is written as the teacher acts as scribe. Conventions of written language such as capital letters, spaces between words, and punctuation marks might be introduced. *Key standards addressed*: Reading, writing

Note: The term *writing* refers to written composition, not handwriting or copying what someone else has written.

Dorothy S. Strickland

Word study

Alphabet knowledge—ability to name and write the 26 letters of the alphabet

Phonological awareness—understanding that words are made up of speech sounds (phonemes)

Phonemic awareness—ability to hear, identify, and manipulate the individual sounds in spoken words. Phonemic awareness is one aspect of phonological awareness

Phonics—use of sound-letter relationships for reading and writing

Curriculum goals: Develops basic understandings about written language.

Teacher involves children in a variety of activities that foster letter recognition, phonemic awareness, and sound-letter correspondence. Recognition of name, own name, and other common words in the environment (such as *stop*), recognition of letters in own name, matching letters, naming letters in ABC books and in the environment, listening for and making rhymes, listening to similarities in the beginning sounds of words, developing an awareness of the alphabetic principle (that a relationship exists between letters and the sounds they stand for).

Key standards addressed: Reading, listening

Guided reading and writing

Teachers work with individual children and small groups in closely guided instruction with texts geared to the instructional level of the learners. Specific strategies are addressed at developmentally appropriate levels (e.g., invented spelling or decoding easy texts).

Curriculum goals: Through differentiated instruction, helps all children access curriculum goals at varied rates, levels, and attention to specific needs.

Teacher selects a book on the instructional level of the children (accessible to them with a minimum of problems). Teacher briefly introduces the story and calls attention to meaning, language, and visual information. Children read on their own as teacher interacts with individual children where needed. Teacher leads discussion and invites responses. Children might reread. Or, teacher might introduce a topic to draw/write about or might call attention to a particular print concept. Children draw/write on their own as teacher interacts with individuals where needed. Children share their compositions.

Key standards addressed: Reading, writing

Independent reading and writing

Children select materials to "read" or "write" on their own. A range of activities might be involved, including "pretend reading" of a book with which they are familiar; looking at and discussing pictures, letters, numbers in books; or actually reading easy material.

Books are accessible so that children can return to those that have been read aloud. Writing materials and alphabet charts are available as resources for written composition.

Curriculum goals: Provides opportunities for children to apply what they have learned in situations that allow for some elements of student choice of what they read and write about.

Teacher might begin with a brief read-aloud or write-aloud. Children select materials to "read" or "write." Teacher circulates and holds brief conferences with individuals. Children are also encouraged to read and write independently at center time and at other free choice times.

Key standards addressed: Reading, writing

library area, many children will attempt to "read" on their own. Thus, a type of scaffolding occurs in a very informal, relaxed manner. By providing multiple copies of the shared text for children to browse on their own, the teacher sets conditions for children to attempt to "read" the book by themselves. The box below shows, in very general terms, how scaffolding might work in reading and writing. The teacher moves from modeling and demonstrating for the children, to collaborating with them, and finally to monitoring and guiding them as they attempt to work independently.

Organizing and managing the language and literacy curriculum

Effective kindergarten teachers offer opportunities for language and literacy development throughout the day. The box on the next page lists some typical opportunities. They range from formal instruction to informal opportunities with an element of choice and individuality.

One of those opportunities is during center time. A "literacy" learning center is any center that includes literacy in some way. (For more on setting up and managing centers, see the Heroman and Copple chapter in this volume.) Here are some examples of language and literacy learning centers appropriate for kindergarten:

- Reading—wide assortment of reading materials (some theme related), class books, charts
- Publishing—writing materials, blank books, alphabet charts, picture dictionaries
- Listening—taped books with print versions, headsets and tape player
- Theme-based (or inquiry)—books, activities, and displays related to themes under study
- Computer—easy games, software programs, word-processing opportunities

---

Scaffolding literacy experiences for children

Read or write aloud teacher models . . . children observe	Read or write along teacher guides . . . children participate	Read or write alone teacher monitors . . . children work independently
Reading		
Teacher reads aloud using books, Big Books, and charts as children observe. She comments aloud about text.	Teacher reads aloud using books, Big Books, and charts as children observe. She invites children to participate at various points during reading.	Teacher provides materials and time for children to select books to "read" on their own. She encourages them to talk about their independent reading experiences.
Writing		
Teacher writes and comments aloud as children observe. She might sound out words to spell them or simply spell them aloud. Makes other comments about the message.	Teacher writes as children observe. She might invite children to suggest letters based on sounds she isolates for spelling, or suggest placement of words, and so on.	Teacher provides materials and time for children to draw and write on their own. She encourages them to share their drawing/writing with others. Is available to assist.

Reading concepts to scaffold: Print carries meaning; Functions of print; Phonemic awareness; Book handling; Directionality; Concept of "word," "letter"; Letter names; Literacy language (e.g., *book, story, title, page, author, illustrator, poem*)

Writing concepts to scaffold: Print carries meaning; Functions of print; Phonemic awareness; Directionality; Concept of "word," "letter"; Letter names; Literacy language (e.g., *title, line, beginning, end, letter, word*)

Dorothy S. Strickland

Opportunities for language and literacy learning

Arrival

Examples: Teacher designates certain activities or centers for exploration. Book reading and play with games and puzzles involving matching words and letters.

Description: Children arrive individually, work independently, and self-select among various familiar materials and activities provided by the teacher, with rules and routines previously established.

Purpose: To practice choosing among various activities. Reinforce and extend previous concepts and skills. Give the school day an orderly and productive beginning.

Organization: Individual children or small (naturally occurring) groups; independent, with some teacher intervention as needed.

Specified language and literacy time

Examples: Teacher reads aloud from a book related to the theme of transportation (read-aloud); children discuss various modes of transportation, recall their own experiences (oral language, vocabulary development), and assist in writing one or two sentences about airplane travel (shared writing). Might focus on any of the curriculum components outlined in the box on page 75; often one or two are combined.

Description: Teacher delivers explicit instruction that is tightly linked to curriculum standards. Might occur more than once per day.

Purpose: To provide intentional, targeted instruction in the skills and strategies of the curriculum.

Organization: Whole group receives ongoing instruction, with small-group differentiated follow-up.

Center time

Examples: Reading and writing opportunities in a variety of centers. Children make use of writing pads for notes and lists provided in the dramatic play area, and utensils for making signs provided in the block area.

Description: Children work at self-selected centers or perhaps rotate from center to center. They have some freedom of choice.

Purpose: To practice working independently. Apply and expand skills and strategies taught during language and literacy time.

Organization: Planning with the whole group, so expectations are clear; for example, the number of children allowed at a particular center is predetermined and visible.

Science and social studies

Examples: Activities that make use of all language arts curriculum components. Children are read to and discuss books about creating an aquarium and how to care for fish. They discuss what they have read and help compose a list of things they must do.

Description: Teacher delivers explicit instruction that is tied to curriculum standards. Often theme-based.

Purpose: To expand background knowledge. Develop vocabulary.

Organization: Whole group, small group.

Share time

Examples: Children describe their activities during center or independent reading time, or activities they engage in out of school. Teacher encourages them to show and explain their writing and drawing, a completed puzzle, or block construction.

Description: Any time designated for children to share personal activities with the group.

Purpose: To prompt children to reflect on something of interest to them and to express that interest in a way that communicates with others.

Organization: Whole group, small group.

• Word study—letter and word study activities such as matching shapes, letters, words; sorting pictures according to rhyme, initial sounds

The centers can stand alone or be combined in various ways; reading and listening, for example, is a frequent combination, as might be publishing and word study.

Assessing language and literacy learning

Effective kindergarten teachers are keen and competent observers. They study what students do every day in various situations. They observe to determine what students can do independently with success. They note areas of growing competence and areas of difficulty. They use what they learn to inform their plans for intervention and curriculum adjustment. Teachers gather information through anecdotal records, checklists, personalized conferences, formal and informal observations, and by systematically collecting work samples. They examine the information to determine how learners are progressing.

Here are some key points to keep in mind about assessment:

Assessments that help examine and document children's abilities to engage in literacy tasks relative to local standards are the most useful.

Multiple sources of information help teachers determine how well each child is progressing, both as an individual and in relationship to the group. They also yield important information about how well the group is progressing as a whole. Each set of information has implications for curriculum adjustment.

Linking assessment with the scope and sequence of curriculum

Earlier, the box on pages 78–79 outlined the essential components, or *scope,* of language and literacy offerings at the kindergarten level. Teachers should address all of these instructional opportunities on a regular basis, either daily or weekly, and by using a variety of literature and focusing on different content. It's best to approach the *sequence,* or order, of instruction through multi-level and differentiated instruction. In multi-level instruction, teachers offer a wide range of opportunities for students to access knowledge and skills within the same lesson. For example, during the shared reading of a Big Book, it is not uncommon for some children to join in on the reading of repeated words and phrases. Others will even point out words or letters that they know. Still others will simply recognize that it is the text on the page that signals what is read aloud.

Effective kindergarten teachers move from easy to difficult, known to unknown, and simple to complex. They provide a range of experience within each of the activities offered in the box on pages 78–79. They observe and track children's development so that they can adjust the scope and sequence of the curriculum for the whole group, and provide more personalized and differentiated instruction for those who need it.

Shown opposite are two examples of assessment within an instructional setting that offers multi-level opportunities to learn. The first is an example of a kindergarten child's written composition. Clearly, this child is able to reflect on a personal experience and both draw and label a credible picture to represent that experience. Collected over time, writing can reveal information that is both important and specific about an individual child's literacy development. The second is a sample observation checklist for assessing children's knowledge about print during shared reading. Checklists of this type yield important information about individual children as well as the progress of the group.

Linking policy and practice

Revisiting kindergarten and its place in a child's overall range of schooling from prekindergarten through grade 12 is a major concern of educators today. Clearly, these concerns go beyond school and classroom practice. Educational policy at all levels of decision making, from national to local, can profoundly affect how educators design and implement developmentally appropriate and

Dorothy S. Strickland

Child's "writing" sample

Child: I am swimming in the pool.

Kindergarten (May)

Source: Reprinted with permission from D.S. Strickland, *Teaching Phonics Today: A Primer for Educators* (Newark, DE: International Reading Association, 1998), 20. Copyright © 1998 International Reading Association.

Checklist for children's knowledge of print

In shared reading, children show understanding of the following concepts:

Book concepts
❐ Books have titles, authors, and illustrators.

Print conveys meaning
❐ Print carries a message.
❐ Illustrations carry meaning but cannot be read.

Directionality
Print is read ❐ left to right, ❐ top to bottom

Concept of word
❐ Words match speech.
❐ Words are composed of letters.
❐ There are spaces between words.

Letter knowledge
❐ Letters in words can be identified and named.

Phonemic awareness
❐ Some words sound the same at the beginning.
❐ The sounds in words are represented by letters.

Literacy language
❐ Certain words (*book, title, author, illustrator, sentence, word, letter*) help people to talk about what they read.

Source: Reprinted with permission from D.S. Strickland & J.A. Schickedanz, *Learning about Print in Preschool: Working with Letters, Words, and Beginning Links with Phonemic Awareness* (Newark, DE: International Reading Association, 2004), 53. Copyright © 2004 International Reading Association.

intellectually stimulating language and literacy kindergarten programs.

Some of the critical issues that require examination at the policy level include: (1) a clear articulation of the language and literacy goals and standards for the kindergarten year in relationship to all the domains of development—social, emotional, physical, and cognitive; (2) the establishment of strong and equal partnerships with prekindergarten and primary grade educators; (3) careful consideration of the need for full-day or half-day kindergarten with a focus on high-quality learning environments; (4) increased attention to quality home-school connections that foster partnership and mutual goals; (5) accountability programs that are developmentally appropriate, are efficient, and that inform instruction; and (6) high-quality, ongoing professional development in literacy learning and teaching.

References

Adams, M.J., B.R. Foorman, I. Lunderg, & T. Beeler. 1997. *Phonemic awareness in young children: A classroom curriculum.* Baltimore: Brookes.

Burns, M.S., P. Griffin, & C. Snow, eds. 1999. *Starting out right: A guide to promoting children's reading success.* Washington, DC: National Academies Press.

Halliday, M.A.K. 1969. Relevant models of language. *Educational Review* 22: 26–37.

IRA (International Reading Association) & NAEYC. 1998. *Learning to read and write: Developmentally appropriate practices for young children.* Joint position statement. Washington, DC: NAEYC. Online: www.naeyc.org/about/positions/pdf/PSREAD98.pdf.

Jimenez, R.T. 2004. Literacy and the identity development of Latina/o students. In *Theoretical models and processes of reading,* 5th ed., eds. R. Ruddell & N. Unrau, 210–40. Newark, DE: International Reading Association.

Neuman, S.B., C. Copple, & S. Bredekamp. 2000. *Learning to read and write: Developmentally appropriate practices for young children.* Washington, DC: NAEYC.

Piaget, J. 1926. *The language and thought of the child.* London: Routledge & Kegan Paul.

RAND Reading Study Group. 2002. *Reading for understanding: Toward an R&D program in reading comprehension.* Santa Monica, CA: Science & Technology Policy Institute, RAND Education.

Seefeldt, C. 2005. *How to work with standards in early childhood classrooms.* New York: Teachers College Press.

Skinner, B.F. 1974. *About behaviorism.* New York: Knopf.

Snow, C., M.S. Burns, & M. Griffin. 1998. *Preventing reading difficulties in young children.* Washington, DC: National Academies Press.

Strickland, D. 1998. *Teaching phonics today: A primer for educators.* Newark, DE: International Reading Association.

Strickland, D. 2002. Bridging the gap for African American children. In *Love to read: Essays in developing and enhancing early literacy skills of African American children,* ed. B. Bowman, 63–71. Washington, DC: National Black Child Development Institute.

Strickland, D. 2004. *Learning about print in preschool settings.* Newark, DE: International Reading Association.

Vygotsky, L. 1962. *Thought and language.* New York: Wiley.

Dorothy S. Strickland

Mathematics in Kindergarten

8

Julie Sarama & Douglas H. Clements

Alex is 5 years old and her brother Paul is 3. Alex bounces over to her father:

Alex: When Paul is 6, I'll be 8; when Paul is 9, I'll be 11; when Paul is 12, I'll be 14 [she continues until Paul is 18 and she is 20].

Dad: Wow! How did you figure that out?

Alex: It's easy. You just go "three-FOUR-five" [she says "four" very loudly and claps her hands at the same time, so that the result is strongly rhythmical and has a soft-LOUD-soft pattern], you go "six-SEVEN [clap!]-eight," you go "nine-TEN [clap!]-eleven." (Davis 1984, 154)

Is Alex gifted, or do all young children have untapped potential to learn—even create—mathematics? What do kindergartners know about mathematics? What might they learn?

Research tells us that children learn quite naturally about number and geometry from their first year of life (Clements, Sarama, & DiBiase 2004). So children come to kindergarten with some knowledge of mathematics. For example, children can count higher, at least verbally, than many traditional curriculum materials have set as their goal for the kindergarten year, and they know quite a bit about shapes (Clements, Sarama, & DiBiase 2004). Further, young children are inter-

ested in situations and activities that are rich with potential for mathematics. Kindergartners' play often involves—at least implicitly—mathematical ideas, such as *classification* (a girl puts blocks away in categories), *magnitude* ("This isn't big enough to cover the table"), *enumeration* (a boy says, "Look! I got one hundred!" and he and a friend count to check his estimate), *dynamics* (a girl makes a flat circular shape out of dough), *pattern and shape* (a boy builds a symmetrical structure with blocks), and *spatial relations* (a girl offers a location or direction) (Seo & Ginsburg 2004).

Unfortunately, children's potential for learning mathematics is not well realized. Even before starting kindergarten, most children in the United States know substantially less about math than do children from other countries. Further, children from low-resource communities have the least knowledge of any group studied. For these children especially, the long-term success of their learning and development requires quality experience during their early "years of promise" (Carnegie Corporation 1998).

In response to the need for high-quality early childhood mathematics instruction, the field has developed research-based content standards, including those specifically for the kindergarten year (NAEYC/NCTM 2002). These standards identify the key concepts and skills children need to gain comprehension and ability in mathematics,

Julie Sarama is a professor in the learning and instruction department and Douglas H. Clements is associate dean of educational technology and a professor in the learning and instruction department, both at the University at Buffalo, State University of New York.

and there are many different means of implementing these standards. In this chapter we outline the concepts and skills, and present recommendations for how teachers can develop kindergartners' mathematic power.

General suggestions for practice

We suggest *organized* instruction for kindergartners. But that does not mean formal mathematics "pushed down" from higher grades. High-quality learning is often incidental and informal, but not unplanned or unsystematic (Clements 2001). Effective programs give children in-depth involvement with mathematical ideas that build their understanding over time; teachers also need to help families extend and develop those ideas outside of school (NAEYC/NCTM 2002). Here are three general suggestions for practice:

Make connections

Much of what understanding is, lies in the connections between ideas. In all activities, especially teacher-directed activities, teachers need to help children connect their informal knowledge to their budding explicit knowledge of mathematics. Children also must connect various mathematics topics to each other. For example, they can connect number to geometry by counting the sides of shapes or by measuring the length of a rug. This helps strengthen their grasp of concepts in both areas as well as their beliefs about mathematics as a coherent *system*. Similarly, linking mathematics to other learning domains such as literacy strengthens both. Most good mathematics activities also develop language and vocabulary. For example, teachers can ask children wearing something red to get in line *first*, those wearing blue to get in line *second*, and so on.

Support play

Long periods of time for play and enriched environments and materials (including manipulatives such as blocks and Legos that invite mathematical thinking) are critical for developing children's mathematics ideas and skills. By closely observing children's play, teachers can meaningfully intervene as needed to further children's learning. If children's block constructions have been routine and uncreative, for example, the teacher might pose challenges, read aloud books illustrating different block arrangements, or post pictures of interesting constructions. The teacher must, of course, determine when intervention is truly called for. It may be useful for the teacher to ask herself whether the social interaction and mathematical thinking are developing or are stalled. If they are developing, the teacher simply observes and leaves the children alone. If children are in conflict or need help clarifying their ideas, then it may be appropriate to step in. The teacher can discuss the experience later with the whole class if that seems useful.

Teachers also support mathematical development in children's play when they help children discuss and clarify their ideas. For example, if two children are arguing over which block construction is bigger, the teacher can help them see that buildings can be big in different ways ("You have a very *tall* building, and Xavier's seems to be very *wide*").

Use appropriate technology

Technology—such as computer programs—is useful in teaching kindergarten mathematics. Wise use of high-quality software helps children think mathematically. Used well, computers offer many advantages. They can help individualize instruction. They provide immediate feedback and patient repetition. They provide manipulatives that are actually easier to use, more durable, and more helpful to learning than physical manipulatives. Computers can present motivating games that involve substantial mathematical thinking. Research shows they complement other hands-on activities to increase learning by kindergartners (Clements & Sarama 2003).

Key mathematics concepts and skills for kindergarten

Standards for kindergarten mathematics can help focus instruction on important ideas and skills. Unfortunately, state standards are not consistent, and some are developmentally inappropriate for young children. Two sources of information provide guidance for appropriate standards. First, the National Council of Teachers of Mathematics' standards document, *Principles and Standards for School Mathematics,* or *PSSM* (NCTM 2000), organizes *content* into five areas: (1) number and operations, (2) algebra, (3) geometry, (4) measurement, and (5) data analysis and probability. The *PSSM* emphasizes that for kindergartners, teaching and learning should focus on number and geometry. Teachers should also provide experiences in the other areas, most often to support number or geometry ideas and skills. Threaded throughout and fully integrated into the content are the mathematical *processes:* communicating, connecting, representing, reasoning, and problem solving.

The second source of information emerged from the Conference on Standards for Prekindergarten and Kindergarten Mathematics Education, which had the goal of finding consensus across NCTM's standards, state standards, research, and the wisdom of expert practice. The resulting book, *Engaging Young Children in Mathematics: Standards for Early Childhood Mathematics Education* (Clements, Sarama, & DiBiase 2004), provides detailed information on standards, children's learning at each year of life, and teaching. The box begining on the next page outlines the book's conclusions about the main instructional goals for kindergartners, which are detailed in this chapter.

Number and operations

Number, including beginning operations (arithmetic), is arguably the most important topic in kindergarten mathematics. To build a strong number sense, children must develop and link competencies in several areas:

Counting. Counting objects is a core competency in mathematics that develops not just as increasing skill, but qualitatively. Children's early numerical knowledge includes four interrelated aspects: (1) learning the list of number words *one* to *ten* and beyond, (2) enumerating objects (i.e., saying number words in correspondence with objects), (3) understanding that the last number word said when counting refers to how many

items have been counted, and (4) "subitizing" (which is discussed in the next section). Children initially learn these four aspects through different kinds of experiences, but their understandings gradually become more connected. Each aspect begins with the smallest numbers and gradually includes larger numbers.

The verbal number words *one* to *ten* are an arbitrary list with no patterns, and children learn these words as they do general language or the ABCs. Rhythms, songs, and other daily activities—such as counting aloud while walking up steps—can help in that learning. To count objects, children learn to coordinate this list of number words with pointing, touching, or moving objects. Doing this ties each word they say in time to an object they count. At first, the objects should be organized into a row for counting; rhythms are often helpful, too. Children must concentrate and try hard to achieve continuous coordination throughout the whole counting effort.

Connecting the counting of objects in a collection to the number of objects in that collection is an important concept for children to learn. It is the necessary building block for further work with number and operations. Initially, children may not know how many objects there are in a collection after having counted them. If asked how many there are, young children typically count again, as if the "how many?" question is a directive to count, rather than a request to tell how many items are in the collection. Although most preschoolers learn that the last number word they say when counting refers to how many items have been counted, some children need their teacher to address this as they begin kindergarten.

To count objects accurately and meaningfully takes children a considerable amount of experience. Large-group activities such as Simon Says ("Simon says jump up 10 times!") are useful, as are games involving number cards, such as Compare/War and Go Fish, and board or path games where children move the number of spaces indicated on the dice or spinner. To extend the learning, teachers can write simple, illustrated directions for the games and send them home with children to play

(continued on p. 90)

Main mathematics topics for kindergartners

Topic	Key concept or skill example
Number	
Verbal counting: Learning the standard sequences of number words helps establish order.	Child counts aloud from 1 to 100, with emphasis on patterns (such as "60, 70" parallels "6, 7"; and "14" to "19" parallels "4" to "9").
Object counting: Creating a one-to-one correspondence between a number word and an item can tell *how many*.	Child counts up to 20 physical items meaningfully.
"Seeing" numbers (subitizing): Instantly "seeing how many" supports counting, comparing, and adding.	Child quickly recognizes groups of one to five objects. Recognizes regular patterns up to 10 objects.
Comparing numbers: Comparing and ordering build on nonverbal knowledge and experience with real collections.	Child uses counting to compare two collections with up to 10 items, using words such as *equal, more, less*, and *fewer*.
Adding and subtracting: Arithmetic can model a variety of real-world situations. Solving problems using informal counting strategies is critical in learning arithmetic.	Child poses and solves word problems using counting-based strategies such as *counting on* (an abbreviated counting method, where instead of beginning at "One," the child begins, say, at "Six" and *counts on* from there: "Six, seven, eight . . . Eight!"). Sums to 10.
Putting together and taking apart number: Another approach to arithmetic is composing numbers as parts to make wholes, and the reverse.	Child sees collections of three and two objects and quickly says that the total is "five."
Geometry	
Shape: Geometric shapes can be used to represent and understand objects in the world around us.	Child recognizes and names a circle, square, triangle, and rectangle in *any size or orientation* (varying shapes for triangles and rectangles).
Putting together shapes: Shapes can be decomposed and composed into other shapes and structures.	Child covers an outline with shapes without leaving gaps, with foresight. Child makes a picture by combining shapes, such as this one.

Julie Sarama and Douglas H. Clements

Topic	Key concept or skill example
Transformations and symmetry: Symmetry can be used to analyze, understand, and create shapes in geometry and art. Transformations such as slides, flips, and turns can determine congruence or analyze movements.	Child identifies and creates shapes that have line symmetry or rotational symmetry. Slides, flips, and turns can be used to determine symmetry or solve geometric puzzles.
Locations and directions: Mathematics can precisely specify directions, routes, and locations in the world.	Child places toy objects in their correct relative positions to make a map of the classroom.
Measurement	
Measuring can be used to specify and compare *how much*.	Child compares the length of two objects using a third object.
Measurement is giving a number to an attribute of an object, such as its length, area, capacity, or weight.	Child measures length with multiple copies of a unit (such as a block).
Patterning	
Patterns give order and predictability. They can be used to recognize relationships.	Child makes and extends linear patterns, such as "ABCABCABC."
Patterns weave through all other topics in mathematics.	Child notices and discusses patterns in arithmetic (for example, adding one to any number results in the next "counting number").
Data analysis	
Classification: Objects can be grouped based on attributes and quantified.	Child sorts a collection of buttons into those with one, two, three, or four holes and counts to find out how many buttons are in each of the four groups.
Graphing: Representing information helps us ask and answer questions.	Child answers questions by making graphs using physical objects (objects such as shoes or sneakers, then manipulatives such as connecting cubes), as well as by drawing picture graphs.

with their families. Situations both real (such as counting for attendance or voting) and fanciful (solving word problems such as "If you got three presents for your birthday and then one more came in the mail, how many would you have altogether?") can also be used to encourage meaningful counting. Using the results of counting helps children to see its practical application.

Subitizing. The fourth core competency of number sense, subitizing, is the skill of "just seeing" how many objects there are in a group. Again, mathematical knowledge develops as qualitative changes in understanding. Children's ability to "see small collections" grows from *perceptual* patterns, to *imagined* patterns, to *numerical* patterns (Steffe 1992). Perceptual patterns are those the child can, and must, immediately recognize when he sees or hears them, such as domino patterns, finger patterns, or auditory patterns (three beats, for example). Later, children develop the ability to imagine such patterns when the image is not physically present. Finally, children develop numerical patterns, which they can operate on, as when they can mentally decompose a five pattern into two and three, then put them back together to make five. All three patterns support children's mathematical growth and thinking, but numerical patterns are the most powerful.

One particularly rich activity is a snapshots game, where children are flashed an image showing some number of objects (such as a card with five dots) then quickly announce that number (Clements 1999a). Many worthwhile variations are possible, including changing the number and arrangement of the objects, having children recreate the arrangement with manipulatives, racing to match the right card to the number announced, or playing on a computer.

Comparing and ordering. Human beings naturally make perceptual judgments of relative quantities. Children need to build on this inherent trait and learn how to match and count to find out more dependably which quantity is *more*. By the end of kindergarten, children typically have linked the counting words into a kind of "mental number line." This allows them to count each of two collections and use their mental number line to de-termine which number comes later on the line, and thus which collection is larger. A card game such as War/Compare can provide practice in this area, as can many other matching and counting activities, including board and computer games.

Finding out *how many more* (or *how many fewer*) items there are in one collection than in another is more challenging, as the language used is complex. To determine how many more, children have to understand that the number of elements in the collection with fewer items is contained *in* the number of items in the collection with more items. That is, they have to mentally construct a "part" of the larger collection (a part that is equivalent to the smaller collection) when that part is not visually present. They then have to determine the "other part" of the larger collection, and find out how many elements are in that other, "left-over amount." Children need considerable experience solving comparing problems and hearing and telling comparing stories.

Most kindergartners can learn to solve these problems by the end of the year. All benefit from talking about them, and can solve them if the numbers are kept small. Children who have limited language abilities can learn to line up two collections side-by-side to aid comparisons. Bilingual children may actually have an advantage on such problems, because they may see the abstract idea that underlies its expression in any language.

Adding to/taking away. Even toddlers notice the effects of increasing or decreasing small collections by one item. Kindergarten children can solve problems such as "four *and two more*" by counting. For example, children would count the objects in an initial collection of four items drawn from a box ("One, two, three, four"), count out two more items from the box ("One, two"), and then count the items of the two collections together ("One, two, three, four, five, six!"). Children naturally use such counting methods to solve story situations, as long as they understand the language used in the story.

Children then build on this solution method for addition/subtraction. For example, when the items are not visually present, they may raise fingers sequentially while saying, "One, two, three,

Julie Sarama and Douglas H. Clements

four, five, six"; then continue on, raising two more fingers, "Seven, eight"; and finally announcing, "Eight!" Children can learn to abbreviate this counting method even further, often during the kindergarten year, given appropriate experience. Rather than raising fingers to count the six imagined items, children can learn to begin at six and simply "count on" from there, saying, "Six, seven, eight. . . . Eight!" Such *counting on* is a landmark in children's numerical development. It is not a rote step: it requires that a child mentally put the six inside the total of eight.

Appropriate story themes that develop the skills of adding to/taking away can be incorporated naturally in children's dramatic play. For instance, teachers and children can create a shop in the dramatic play area where the shopkeeper fills orders and asks the customers for money. Card games such as War/Compare can be changed into Double War, in which each child flips over two cards and the highest sum wins. Many other games are available (see Kamii & Housman 1999, and the resources in the box opposite) and are useful for individualizing learning in this area.

Putting together and taking apart numbers. Another way to add or subtract is by combining and separating. These processes bring together two aspects of children's early numerical knowledge (counting and subitizing), and they strengthen children's concepts of *parts* and *wholes*. For example, children can develop the ability to recognize that the numbers 2 and 3 are "hiding inside" 5, as are the numbers 4 and 1. Working with objects, kindergartners can learn to separate a group of objects into parts in various ways and then count to produce all of the number *partners* of a given number (for example, they can separate six objects into 5+1, 4+2, and 3+3). Children can work with objects within a story context, for example. The number 6 can be presented as six animals in a field that need to go into two different pens, or six cars into two different parking lots.

Two kinds of special patterns are especially powerful and easy for children to see: *doubles* (such as 3+3), which eventually allow access to combinations such as 3+4 (one more than 3+3);

and *fives* (such as 6 made as 5+1; 7 as 5+2), which allow for decomposition into fives and tens. Such strategies develop children's number sense but also meet another major goal in early childhood mathematics—strategic reasoning. Snapshots activities such as presenting two groups of dots, like the activities described earlier under subitizing, can help develop these abilities.

Geometry

Geometry and spatial reasoning are inherently important because they help children understand the spatial composition of their world (NCTM 1989). Two mathematical ideas that are particularly important for kindergartners are the shape of

| **Sources for games, and more** |

www.nctm.org—National Council of Teachers of Mathematics. See especially the "Teacher's Corner" and "Family Corner" sections.

http://standards.nctm.org—The math standards *Principles and Standards for School Mathematics* and many activities, Web-based software environments, and videos.

www.naeyc.org/about/positions/mathematics.asp—Early Childhood Mathematics: Promoting Good Beginnings. A joint position statement of the National Association for the Education of Young Children (NAEYC) and the National Council of Teachers of Mathematics (NCTM).

www.ed.gov/pubs/EarlyMath—Early Childhood: Where Learning Begins—Mathematics. Mathematical activities for parents and their 2- to 5-year-old children. Online information for parents from the Department of Education. Also see **www.figurethis.org/** and **www.lhs.berkeley.edu/equals/equals.html.**

www.mathperspectives.com—Mathematical Perspectives. Mathematical Perspectives Teacher Development Center provides preK to sixth grade mathematics educators with tools, strategies, and assessments that will ensure that all children are successful in the study of mathematics and are able to use mathematics to solve problems and to think and reason mathematically.

objects and the shape of their environment (locations/directions).

Shape. Children begin to form concepts of two-dimensional shapes during their prekindergarten years. For example, most children can recognize and name some familiar two-dimensional shapes by age 4. But, sadly, their classroom experiences too often do not add much to their knowledge in the early grades (Clements 2004; Lehrer, Osana, & Jenkins 1993). Kindergarten children can learn richer concepts about shape if their educational environment includes the following four key features:

First, children should experience many different examples of a shape (lots of different triangles, for example), so they do not form narrow ideas about any class of shapes. Comparing examples (triangles) with nonexamples (chevrons or kites) focuses children's attention on the critical attributes of shapes and prompts discussion. Second, these discussions about shapes and their characteristics (sides or angles, for example) should encourage the development of language that children can use to explain why a shape does belong ("It has three straight sides") or does not belong ("Its sides aren't straight") in a certain shape class.

Third, children's learning should cover a wider variety of shape classes than just the traditional ones of circle, square, triangle, and rectangle. Children should encounter examples of these four shapes, but with variations in orientation, size, and so on (including squares as examples of rectangles), as well as but not limited to semicircles, quadrilaterals, trapezoids, rhombi, and hexagons. The mistaken notion that a square is not a rectangle, for example, is rooted by age 5 (Clements & Sarama, in press).

Fourth, teachers should challenge kindergartners with interesting tasks that promote reflection and discussion. Children can build models of shapes, explore a shape hidden in a "feely box," form shapes with their bodies, and play group games such as I Spy ("I spy something with four sides all the same length").

Putting together shapes. Young children move through levels of competence as they learn to compose and decompose two-dimensional figures. First they gain the ability to combine shapes into pictures, then to synthesize combinations of shapes into new shapes ("composite" shapes). Kindergartners can develop these abilities through free play with various shape sets (building blocks, tangrams, pattern blocks) and solving pattern block or tangram puzzles.

Children need many rich experiences identifying, describing, and putting together three-dimensional figures, too. Manipulation and play with solids should lead to discussions of their overall shape ("It's like an ice-cream cone") and attributes ("All these are round and roll"). Building with blocks helps children learn about three-dimensional figures; construction activities involving foldout shapes of solids (or "nets") can help children learn to discriminate between two- and three-dimensional figures.

Transformations and symmetry. Kindergarten children may be limited in their ability to mentally transform shapes (e.g., move shapes with slides, flips, or turns), but they can do so in solving simple problems. For example, they can "see" that a shape will fit in a puzzle if it is flipped upside-down. Further, they can learn to slide, turn, and flip objects (physical or virtual). A curriculum rich with such experiences, including physical manipulatives and computer tools, helps them develop skills of mental imagery.

Recognizing and constructing symmetric figures is well within a kindergartner's reach. Flipping shapes will help children determine whether shapes are symmetric, and they can create designs with different kinds of symmetry (such as line or rotational) with manipulatives and other art media. Kindergartners can learn to draw the other half of a geometric figure to create a symmetric figure and identify lines of symmetry. Computer environments, in which children need to think abstractly and give concrete and precise commands, can be particularly helpful in learning symmetry and transformations (Clements et al. 2001).

Locations and directions. Children have considerable intuitive knowledge of the shape of their environments. With guidance, they can learn

Julie Sarama and Douglas H. Clements

to reinterpret in mathematical terms their informal knowledge about getting around, for example, in places such as their school or neighborhood. For example, they can talk about walking straight 20 steps down a hall, then turning right, then walking 50 steps to the large motor area. They can learn beginning ideas about direction, perspective, distance, symbolization, and location.

Age 5 to 6 is a good time to provide informal experiences with locations and directions— especially those that emphasize building imagery from physical movement—and to introduce simple maps (Clements & Sarama, in press). For example, children might use blocks to make a model of their classroom. Or they can draw or use blocks and toys to make simple maps of routes they travel around the school or playground.

Measurement

Young children naturally encounter and discuss quantities, such as comparing clay "snakes" to see whose is longer (Seo & Ginsburg 2004). They compare two objects directly and recognize equality or inequality. At about kindergarten age they are ready to learn to measure, connecting number to the quantity.

Children should learn to measure with meaning, through experiences that emphasize problem solving and thinking rather than in rote procedures. Initially teachers should use informal activities to establish the attribute of *length*; develop concepts such as *longer, shorter,* and *equal;* and teach strategies such as *comparison*. Children should make comparisons for a purpose, as in comparing the lengths of two objects in order to solve a problem. For example, a teacher might ask, "Is our doorway wide enough for that table to go through?"

Many curricula teach measurement through a set sequence—children compare objects directly, then measure them with nonstandard units such as paper clips, and *then* measure them with standard units. But following this traditional sequence rigidly may not be best. As long as the tasks and interactions with teachers and peers emphasize meaningful use, children benefit from using rulers as well as manipulable standard units (such as

centimeter cubes) as their measuring ideas and skills are developing (Clements 1999b). Teachers can help children begin to develop concepts and procedures such as starting at zero and focusing on the lengths of the units rather than only on the numbers on the ruler.

Patterning and algebraic thinking

Algebra begins with a search for patterns. Identifying patterns helps bring order and predictability to seemingly unorganized situations and allows us to generalize beyond the information we have. In kindergarten, children can learn to extend and create simple linear patterns. They can learn to recognize the relationship between patterns with non-identical objects or between different representations of the same pattern (such as between visual patterns and movement patterns). Beginning in kindergarten, children learn to identify the core unit (AB as an example) that either repeats (ABABAB) or "grows" (ABAABAAAB), and then use it to generate both of these other types of patterns.

Preschoolers can engage in rhythmic and musical patterns, even complex ones such as "clap, clap, slap; clap, clap, slap." They can talk about these patterns, too, representing the patterns with words. In kindergarten, children enjoy adding physical movements to the same patterns, so "clap, clap, slap . . . " is transformed to "jump, jump, fall down; jump, jump, fall down" and soon symbolized as an AABAAB pattern—symbolism that kindergartners can learn to hear and describe verbally. And they will intentionally re-create and discuss patterns in their artwork. Kindergartners can learn to describe such patterns with numbers ("two of something, then one of something else"). These are actually the first clear links among patterns, number, and algebra.

Data analysis: Classification and graphing

Data analysis contains one big idea: asking and answering questions. To do this, children classify, organize, represent, and use information. The developmental continuum for data analysis includes growth in classifying and counting and in data representations. Children initially learn to sort objects and quantify their groups. After children gather data to answer questions, their first representations often do not use categories. Their interest in data is on the particulars. For example, they might simply list each child in their class and his or her response to a question, and then learn to classify these responses and represent data according to categories during the kindergarten year.

To develop classifying and graphing abilities, teachers might ask children to sort a collection of buttons into those with one, two, three, or four holes, and then to count to find out how many buttons they have in each of the four groups. To do this, children focus on and describe the attributes of objects—classifying according to those attributes—and quantify the resulting categories. Children eventually become capable of simultaneously classifying and counting; for example, they learn to count the number of colors in a group of objects.

During the kindergarten year, teachers can foster children's skill progression from recording particular data (such as counting how many sneakers are in the classroom) to classifying data (how many of those sneakers are red vs. not red) to representing data (using graphs to represent sneakers that are red and not red). Children should start graphing by using the physical objects being studied (sneakers, for instance), then progress to working with abstract manipulatives such as connecting cubes to represent different items. They can then move on to creating picture graphs, and finally to bar graphs with grid lines signifying different quantities. By the end of kindergarten, most children typically can compare parts of the data, make statements about the data as a whole, and generally determine whether the graphs answer the questions posed initially.

Mathematics help us make sense of our world. Early childhood is a good time for children to become interested in counting, sorting, building shapes, patterning, measuring, and estimating. Quality kindergarten mathematics is not elementary arithmetic pushed down onto younger children. Instead, it invites children to experience mathematics as they play in, describe, and think about their world.

References

Carnegie Corporation of New York. 1998. *Years of promise: A comprehensive learning strategy for America's children.* Online: www.carnegie.org/sub/pubs/execsum.html.

Clements, D.H. 1999a. Subitizing: What is it? Why teach it? *Teaching Children Mathematics* 5: 400–5.

Clements, D.H. 1999b. Teaching length measurement: Research challenges. *School Science and Mathematics* 99 (1): 5–11.

Clements, D.H. 2001. Mathematics in the preschool. *Teaching Children Mathematics* 7: 270–75.

Clements, D.H. 2004. Geometric and spatial thinking in early childhood education. In *Engaging young children in mathematics: Standards for early childhood mathematics education,* eds. D.H. Clements, J. Sarama, & A.-M. DiBiase, 267–97. Mahwah, NJ: Erlbaum.

Clements, D.H., & J. Sarama. 2003. Strip mining for gold: Research and policy in educational technology—A response to "Fool's Gold." *Educational Technology Review* 11: 7–69.

Clements, D.H., & J. Sarama. In press. Early childhood mathematics learning. In *Second handbook of research on mathematics teaching and learning,* ed. F.K. Lester, Jr. New York: Information Age.

Clements, D.H., J. Sarama, & A.-M. DiBiase, eds. 2004. *Engaging young children in mathematics: Standards for early childhood mathematics education.* Mahwah, NJ: Erlbaum.

Clements, D.H., M.T. Battista, & J. Sarama. 2001. *Logo and geometry.* Journal for Research in Mathematics Education Monograph Series, vol. 10. Reston, VA: National Council of Teachers of Mathematics.

Davis, R.B. 1984. *Learning mathematics: The cognitive science approach to mathematics education.* Norwood, NJ: Ablex.

Guberman, S.R. 2004. A comparative study of children's out-of-school activities and arithmetical achievement. *Journal for Research in Mathematics Education* 35: 117–50.

Kamii, C.K., & L.B. Housman. 1999. *Young children reinvent arithmetic: Implications of Piaget's theory.* 2d ed. New York: Teachers College Press.

Lehrer, R., H. Osana, C. Jacobson, & M. Jenkins. 1993. *Children's conceptions of geometry in the primary grades.* Atlanta, GA: American Educational Research Association.

NAEYC & NCTM (National Council of Teachers of Mathematics). 2002. *Early childhood mathematics: Promoting good beginnings.* Rev. ed. Joint position statement. Washington, DC: NAEYC. Online: www.naeyc.org/about/positions/mathematics.asp.

NCTM. 1989. *Curriculum and evaluation standards for school mathematics.* Reston, VA: Author.

NCTM. 2000. *Principles and standards for school mathematics.* Reston, VA: Author..

Seo, K.-H., & H.P. Ginsburg. 2004. What is developmentally appropriate in early childhood mathematics education? In *Engaging young children in mathematics: Standards for early childhood mathematics education,* eds. D.H. Clements, J. Sarama, & A.-M. DiBiase, 91–104. Mahwah, NJ: Erlbaum.

Steffe, L.P. 1992. Children's construction of meaning for arithmetical words: A curriculum problem. In *Implicit and explicit knowledge: An educational approach,* ed. D. Tirosh, 131–68. Norwood, NJ: Ablex.

Science in Kindergarten

Ingrid Chalufour & Karen Worth

It's Monday morning. Twenty kindergarten children are sitting in a circle as their teacher, Derek, presents them with an interesting challenge:

"I'm wondering how many ways you can think of to change the size and shape of your shadows. You'll all have a chance to work in our shadow theater this week, and then we'll talk about what you've discovered. There are paper and markers for you to keep track, and I'll be around to record your ideas, as well."

The children have been exploring shadows for three weeks—outdoors on the playground, indoors with flashlights and different objects, and with a small shadow box. A shadow theater, a sheet hung from the ceiling with a gooseneck lamp on one side, was introduced the week before. The children are very excited to use their bodies and puppets to make shadows. This week, Derek wants the experimentation to be more intentional, so he gives the children this challenge at the beginning of choice time.

During the week, the children explore the shadows they can make. Derek spends quite a bit of time with them observing, commenting, and asking questions. "How do you think you could make your shadow very small?" "What do you think would happen if we moved the lamp over to this side?" "Might your shadow look like a rock, just sitting there?" "You might like to

draw what your shadow looks like when you stand sideways like that." "Let's write down what you did and where the lamp was."

By the end of the week, there are many pictures with captions on the wall near the theater—pictures the children have drawn and photographs Derek has taken with his digital camera. These images become the focus for the science talk at the end of the week, after the children have pursued some of their ideas about shadows and how they change.

Over the weekend, Derek will produce a documentation panel with the pictures, the children's captions, and the ideas they have come up with. Derek plans to wrap up the shadow work the following week with a shadow theater presentation for families and other classes.

In another classroom, in the spring, Katie and her kindergartners have been studying plants and how they grow:

While they watch grass sprouting and trees budding on the playground, they're growing a variety of things in the classroom. Windowsills and shelves are covered with potted plants, narcissus bulbs, garlic pieces, and carrot tops. The 21 children are gathered on the rug for their morning meeting, and 11 small foam trays are placed around the circle so the children can closely inspect the seedlings while they talk. The children are talking about what has been happening to the seedlings.

Katie begins by reviewing the chart of observations from the previous week and then asks, "How

Ingrid Chalufour is a senior developer at Education Development Center, Inc. Karen Worth is a senior scientist in the Center for Science Education at Education Development Center, Inc., and an instructor of elementary education at Wheelock College.

have our seedlings changed since last week?" The children are eager to share their observations. "They're longer." "There are green leaves coming out on these." "This one is getting lots of things at the bottom." Katie writes their comments down on a chart with the date as she encourages specifics. "How do you know they're longer?" "Let's look at those leaves. The leaves on the kidney beans look different from the leaves on the lentils, don't they? How would you describe the difference?" "Does anyone know what we call the growth at the bottom of a plant? . . . Yes, it's called 'the roots.'"

Jamal is very interested in the growth of the seedlings. Katie decides it's time to begin measuring them. She asks Jamal to get the measurement basket, which has string, tape measures, and rulers in it. She quickly makes a chart they can use to record length over time. The children start filling in the chart by measuring three of the seedlings, then marking their length in inches on the chart in a column with the date on it. "I wonder how long these will be the next time we measure them?" "Do you think the kidney bean will always be the longest one? . . . What other changes do you think will happen?"

At the end of the discussion, Katie sets the stage for the day's choices. "There are several things you can do with these seedlings during choice time today. I'd like you to do a drawing in your journal. Draw the same seedlings you drew last time. I'll place the word cards at the table with your journals so you can use them to label your drawings. I'd also like some of you to do more charting of the seedlings' lengths. I think we could chart the growth of the bulbs, garlic, and carrots, as well." The children eagerly choose activities and choice time begins.

These examples give brief glimpses into the world of science teaching and learning that can and should take place in kindergarten classrooms. Three important questions must be answered in order for this teaching and learning to take place: What science should be taught? How should science curriculum be structured? How should it be taught? These questions lead to other questions: How much science should children do? What are the key instructional strategies teachers can use to promote learning? How can science fit into a program, given the typical kindergarten focus today on mathematics and literacy? The answers

to some of these questions will be found in the following pages.

What science should we teach?

The National Science Education Standards (National Research Council 1996) and the *Benchmarks for Science Literacy* (AAAS 1993) describe what students should know and be able to do in science. These documents have provided guidance to many educators for a decade, but neither one addresses the kindergarten year; both start with first grade. Since the publication of these documents, a growing number of states have developed standards both for the preschool years and for kindergarten. However, given the current emphasis on mathematics and literacy, and the reality that science has never been a significant part of programs for young children, many of these standards do not include science. With little guidance for teachers and few expectations from the school system, the science teaching in kindergarten is often just a science table in a corner of the room with a few objects for children to look at or individual activities that they can do during choice time. The science that happens is often focused on the study of living things—classroom pets, plants, and nature walks—and it neglects the physical sciences. In too many classes science is not taught at all.

What follows is a framework for thinking about science content in the kindergarten classroom. There are many ways to organize the content of science for any level. We have chosen to turn to the national documents, the research on cognitive development, the practice of expert educators, and our own experience in the development of science curriculum materials. We have based the framework on five content areas: inquiry, life science, physical science, earth science, and space science.

Inquiry

Perhaps the most important area of science content is inquiry. In science, *inquiry* refers to the diverse ways in which scientists study the natural world and propose explanations based on the

Ingrid Chalufour and Karen Worth

evidence derived from their work. Inquiry also refers to the activities of students in which they develop knowledge and understanding of scientific ideas, as well as an understanding of how scientists study the natural world (National Research Council 1996).

The box opposite lists important inquiry skills that kindergarten children must be given the opportunity to develop. They should be able to perform these skills at a simple level by the end of kindergarten. The two vignettes that opened this chapter include many examples of children using these skills as they explore shadows and the growth of seedlings.

One often sees such lists of inquiry skills in science programs and frameworks. They are frequently accompanied by the suggestion that the simpler skills of exploration, observation, and description and simple tool use are the most appropriate for younger children, and that the skills of investigation and experimentation and the more analytic synthesizing skills can only be learned as children get older. We suggest that kindergarten children can and do use *all* of the inquiry skills, but at a kindergarten level.

This is not a list of skills to be taught in isolation. Instead, it provides a practical guide for teachers to use as they design science experiences for children. Whatever the topic of study, all of the skills are used in the process of pursuing that study. In the flowchart on the next page, the inquiry skills are placed in a context, demonstrating that children's inquiry is a process, or a set of stages. The stages follow one another, with the arrows in the diagram suggesting that children will move back and forth between different stages depending on their interests, the challenges that arise, and the guidance of teachers.

Inquiry is about questions—but it is hard for children to ask questions about something if they haven't had a chance to get to know the thing or the event, whether it is shadows, seeds, snails, or water flow. So the first stage in the framework is to *notice, wonder, and explore.* This is a time for children to play, to see what they already know, to mess about in a rich environment with little direct guidance or structure. As children explore, they

Important inquiry skills

As a result of their science experiences, kindergarten children should develop their abilities to:

- Raise questions about objects and events around them
- Explore materials, objects, and events by acting upon them and noticing what happens
- Use all senses to make careful observations of objects, organisms, and events
- Describe, compare, sort, classify, and order in terms of observable characteristics and properties
- Use a variety of simple tools to extend their observations (a hand lens, measuring tools, eye droppers, a balance)
- Engage in simple investigations including making predictions, gathering and interpreting data, recognizing simple patterns, and drawing conclusions
- Record observations, explanations, and ideas through multiple forms of representation including drawings, simple graphs, writing, and movement
- Work collaboratively with others
- Share and discuss ideas and listen to new perspectives

Source: From K. Worth & S. Grollman, *Worms, Shadows, and Whirlpools: Science in the Early Childhood Classroom* (Portsmouth, NH: Heinemann; Newton, MA: EDC; Washington, DC: NAEYC, 2003), 18. Reprinted with permission from Education Development Center, Inc. (EDC).

ask questions through words or actions. They may be struck by a particular idea or question, such as, "I wonder what will happen if I shine the flashlight on the car from the block corner?" These questions may lead them to *take action and extend questions,* the second stage in the framework.

It may not be possible to investigate many of the questions children raise. "Why does the seedling come out of the seed?" cannot be explored directly. "What is the name of this plant?" will not lead to lengthy discussion. But "What does the seedling need to grow?" has the beginnings of a rich investigation. At this stage, children often need adult guidance to begin to *focus observations*

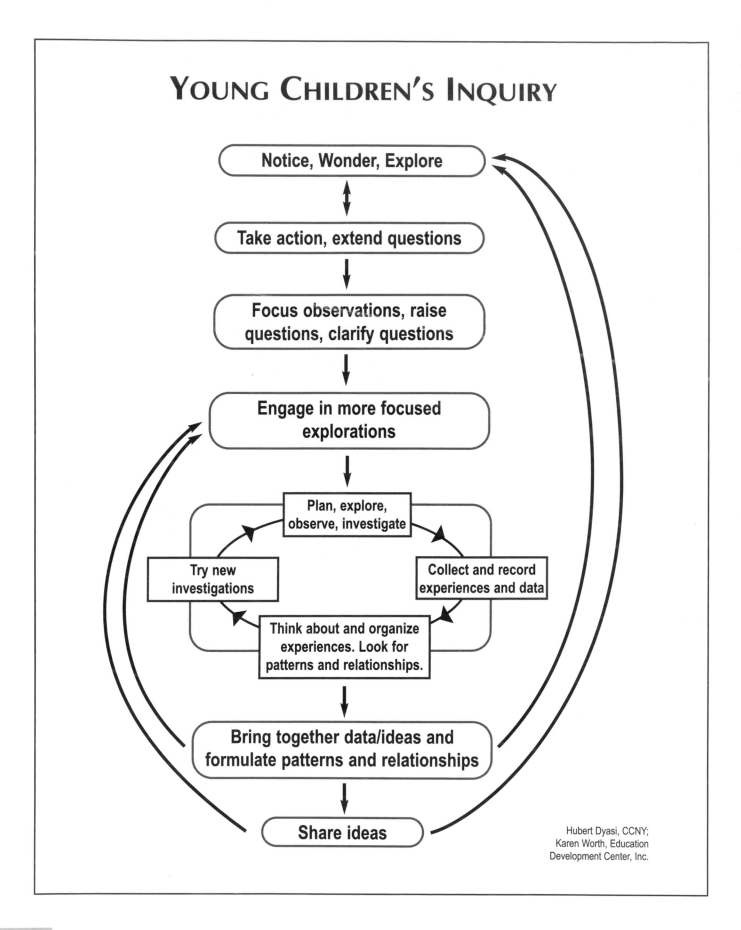

YOUNG CHILDREN'S INQUIRY

Notice, Wonder, Explore

Take action, extend questions

Focus observations, raise questions, clarify questions

Engage in more focused explorations

Plan, explore, observe, investigate

Try new investigations

Collect and record experiences and data

Think about and organize experiences. Look for patterns and relationships.

Bring together data/ideas and formulate patterns and relationships

Share ideas

Hubert Dyasi, CCNY;
Karen Worth, Education
Development Center, Inc.

Ingrid Chalufour and Karen Worth

and raise/clarify questions. They need to be encouraged to make some predictions about what might happen.

When children *engage in more focused explorations,* they are entering the experimental phase of inquiry. Given the right materials and teacher support and guidance, kindergarten children can do focused investigations. The framework presents this as a circular process, one that can go around and around. Children may explore a question for a long time, with their explorations leading to new questions and new investigations.

When children have a good deal of experience and begin to form some ideas, they need to step back from their hands-on investigative work, review and reflect on what they have done, and *bring together data/ideas and formulate patterns and relationships.* Young children's explanations and generalizations may be quite simple and naïve. What is important is that they draw from the experiences they have had and the data they have collected. New ideas in science are built on the knowledge of others.

The important last step of the framework is to *share ideas.* This is a time when children are encouraged to share what they have done, relate it to what others have done, discuss, and debate.

Yet inquiry skills cannot be acquired in a vacuum. Children need to inquire into something. So we turn to a list of basic ideas and topics in the four remaining content areas—life science, physical science, earth science, and space science.

Subject matter

Educators do not completely agree on the appropriate science subject matter for the kindergarten year. The criteria we use in developing science curriculum materials follow below. We include concepts or topics if they are:

- Drawn from the life, physical, and earth/space sciences as they are experienced by children in their daily lives
- Based on important science ideas
- Developmentally appropriate
- Accessible to children's direct exploration

- About things/events that children can explore deeply and over time
- Engaging, challenging, and fun

Topics such as dinosaurs, the solar system, or rain forests do not meet all of these criteria and are not appropriate for kindergarten science study. They are examples that are not drawn from children's lives and are not accessible to children's direct exploration. In addition, the underlying science of the history of the Earth, the structure of the solar system, and the complex interactions of the rain forest require a level of abstract thinking more appropriate for older students.

Applying the criteria yields the concepts and topics shown in the box on the next page. This list, however, is not intended to dictate what content must be covered in kindergarten. Rather, its purpose is to guide teachers, schools, or districts in choosing topics for a strong year-long program. Such a program must:

- Reflect the nature of the local environment and community
- Provide experiences drawn from the different content areas (not just from life science)
- Be limited enough to allow for in-depth inquiry in each topic

Further, the questions accompanying each topic or concept are simply to suggest the kinds of questions that children might explore. In many cases, especially in life science, a number of concepts might be part of a single study.

State standards may be more numerous and specific than the broad ideas outlined here but most will fit within one or another of these very basic ideas and topics. If state standards include other content, teachers will need to use the criteria provided to determine the most age-appropriate topics.

The big ideas

A carefully designed science program includes more than specific content. There are major understandings or ideas in science—sometimes called its *unifying concepts* or *big ideas.* These may not be taught directly, but should be the basis for curricu-

Key concepts and topics for the kindergarten year

Life science

Physical characteristics of living things

The basic needs of living things

Simple behaviors of living things

Relationship between living things and their environments—*What living things are there outside the classroom? What do they look like? How do they compare? What do they need to survive?*

The life cycle—*What happens to a seed as it grows and develops? What things make a difference in how it grows? What changes do animals go through as they grow?*

Variation and diversity—*What are all the living things we can find in a small plot? Are they the same? Are they different?*

People—*How are we all alike? How are we different? What do our senses tell us?*

Physical science

Properties of objects and materials

- Properties of solids—*What are the properties of our rocks? What are the properties of the soils? What are the properties of the leaves we collected? What are the properties of the different blocks we are building with?*

- Properties of liquids—*How does water move? How can water go up? What are drops like? How do they move? What happens to water when it is left in an open container? Frozen?*

Position and motion of objects—*How far will the ball go when it rolls down different ramps? What difference does it make if a ball is large or small? Heavy or light?*

Properties and characteristics of sound—*What kinds of sounds do different things make? How can sound be made louder? Softer? How can the pitch of a sound be changed?*

Properties and characteristics of light—*What happens to a shadow when a light moves? How many different shadows can be made with a light and an object?*

Earth science

Properties of Earth materials—*What is the ground like outside our classroom? What is in the soil?*

Weather—*What are the features of weather, and how can they be measured? What are the patterns of weather over a week? A month? A year?*

Space science

Patterns of movement and change of the Moon and Sun—*How does the Sun move across the sky? Is it the same every day? How does the shape of the Moon seem to change? Is there a pattern?*

Ingrid Chalufour and Karen Worth

lum planning. For kindergarten children, these big ideas include looking for patterns, seeing relationships, noticing change, identifying cause and effect, and seeing how form is related to function.

Attitudes and dispositions

Finally, a rich kindergarten science program supports the development of certain attitudes and dispositions that are important in all areas of learning. These include:

- Curiosity
- Seeing oneself as a learner of science
- Respect for life
- Willingness to take risks
- Perseverance
- Respect for evidence
- Willingness to collaborate

How should science curriculum be structured?

Let us look back at the two vignettes and see how these four components of a rich science program—inquiry, subject matter, big ideas, and attitudes—come together in curriculum.

Putting it all together

In the first vignette, Derek has gone to his state standards and selected light and shadow as his subject matter. He has identified these concepts: light travels from a source; light can be blocked by objects; when light is blocked by something, there is a shadow; and the size and shape of shadows change if the light source or object is moved. Katie has chosen plants as her subject matter. She has identified that plants have a life cycle, plants have basic needs that must be met if they are to survive, plants develop and grow in predictable ways, and there is variation in the way seeds grow.

Derek and Katie have provided the children with many materials that allow them to inquire. In Derek's class, the children explore and notice what shadows and lights do, both indoors and outdoors. They describe what is happening and

talk about their ideas. They use shadow boxes and the theater for simple investigations that follow up on their own questions and respond to Derek's challenge. Representation (drawing, writing, making models) is a constant part of the children's work, as are the science talks that help them draw out their ideas and conclusions. Katie's classroom is also engaged in a study that is taking place indoors and outdoors with many different kinds of plants. They are using simple tools—the magnifier and measuring tools—as part of their investigation of the growth of seedlings. As they collect and record their observations using graphs, drawings, and words over a couple of weeks, they continuously analyze the data looking for patterns and relationships, and they talk about their thinking.

Derek keeps the big ideas in mind as he interacts with children during their investigations and guides the science talks. He asks the children about relationships—in this case, the relationship between the light and the objects they are using and the shadows. Together he and the children wonder about cause and effect—what causes a shadow's size and shape and how they can control the effect. Katie considers the patterns of growth the children are watching. Rather than just naming parts of the plant, she talks about change—how the plants are changing and what functions new parts might serve and the relationship between form and function.

Finally, the materials and the events invite the children to question, to develop important attitudes and dispositions such as curiosity, a sense of themselves as science learners, perseverance, and collaboration. As Derek and Katie pose questions and challenge children to develop and share their own ideas, they are creating an environment in which learning science is an active and rigorous process that everyone can do, and a process that is based in the data they collect. This environment and culture also support children as they try out new actions and ideas. Children discover that sometimes things fall down or a light goes out, and they have to start again. They learn that they must work together—to investigate different shadows, one person has to hold the flashlight while another moves the object.

A simple framework

Each science study or investigation takes on a life of its own based on the content and the topic that is selected. But a science study has a simple structure that is useful to consider: engagement, focused exploration, extending the investigation through books and other media, and connecting to home and community.

Most studies begin with time for children to *become familiar* with the materials and events they will explore more deeply and pose some initial questions. A science study then moves on to *more focused exploration,* where the teacher challenges children to go deeper, to build understanding, and to document their work. Guided by the goals she has set, the teacher creates a focus using a child's question or one of her own.

> The teacher's guidance of children's hands-on explorations is essential to the success of any science investigation.

A third part of this framework lies in the use of books and other media to *extend and enrich the firsthand experience.* Once they have grown seeds and studied the plants outside their classroom, children may be transported to a different plant world with a book on the giant redwoods. Once they have explored what the plants in their neighborhood need, they can read about desert plants and how they survive to learn more about basic needs and habitats. Reading a story about a scientist helps them to understand how scientists inquire.

Finally, the structure of a science study includes the *interplay between classroom, community, and home.* If science consists of activities only in the classroom, children will be less likely to see themselves as learners of science outside the classroom. Children and teachers can take trips to a plant nursery or science museum. Parents and community members with experience and expertise can be invited into the classroom. Teachers can send children home with letters that offer simple ways to support continued investigation at home.

How should science be taught?

Teaching inquiry-based science carries particular responsibilities for the teacher. Derek and Katie both demonstrate a variety of roles that promote science learning. They are both clear about the goals they have for learning and how their actions relate to those goals. They also have embedded the skills and the attitudes of inquiry into the daily routine of their classrooms. The children actively investigate. They record and discuss their experiences and observations. Teachers who engage a class in science inquiry play the following four roles:

Designing a science-rich environment

Direct hands-on exploration lies at the heart of inquiry, and effective teachers design the learning environment to stimulate and support children's exploration. To create this learning environment, teachers begin by making decisions about the central concepts. For example, a teacher may decide to focus on properties of liquids and, more specifically, on water flow and water drops. Then they select materials, carefully create spaces for exploration, and design the schedule.

Selecting materials. The materials for children's exploration must connect directly to the core science learning goals. This means that teachers may have to remove materials as well as add them. Children may not be able to focus on the science of water flow when there are dolls and dishes in the water table. Materials must be plentiful, too. For example, each pair of students needs a flashlight to work with light and shadows. Basic science tools such as magnifiers, measuring instruments, and containers should be part of all classrooms.

Teachers also need to consider what materials to provide for documentation and representation. Books and other resources, such as pictures or posters, strategically placed around the room stimulate children's inquiry and provide them with needed information.

Ingrid Chalufour and Karen Worth

Teachers may worry, "I can't get all the materials needed for science."

With time and money limited, it can be difficult to get the varied materials needed for science inquiry. However, many of the materials of science are free or inexpensive. Nearby recycle centers are very useful. Printing stores, lumber yards, brick and gravel companies, and other businesses often will give away remainders and scraps. Members of the community might donate materials or money. Laboratories, science centers, colleges, and even high schools might give or loan materials. Libraries and the Internet offer free media resources.

Creating space for exploration. There are several ways to think about space. Teachers might have to temporarily rearrange a room in order to provide adequate space. For example, Derek uses his block area for the shadow theater. Katie dedicates several parts of her room to science so more children can participate. She puts the seedlings on one table and potted plants on the windowsill. Children keep track of the sprouting carrot tops and the potato on another table. It is also important to think about the way that display space can serve to stimulate and inform children's work. Posters, pictures, charts, documentation panels, and representations displayed at children's eye level help them revisit and build on their previous work and lead to new investigations. Finally, it is important to think about space beyond the classroom. Teachers extend children's learning by making connections between classroom investigations and the immediate environment of the school or community.

Teachers may express the concern, "I don't have any space to do this."

Many classrooms are small. Some have limited wall space. There may be only blacktopped playgrounds outside the school. However, any room can temporarily be rearranged, borrowing from one area to add to another. Displays can be set up on the back of a cabinet or on an extra easel. Checking beyond the school yard can turn up places to expand investigations.

Designing the schedule. In-depth investigations take time. It can take weeks, even a month or two, for children to engage deeply with a topic and build new understandings. Some studies—such as weather patterns or how the world outside changes from season to season—can last all year. Regular choice times— at least 45 minutes of uninterrupted time—allow children to get engaged, see through an exploration, and spend some time representing their experience. Children also need regular opportunities to share their experiences and explore the patterns that emerge as they put a series of experiences together. This can happen at morning meetings, at circle time, and in small groups during choice time.

Teachers may worry, "I have to cover so many things. I have no time for science."

Classroom time pressures are very real. The emphasis on standards and basic skills in literacy and mathematics encourages teachers to view the daily schedule as a series of subject-specific activities. But time might be best spent by integrating competing demands. Katie's teaching is a good example. She makes science central to her kindergarten day. She emphasizes the role of documentation. The children chart, make observational drawings, and label. They learn the concepts of print, the connection between sound and print, and how to use print to label and explain their experiences and ideas. The children also have a variety of books available—from instructional books on how to grow plants to fiction such as *The Carrot Seed* (by Ruth Krauss). Katie also incorporates appropriate mathematics learning into the data-collection process. The children measure and discuss the seedlings. In the process, they build a vocabulary for discussing relative size and shape. They develop an understanding of numbers, number patterns, relationships, and the use of measurement to provide comparative data.

Guiding children's hands-on explorations

The teacher's guidance of children's hands-on explorations is essential to the success of any science investigation. While the environment does a lot of the work, the teacher's encouragement, guidance, probing, and challenges are vital to children's learning.

Setting the stage. A teacher's introduction to the day's science activities helps children focus on important science concepts. Ways to do that include these:

• Use documents from the previous day. Katie's children's growth charts provide opportunities to stimulate new investigations or extensions of previous experiences.

• Show children new materials and ask what they might do with them. "I have these new blocks. Feel them. What do you think you might build with these?"

• Offer a challenge. Derek introduces the shadow theater and challenges the children to make different shadows. A new investigation is launched.

Closely observe children's engagement. Once children begin to work, teachers need to watch their interactions with the materials and each other. These observations form the basis for selecting interventions that are relevant to what the children are doing and thinking and that improve their understanding. For example, Derek observed his children looking at the shadow of the flag pole in the playground and suggested they might look at it at different times of the day to see if it stayed the same.

Maximize engagement. Early in a topic, teachers need to notice who is engaged and who is not. Teachers should provide encouragement to any children who remain unengaged after several days. With knowledge of the children's interests, learning styles, background knowledge, and experiences, teachers can attempt to connect them with the exploration. Children who are reticent to interact with the materials might feel more comfortable taking on a documentation role at first. Others may need help learning to use the materials. Or, the teacher may need to add materials so that more children can be engaged.

Focus attention on the science. Teachers can use strategic comments or questions to help children focus on the science they are experiencing. "I notice that the roots of your seedlings are different lengths." Or, "I wonder how you made the shadow of the crayon look shorter." These kinds of comments heighten the children's attention to their science experience.

Extend children's learning. When the teacher's goal is to extend the exploration, these interactions will go further. For example, Katie might ask a child to measure the roots of the seedlings every other day to see what happens. Derek might select several objects and then ask a child to make three differently shaped shadows with each.

Deepening children's understanding

Experiences are the basis of science learning, but reflection on those experiences is what leads children to modify any previous naïve beliefs to form more sophisticated theories. Representation and discussion are two primary ways to encourage children's reflection.

Representation. The use of various media to reflect on and communicate experiences, observations and ideas is termed *representation*. Children learn to communicate in a variety of ways when they have regular opportunities to represent their experiences and ideas. Representation gives children a chance to reflect on a recent experience. They can think about the elements that were important to them, and ultimately gain new understandings of the science they are exploring (Wells 1986). Teachers encourage representation by:

• Making representation a regular part of the classroom routine

• Selecting materials that allow for an accurate representation of the object or experience and that provide opportunities for movement and story telling

• Providing easy access to materials where the science exploration takes place

• Building special times for representation into the schedule

• Valuing all children's work

• Talking with individuals about what they have done

Teachers may say, "But my children can't write."

Even at the beginning of the year, all kindergarten children can put something down on a piece of paper or in a science notebook. They can draw, they can begin to label drawings, and they can start to put letters down for words. The desire to represent the science work they have done may motivate some children to develop and use initial writing skills.

Discussions. A group discussion stimulates and makes explicit the thinking processes that underlie inquiry. They help build a shared vocabulary and encourage collaboration. Teachers can engage small groups in retelling the steps in their investigation, analyzing the data they have collected, or solving a problem. In large groups, children can share experiences, compare and contrast what they have found out, try out a new explanation, and ask a new question. Teachers guide meaningful conversations by:

- Keeping the dialogue open ended, accepting all contributions
- Maintaining a focus on the important science concepts that are being explored
- Probing for additional observations, more specifics, and alternate points of view
- Asking children: "Why do you think?" "How do you know?"
- Giving children time to think before expecting them to speak
- Using children's work and teacher documentation to encourage children to think back on what they have done and ideas they may have
- Asking children to comment on and question each other's experiences and ideas
- Avoiding explaining the science or looking for a right answer

Teachers may protest, "My kids won't sit still and don't listen to one another."

Children need to learn discussion skills and norms. They need to be taught explicitly how to listen and how to ask a question of another child. Sitting in a circle facing one another sets the stage. Discussions should be kept short at the beginning of the year. When children have discussions regularly, their participation will increase over time.

Using ongoing assessment to inform teaching

Children's engagement and learning is contingent on the relevance of what is being taught, and whether the learning opportunities match the level of their skills and understanding. Teachers can build a relevant curriculum through ongoing assessment. Important considerations include these:

What do you expect the children to do and learn? An essential step in assessing teaching and learning is to identify the learning goals related to each topic. These include both the conceptual learning goals and the inquiry goals.

How will the children display new understandings and skills? Children's understandings are best revealed as they explore, represent, and talk. Their ideas are often evident in their interactions with materials. For example, what process does a particular child go through to make a shadow smaller? Does he go through a lot of trial and error before he finds a successful strategy? Is he able to use past experiences to come to a solution quickly? Children's understandings are also revealed in their representational work. Have they included all of the parts of their seedling in their drawings? Can they talk about the seedlings' parts using accurate terms for the roots, stem, and leaves?

> Children's understandings are best revealed as they explore, represent, and talk.

What questions are revealed in their work? Ongoing assessment is sometimes called "formative" assessment because the knowledge the teacher gains from the assessment helps him to determine what to do next. Often the assessment will uncover questions children are asking, in action or in words, which can then be used as the focus for another investigation. For example, while the children are investigating ways to change the size of shadows, Derek might observe that they show their interest in the varying shadows by using different materials. They may be curious about the materials that do or do not let some light through. This might serve as an excellent investigation for the future. Or, the teacher may realize that children are still struggling with a concept and need more time before moving on.

❖ ❖ ❖

Science is very important for kindergarten children for many reasons. Young children are naturally curious about their environment and are struggling to make sense of the world around them. A good science program engages all children in a way that builds on this natural curiosity, supports their attitudes and dispositions toward learning, and fosters inquiry skills. In addition to setting the foundation for later science learning, science investigations support other curriculum areas by providing many opportunities for developing literacy skills, applying mathematical ideas, and working together.

In this chapter, we have looked at appropriate goals for kindergarten children in science knowledge and abilities. We have emphasized the need for in-depth, long-term science studies that provide all children with the opportunities they need to develop an understanding of ideas and the nature of inquiry. We have looked at the teacher's role, highlighting the importance of the learning environment; the strategies that guide and challenge children's hands-on work; and perhaps most important, the strategies that teachers use to help children reflect on their experiences and develop science reasoning through discussion, representation, and documentation.

References

AAAS (American Association for the Advancement of Science). 1993. *Benchmarks for science literacy*. New York: Oxford University Press.

National Research Council. 1996. *National science education standards*. Washington, DC: National Academies Press.

Wells, G. 1986. *The meaning makers*. Portsmouth, NH: Heinemann.

Worth, K., & S. Grollman. 2003. *Worms, shadows, and whirlpools: Science in the early childhood classroom*. Portsmouth, NH: Heinemann; Newton, MA: EDC; Washington, DC: NAEYC.

Ingrid Chalufour and Karen Worth

Social Studies in Kindergarten

Gayle Mindes

Sally, a kindergartner, falls on the playground, skins her knee, and starts crying. Estelle, an eighth-grader, rushes to comfort Sally and take her to the nurse. How did this friendship develop? Ms. Trumpet, the kindergarten teacher, began the school year by establishing "big sister, big brother" relationships for each of the 25 kindergartners in her urban classroom, where most children have not had preschool experience. Eighth-graders read to their "little brothers and sisters" and orient them to "school." Social studies in action ... the school as community.

Social studies is the exploration of people's interactions in and with their social and physical environments. The content and process of the social studies originate in the traditional social sciences: anthropology, archaeology, economics, geography, history, law, philosophy, political science, psychology, religion, and sociology (NCSS 1994). In kindergarten, the main focus of social studies is to foster a child's awareness of self in the social setting (NCSS 1984). Young children begin to understand the larger world through their understanding of themselves and their individual experiences. Thus, in kindergarten the content focuses on self and the child's relationship to family, school, and community.

Traditionally, elementary social studies content follows a developmental path. A person be-

gins with a basic understanding of self and, in later years, develops a sense of place in a community and in the formal structures of human societies. The content in later grades gradually includes a focus on state and nation, such as state and country governments. Similarly, the basic understanding in preschool and kindergarten of how actions affect the individual child develops in later grades into an understanding of cultural norms, mores, and value systems. Today, the curriculum varies somewhat from the traditional focus, to include international topics. This recognizes children's increased exposure to global issues, and helps develop a multicultural understanding.

According to the National Council for the Social Studies, "the primary purpose of social studies is to help young people develop the ability to make informed and reasoned decisions for the public good as citizens of a culturally diverse, democratic society in an interdependent world" (NCSS 1994, 3). Thus, even as far back as the 1830s, the processes of social studies have focused on teaching citizenship and the democratic procedures of civil society. When that is the case, the overall content of social studies education is often reduced to an appreciation for citizen rights and responsibilities, the nation's core documents (such as the Declaration of Independence, the Constitution), and symbols such as the flag and patriotic songs (Oakes & Lipton 2003). Even with this political responsibility to educate citizens,

Gayle Mindes is a professor of teacher education at DePaul University.

schools in recent years have reduced the time they devote to social studies in favor of reading and mathematics. This erosion of content also leads to randomness in the selecting of topics schools will cover—maybe stories about "our neighborhood helpers," sporadic development of character education, certainly lectures on "the rules of our room."

Yet teachers know that in addition to teaching literacy and mathematics skills they must cover other important areas in social studies, including assisting children in social/emotional growth; seeking an antibias approach to values and avoiding overemphasis on "holiday" curriculum; collaborating with parents; and fostering the development of integrity in individuals and groups of children (Mindes & Donovan 2001). Fortunately, the social studies offer rich content and processes for problem solving, multicultural understandings, and critical thinking that can encompass multiple learning domains.

Developing the school self

The "school self" is the competent learner who knows when to work responsively as an individual, how to work independently, and how to reflect on tasks and accomplishments. This school self begins to develop during the preschool years, when most young children first experience a "school" setting. For children who have attended preschool, kindergarten continues this early socialization. The social demands of school will become more complex and formal for children in kindergarten.

A number of children in the United States, however, come to kindergarten with no preschool experience. According to one study, some 19 percent of children are not in any type of care outside of the home in the year before kindergarten entry; of those children who are in outside care, about 30 percent are not in formal center-based programs as their primary child care arrangement (West, Denton, & Germino-Hausken 2000). For many children, then, kindergarten is their first experience with formal group interaction. Others not enrolled in preschool may not

have "school" experience per se, but they may be veteran church-goers or play group participants and so have some familiarity with structures requiring quiet times, discussion times, and free play times.

Regardless of their experiences before kindergarten, all children must build upon prior knowledge and learn how to perform in school. A child's school self acts as a member of the classroom community, respecting the rules for group activities and the rights of classmates. The activities that kindergarten teachers plan at the beginning of the year for "getting to know you" and the ways in which the class will interact, transition, pass papers, or store materials help children begin to understand political science—the democratic principles of decision making and civic participation. With experience in school, children learn the basics of appropriate behavior and cooperative decision making. As the kindergarten year progresses, they take on more responsibility for their decisions about personal learning and contributing to the group life of the classroom.

Community building

Community-building activities involve children in creating rules for classroom behavior. Teachers can develop the *community of learners* by planning collaborative learning activities that offer multiple entry points. For example, in a thematic unit on banking, some children will read books about banks, some will visit selected Internet sites for information, and others will interview parents, school personnel, and neighbors about their experiences with banking. Then, through class discussions, the teacher gives children the opportunity to sharpen their research skills, appreciate diverse perspectives, and listen for different viewpoints.

Such activities are a natural part of the social studies and the democratic practices of our nation. Through these activities, young children learn a range of social skills that enable them to:

- Approach others positively
- Express wishes and preferences clearly
- Assert personal rights and needs appropriately
- Avoid intimidation by bullies

- Express frustration and anger appropriately
- Collaborate with peers easily
- Participate in discussion and activities
- Take turns
- Show interest in others
- Negotiate and compromise with others
- Accept and enjoy people of diverse backgrounds
- Employ appropriate nonverbal greetings and communications (McClellan & Katz 1997)

The teacher who embraces a community-building and shared decision-making approach to teaching commits to developing democratic learning processes in the classroom—focusing on cooperation, real-life problem solving, and the use of flexible and open learning sources. The teacher uses dialogue to explore the diverse ideas of the kindergartners and their feelings within the group. This builds learning processes that involve everyone and results in deep, caring, responsive, and meaningful relationships with children; celebrates the achievements of all learners as well as the group; and honors a spirit of diversity (MacNaughton & Williams 2004).

In the inevitable times when children are in conflict with one another, both teacher and children must consider, propose, and negotiate certain key elements in the classroom community. The children involved in the conflict must appreciate and see the problem from both or all sides, come up with possible solutions, find a solution that everyone agrees to try, implement and evaluate the solution to see whether it works, and apply what they've learned to future conflicts (Levin 1998).

A great deal of social studies content can be found in the everyday events of the classroom. Through the daily activities of classroom community building, teachers develop kindergartners' abilities to participate in group decision making, establish rules and consequences, express opinions in a public setting, collaborate with others, and respect public space in the classroom (Bickart, Jablon, & Dodge 1999). For example, teachers might begin a December discussion about holiday celebrations of the season—Christmas, Hanukah, Kwanza—and a conversation about those families who do not have holidays to celebrate (for example, those who are Buddhist). With some assistance from the teacher, the class could decide how to be respectful of the celebrations of some people, while not imposing traditions on others. In this way, young children gain sensitivity to the diverse belief structures within the class and knowledge of these cultural celebrations in the natural setting of the class community. Teachers can also help children to appreciate differences in peers and others. The class can compare their own rituals with those of other cultures, or talk about differences in the way people communicate (Bickart, Jablon, & Dodge 1999).

Many teachers have found class meetings to be an effective tool in community building (Vance & Weaver 2002). In class meetings, children can listen to the ideas and opinions of others, or perhaps enact role plays to resolve conflicts. For example, if a child believes that the boys are picking on the girls, the child might bring the problem to the class meeting. The teacher opens up a discussion in a comfortable place, such as the circle.

Before the discussion begins, the class reviews the rules for meetings: (1) The child bringing the problem forward clearly presents the concern and makes sure everyone understands it. (2) Those taking part in the discussion raise their hands to speak, listen politely to others' opinions, and are respectful of all opinions. (3) The teacher (or child facilitator) sums up the opinions and possible solutions to the problem. (4) The class agrees by consensus on a solution.

Character education

Character education is another area that teachers can focus on through social studies content. Kindergarten experiences help children develop an awareness of certain character traits that help people to function well in society—honesty, caring, and fairness, as examples. In turn, this awareness helps children develop into good citizens. The National Council for the Social Studies divides the values related to the promotion of the common good into four major categories: beliefs concerning societal conditions and governmental responsibilities, individual responsibilities, individual rights, and individual freedoms (Jarolimek 1990). Specific values often identified and included in this foundation for good citizenship are kindness, courtesy, honor, courage, and respect for the rights of individuals. The social studies curriculum fosters even more values, including honesty, helpfulness, fairness, justice, conviction, sound use of time and talent, tolerance, family pride, and the rights of equal opportunity (Mindes & Donovan 2001).

The values that unite and divide society about the rights, responsibilities, and experiences of individuals within and across the community influence the development of kindergartners and become a part of the daily social studies curriculum. The ways in which a kindergarten teacher preserves the common good while respecting and promoting the role of each child as a self-described individual set the stage for individual success and appreciation for diversity as a part of school life.

> The school experience is crucial in developing children's social behaviors and values.

Children's awareness of relevant character traits begins, naturally, in their family, although the traits may not be formally labeled. For example, children often learn to share with siblings but do not label that as "fairness." They learn in kindergarten how family values relate to the expectations of society.

In responsive school settings, families' home cultures influence the curriculum. Family values become the starting point for the social and ethical orientation of the classroom. This helps children negotiate the differences between their lives at home and in school. While experiences in both settings shape children's characters, the school experience is crucial in developing children's social behaviors and values.

Teachers must recognize, however, that our society is multicultural and that no one set of values can be imposed on children. To be effective, sensitive teachers learn the histories and experiences of the school's community and of each child's family. One way in which teachers acquire this cultural knowledge is by communicating regularly with parents. For many parents, their social class, immigration status and reasons for emigrating, and experiences with the dominant culture influence how they approach teachers and school. Teachers must respect parents' attitudes while encouraging two-way communication. Teachers who recognize family diversity can greatly ease children's transition into kindergarten and the world of school. Unfortunately, teachers may also have to address racism, sexism, and other forms of prejudice that diminish the experience of children and parents at their school. To mitigate the effects of prejudice, teachers who use a *culturally relevant pedagogy* (Ladson-Billings 1994) are those who make connections with home and community culture so that children see themselves in the larger social context as empowered members of society.

To teach children about values and ethical behavior, teachers first must examine their own beliefs and preconceived notions. Kindergarten teachers must remain current with the labels of cultural and social groups whose relationships and social values change (Ramsey 2004). For example, the once common expression "broken family" is not appropriate today.

What does our society value? The answer is often material goods. Children themselves can reach and be affected by this negative conclusion. They notice social class differences by observing clothes, homes, possessions (Ramsey 2004), vacations, and household help (or its absence). When teachers take an *antibias* approach to curriculum, it can help them be aware of differences in social class and values. Such teachers aim to treat all children and their families with dignity and respect. They actively recognize and work against the "personal and institutional behaviors that perpetuate oppression" (Derman-Sparks 1989, 3). Kindergarten teachers who use an antibias approach in their teaching then have it to use as a starting point for choosing their social studies content, the first step in curriculum planning.

Planning the curriculum

An integrated, theme-based approach can help children acquire tools for learning:

> As children pose questions, conduct research, engage in discussions, and present their findings, they learn to think critically and make connections between what they are learning and their own lives. In-depth studies of topics related to self, family, and community give vitality to the familiar, and encourage children to go beyond the superficial in their research efforts. (Dodge, Jablon, & Bickart 1994, 352)

This philosophy of curriculum construction is based on the principles of developmentally appropriate practice (Bredekamp & Copple 1997), particularly:

• To provide a broad range of content across traditional disciplines in a socially relevant, intellectually stimulating, and personally meaningful way

• To be mindful of each child's knowledge base

• To use a cross-disciplinary approach to curriculum while providing opportunities for subject-matter focus

• To incorporate technology judiciously in support of the construction of knowledge by children

The NAEYC principles reflect best practices. Teachers can use these principles as a guide when they select their content, strategies, and instructional materials.

Choosing the content

Teachers planning a social studies curriculum should first review the field's professional standards, which organize the content into 10 themes: Culture; Time, Continuity, and Change; People, Places, and Environments; Individual Development and Identity; Individuals, Groups, and Institutions; Power, Authority, and Governance; Production, Distribution, and Consumption; Science, Technology, and Society; Global Connections; and Civic Ideals and Practice (NCSS 1994). These themes lend themselves to a variety of interesting topics that can foster critical thinking, problem solving, and knowledge acquisition in children. Teachers can also review their state standards for more ideas for content themes.

In the preschool and kindergarten years, social studies offers a structure for broad, theme-based content. This content is organized around a topic, offering children multiple entry points and many opportunities for investigation. Kindergartners begin with a study of self, family, school, and community. The class may study topics including our school; my family; aspects of children's neighborhoods such as houses and businesses; and rich thematic units such as the study of food, clothing, shelter, childhood, money, government, communication, family living, or transportation.

In respect of an antibias approach, teachers should carefully include relevant holidays, special occasions, and ethnic customs in their curriculum in order to promote multicultural understandings. Unfortunately, many teachers have used and continue to use a "tourist" approach toward multiculturalism. This approach misuses holidays, special events, folktales, and representational music and art by presenting simplistic, isolated activities such as cooking ethnic foods without meaningful discussion, hanging travel posters, or only discussing African American accomplishments during Black History Month (Henniger 2005).

To be culturally responsive, teachers must reflect on personal cultural backgrounds and values, learn about cultures different from their own, take concrete actions to include diversity in the literature and activities of the classroom, and find ways to accommodate diverse values within the classroom (Bromer 1999). The following questions can aid in such reflection:

• Am I respectful and accepting of each child's gender, race, sex, capabilities, culture, and linguistically diverse background?

• Do the literature, resources, and materials in my classroom reflect the diversities, cultures, and languages of all the children?

• Does the curriculum that I offer celebrate diversity?

• Do I encourage families to maintain their culture and first languages?

• Do I integrate the various traditions, values, history, interests, games, music, art, languages, and families into my curriculum and programs where appropriate?

• Do I encourage many opportunities for cooperative learning? (Eliason & Jenkins 2003)

Building on the everyday aspects of social studies—classroom community building and respect for diversity—kindergarten teachers choose content that supports state standards in a variety of ways. Teachers focus on this content through a number of different strategies, often integrating multiple curricular areas.

Choosing the strategies

The integration of different curricular areas works particularly well with social studies, since the content lends itself to broad theme-based discussions about self, family, school, and community. This type of learning naturally includes multiple learning domains. For example, children who study transportation systems can explore the physics of building a bridge and also engage in literacy learning by creating traffic signs. Many of these class investigations will cover multiple standards and incorporate several themes.

A project approach. Teachers who focus intensely on a theme may find a project approach useful. Thematic, project-based curriculum should build on what children already know, develop concepts of social studies rather than focus on isolated facts, provide hands-on activities, concentrate on content and processes relevantly throughout the year, and capitalize on child interest (Katz & Chard 2000). Using the "big ideas" of social studies—that communities have structures, for example—teachers can offer an integrated curriculum that organizes instruction into child-friendly chunks that carry adult-important ideas. Another commonly developed big idea in kindergarten is the investigation of self (Who am I?). This investigation typically occurs near the beginning of the year and often highlights the growing competencies of kindergartners.

Thematic curriculum gives kindergartners the opportunity to use their budding research skills for observing, reading, writing, interviewing, and computing to pursue their own interests. They can do this through the broad nature of the inquiry process. Project- and theme-based teaching lends itself to individual and small-group activities, although they usually also include large-group summarization and culmination projects.

Cooperative learning. Through small-group activities, and with an investment of time and effort, teachers can develop children's understanding of cooperative learning. This important strategy helps children to learn cooperative problem-solving behaviors, including expressing and rationalizing one's own ideas, listening to others, and discussing different viewpoints and solutions (Morris 1977). While children are learning how to work with others, they must learn to be responsible for their own behavior—an often difficult task for kindergartners. However, for children to truly participate in cooperative learning experiences, they must be able to recognize how their own actions both positively and negatively affect the group.

Teachers can lead activities that promote cooperative learning, such as dividing the class into groups and giving the children a concrete task or a problem to solve (such as making pumpkin cookies or creating a mural that shows daily class activities). Then teachers can go on to more abstract problems such as: "The United States has many important symbols—the flag, the seal, the Pledge of Allegiance. If we were going to represent our kindergarten, what kind of symbol would we choose?" Through these group experiences, class members routinely engage in active learning—gaining knowledge and skills that build on prior knowledge, resulting in new knowledge. Through class dialogue, children clarify and explore new understandings and improve academic achievement (Cohen 1994). Cooperative learning is also ideal for implementing a project- or theme-based approach to curricula.

Critical thinking. Besides cooperative learning, kindergarten teachers can include activities that promote critical thinking as part of an investigation into social studies topics. When these activities are part of broad-based themes, they can lead to activities that touch on multiple learning domains and reinforce important concepts.

Gayle Mindes

These questions can help teachers identify opportunities for children's investigations: What do the children already know about the subject? Can they conduct firsthand observations? What artifacts are available for children to observe (photos, maps, blueprints)? Are there collections they can gather? Can the children conduct interviews? Are there experts on the topic who can visit the classroom? Are there read-aloud books available on the topic? Are there books that children can read independently? Are there suitable audiovisual or Internet materials? Are there songs that relate to the subject? What are some open-ended questions that apply? (Bickart, Jablon, & Dodge 1999)

Representation. Once children finish their investigations, teachers can offer opportunities for them to represent their learning through documentation and projects. For instance, the class may decide to illustrate their new understanding of how bread is made with a mural showing the process from harvest to table. Teachers can also explore with children the many different ways to present data. Some might be mathematical, such as charts, graphs, and maps; they may create other representations through dramatic play or organized skits. Another approach to graphically representing the themes children investigate is a "web" of ideas. The box below shows an example of webbing that demonstrates how the topic of "Family" might appear.

K-W-L. After children represent their learning, teachers should guide them to think about the questions they had at the beginning of their investigations to assess whether they have found answers. The "K-W-L" strategy is one way to do this. At the beginning of the investigation, children are asked the questions, "What do we **K**now?" and "What do we **W**ant to learn?" At the end of the project, they reflect by asking, "What have we **L**earned?" In the box below is an example related to an investigation of "Where does our food come from?"

Example of an idea web

important people who don't live with me

things we like to do at home

other important people at home

celebrations in our family

brothers and sisters

grandparents — parents — **Family**

where we live

Example of the K-W-L strategy

What do we **K**now?
Food comes from the grocery store.
There are many kinds of grocery stores.
Sometimes food comes from open air markets.
Sometimes families grow some foods.

What do we **W**ant to learn?
How does the food get to the grocery store?
Where does the food come from?
How long can the food stay in the store before people buy it?

What have we **L**earned?
Trucks deliver the food to the grocery store.
Some food is grown in our community.
Some food flies on a plane before getting to the truck.
Large warehouses store food before it goes to the grocery store.

Choosing instructional materials

Teachers rely heavily on instructional materials when they put their chosen teaching strategies into practice. A textbook or kit of books that focuses on typical kindergarten themes is often the basic instructional material in classrooms. But quality children's literature may be more useful when social studies is taught through the investigation of broad themes.

Kindergarten teachers can consult school librarians and various other sources in order to develop booklists that help children understand different topics. *The Horn Book* magazine and guide, which review children's books, are useful print sources (www.hbook.com). There are also many sources of information about children's literature on the Internet.

> Trips can be as simple as walks around the neighborhood, or as elaborate as outings to community agencies and businesses.

Besides texts, many other materials support theme-based or integrated instruction, including open-ended props typically used in sociodramatic play (Fromberg 1995). Other social studies materials include maps, globes, time lines, and computers. Kindergartners can use children's computer software programs that focus on data collection and organization, such as Kidspiration (www.inspiration.com) or Timeliner 5.0 (www.tomsnyder.com), as well as various data presentation tools, such as Kidpix 4.0 (www.broderbund.com). Classrooms with Internet connections can also use online informational resources designed for children.

Materials should reflect and offer information about people of all cultures, represent people of color, and include people with exceptionalities. While the idea that groups of people may have different but equally valid interpretations of the same event is overly sophisticated for kindergartners, teachers can help children begin to understand this by encouraging them to think about how individuals and groups experience things differently. Teachers can examine materials carefully, avoid stereotypical roles and language, and include concepts of gender equity (Morrison 2004).

Finally, social studies content naturally lends itself to field trips. Trips can be as simple as walks around the neighborhood, or as elaborate as outings to community agencies and businesses. Through their firsthand experience, children are able to:

• Encounter adult models in the world of work

• Observe social systems such as banking, garbage collection, traffic control, fire and police protection

• Use scientific methods and gain skills in observing, collecting information, making inferences, and drawing conclusions

• Use the methods of the historian as they examine the past, such as collecting oral histories or examining artifacts from their grandparent's time

• Experience knowledge together as a group that can later be translated to class drama, music, and art projects (Seefeldt & Barbour 1998)

Children can also take virtual trips through the Internet. Many sites will be useful for particular local topics, too. (For an extended list of print, multimedia, and online resources for teaching and learning about social studies, see Mindes 2005.)

Assessing and documenting learning

Particularly useful methods for assessment in the social studies rely on teacher observation supported by checklists and rubrics. Child-developed rubrics, data summaries, and the products of children's investigations are other important ways that teachers can assess and document learning. This evidence can include document panels, notebooks, paintings, collages, maps, and constructions and models in various media.

In short, the holistic teaching approach to social studies requires evaluative techniques that span the curricula (as described in the Gullo chapter in this volume).

Kindergarten social studies content includes a socialization to the world of school, a development of a sense of civic responsibility, and an introduction to basic democratic processes. This socialization occurs in a classroom setting that supports diversity and cooperative learning strategies. The broad questions that kindergartners have about themselves and their social world drive the curriculum, within the context of national and state standards. Effective teaching and evaluation approaches are holistic, such as comprehensive theme-based investigations that focus on kindergartners' acquisition of skills of inquiry and documentation.

References

Bickart, T.S., J.R. Jablon, & D.T. Dodge. 1999. *Building the primary classroom: A comprehensive guide to teaching and learning.* Washington, DC: Teaching Strategies.

Bredekamp, S., & C. Copple, eds. 1997. *Developmentally appropriate practice in early childhood programs.* Rev. ed. Washington, DC: NAEYC.

Bromer, J. 1999. Cultural variations in child care: Values and actions. *Young Children* 54 (6): 72–78.

Cohen, E.G. 1994. *Designing groupwork.* 2d ed. New York: Teachers College Press.

Derman-Sparks, L., & the ABC Task Force. 1989. *Anti-bias curriculum: Tools for empowering young children.* Washington, DC: NAEYC.

Eliason, C., & L. Jenkins. 2003. *A practical guide to early childhood curriculum.* 7th ed. Upper Saddle River, NJ: Prentice Hall/Merrill.

Fromberg, D.P. 1995. *The full-day kindergarten: Planning and practicing dynamic themes curriculum.* 2d ed. New York: Teachers College Press.

Henniger, M.L. 2005. *Teaching young children.* 3d ed. Upper Saddle River, NJ: Prentice Hall/Merrill.

Jarolimek, J. 1990. Social studies for citizens of a strong and free nation. In *Social curriculum planning resources,* 31–32. Washington, DC: National Council for the Social Studies.

Katz, L.G., & S.C. Chard. 2000. *Engaging children's minds: The project approach in education.* 2d ed. Stamford, CT: Ablex.

Ladson-Billings, G. 1994. *The dreamkeepers: Successful teachers of African-American children.* San Francisco: Jossey-Bass.

Levin, D.E. 1998. *Remote control childhood? Combating the hazards of the media culture.* Washington, DC: NAEYC.

MacNaughton, G., & G. Williams. 2004. *Teaching young children: Choices in theory and practice.* Maidenhead, Berkshire, England: Open University Press.

McClellan, D., & L. Katz. 1997. *Fostering children's social competence: The teacher's role.* Washington, DC: NAEYC.

Mindes, G. In press. *Assessing young children.* 3d ed. Upper Saddle River, NJ: Prentice Hall/Merrill.

Mindes, G. 2005. Print, multimedia, and online resources for teaching and learning about social studies. *Beyond the Journal.* Online: www.journal.naeyc.org/btj/200509/PMOResources.asp.

Mindes, G., & M.A. Donovan. 2001. *Building character: Five enduring themes for a stronger early childhood curriculum.* Needham Heights, MA: Allyn & Bacon.

Morris, R. 1977. *A normative intervention to equalize participation in task-oriented groups.* Unpublished doctoral dissertation. Stanford University. [quoted in Cohen 1994, 53–54]

Morrison, G.S. 2004. *Early childhood education today.* 9th ed. Upper Saddle River, NJ: Prentice Hall/Merrill.

NCSS (National Council for the Social Studies). 1994. *Expectations of excellence: Curriculum standards for social studies.* Silver Spring, MD: Author.

Oakes, J., & M. Lipton. 2003. *Teaching to change the world.* 2d ed. Boston: McGraw-Hill.

Ramsey, P.G. 2004. *Teaching and learning in a diverse world: Multicultural education for young children.* 3d ed. New York: Teachers College Press.

Seefeldt, C., & N. Barbour. 1998. *Early childhood education: An introduction.* 4th ed. Upper Saddle River, NJ: Prentice Hall/Merrill.

Vance, E., & P.J. Weaver. 2002. *Class meetings: Young children solving problems together.* Washington, DC: NAEYC.

West, J., K. Denton, & E. Germino-Hausken. 2000. *America's kindergartners* (NCES 2000-070). Washington, DC: National Center for Education Statistics, U.S. Department of Education.

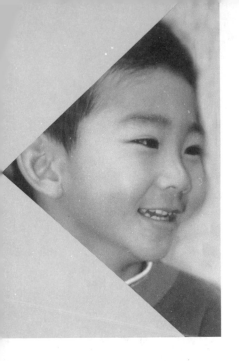

Creative Expression and Thought in Kindergarten

11

Mary Renck Jalongo & Joan Packer Isenberg

Every morning in Shayna's kindergarten, the routine is just the same—each child picks up a folder filled with pages to color, numbered dots to connect, and phonics workbook pages to complete. Shayna already knows her colors, numbers, and initial consonants and, as she impatiently plows through her work, she softly chants, "Boring, boring." A classmate seated next to her responds to the rhythm of her words by tapping a crayon on the table. Several more children soon chime in, unaware of the effect those words and sounds have on their teacher. The next day, Shayna's parents are called to the school for a conference because their child had "started a revolt in kindergarten."

As early childhood educators who have written about children's creative development for more than a decade, we interpret this incident quite differently. These kindergarten children had not conspired to make their teacher look bad; rather, they were pleading for a chance to move beyond mindless busywork. In short, they were calling out for opportunities to think creatively. In this chapter, we will examine creative thought and expression in kindergartners from the perspective of contemporary cognitive psychology. We will also identify the characteristics of learning experi-

Mary Renck Jalongo is a professor in the department of professional studies in education at Indiana University of Pennsylvania. Joan Packer Isenberg is a professor and associate dean for outreach and program development in the College of Education and Human Development at George Mason University.

ences that support creative thought, growth, and expression in kindergarten students, and that meet national standards. Finally, we will suggest research-based ways that adults—parents, families, teachers, and administrators—can support the kindergarten child's creative growth and development.

How is creative thought and expression manifested?

A class of early childhood education majors were assigned to interview a young child about drawing and writing, obtain a sample of the child's work, and bring it to class for discussion. One of the drawings appeared to be an adult's attempt to draw childishly. Before class, the professor spoke privately with the student who had submitted it. The student confirmed what her professor suspected and then wondered aloud, "But how could you tell?" Without sharing any details of the incident, the forged drawing was later shown to a large group of experienced kindergarten teachers. Not one of them was fooled. It was easy to distinguish between child and adult drawings, they said: the lines in a young child's drawings would be less controlled, the person in the drawing would appear to be floating on the page, and the drawing would look fresher, more original—certainly not a stereotypical stick figure.

These teachers were describing a young child's budding creativity, which is stronger in unique ideas than in controlled techniques for expressing those ideas (Fishkin & Johnson 1998). Kindergarten teachers realize this, but often the curriculum fails to reflect such understandings. In fact, most kindergarten curriculum has it backward: Children are given the ideas—the help they need the *least*—when they are asked to copy, trace, or imitate a model. Children rarely get the help they need *most*—coaching in techniques—because many adults assume that this would somehow compromise the child's creativity. Actually, mastering techniques gives children greater skill in expressing their creative ideas. A look at the artwork produced by children in programs using the Reggio Emilia approach, or at the impressive musical achievement attained by children in the Suzuki method, serves to remind us that training in technique can yield positive results without compromising creativity. Creative thought and expression is a form of "regulated curiosity" that combines intensity with playfulness (Kashdan & Fincham 2002). An artist's behaviors may be inspired, yes, but they are also planned, and techniques are controlled and practiced.

Stated plainly, many educators' ideas about creative thought and expression are outmoded (Jalongo 2003). To illustrate, let's consider three widespread misunderstandings about young children's creativity.

Myth 1: Creativity is limited to the arts

One pervasive assumption about creative thought and expression is that it is exclusively about the arts. Yet brilliance in any field is connected with creative thought and expression, for these are the ways of knowing that raise performance in all disciplines to the highest levels. Across the curriculum, it is important to allow children to select an interesting line of inquiry, engage in it fully, implement and revise ideas, and critically evaluate the results. If a 5-year-old is trying to fashion a lion puppet out of a sock and a collection of buttons, yarn, and fabric, the child has a goal in mind and many choices to make along the way. In order to succeed, the child will need to evaluate each decision: "What sort of eyes should my lion have and how can I make him look fierce? . . . This yarn could work for the mane, but how will it move and how do I attach it? . . . How will I use my voice and movement to make my puppet come alive?"

Myth 2: Creative thought and expression focus primarily on feelings

Popular opinion holds that creative thought and expression focus primarily on feelings and are valuable for their ability to provide an emotional release. However, creative thought and expression focus every bit as much on thinking—notably on the discovery of interesting problems and engagement in problem-solving processes—as they do on feelings. The behavior of Tamyra, a kindergarten child with leukemia, offers an illustration of this point:

> Tamyra's illness requires frequent hospital stays and she participates in the activity program there. As she draws a picture, Tamyra thinks out loud: "I'm gonna draw a princess—no, a fairy. Look, here's a pink crayon with the point still on. I'll give her a pink dress and make her wings kinda blue, kinda silvery. There! I'm done." With that announcement, the child artist turns her head to the side and leans down close to her drawing, as if listening, then reports, "She says she *had* a magic wand but she lost it to a wicked witch." Tamyra's drawing stimulates a discussion about magical powers among the other children who are participating in the hospital's activity program.

Tamyra's pink fairy drawing is a perfect example of creative expression. Although strong feelings were linked with the experience, there was much more to it than that. Tamyra used internal thought processes to plan her drawing and language to talk about it; she used crayon techniques to solve the puzzle of how to make the wings look transparent and iridescent; and she drew upon her prior knowledge of fantasy to imagine a fairy. Ultimately, the lives of Tamyra and her family, her fellow patients, and the health care professionals were touched by the comments and conversation about that imaginary persona brought to life and proudly displayed on the bulletin board.

Myth 3: Creativity is free, natural, and innate and cannot be taught

Imagine the following two kindergarten classrooms. In the first, Mrs. Marten believes that a teacher's main responsibility is only to provide a supply of new and unusual materials. Her classroom is in a constant state of disarray. In the second, Miss Hernandez worries that parents will not think their child's work is good enough, and she stays after school to "improve" her students' work with tape and glue.

As these situations illustrate, there is a tendency toward one extreme or the other regarding kindergarten art. Teachers often are laissez-faire and provide no instruction in technique, or are overly controlling and prevent children from using their own ideas. The problem with the first situation—an "all-process" approach—is that the activities are not linked to learning goals and are frivolous and expendable. The problem with the second situation—an "all-product" approach—is that the activities simply consist of assembly line tasks that may not even result in the child's own work. If a project fails to break stereotypes and allow for the expression of originality, it has nothing to do with art.

In kindergarten, most children are learning to use some basic tools for creative expression— paints and brushes, simple musical instruments, toys for dramatic play, props to combine with creative dance, and computer software. Learners need both freedom and structure, not one or the other. They also need material resources, learning opportunities, enthusiastic role models, and diverse experiences across the disciplines in order to discover their gifts and put innate talents to work. Above all, they need to learn to use work habits that develop talent and will serve them well throughout life: habits such as persistence, deliberate practice, and collaborative approaches.

Fostering creative growth in the kindergarten child

Classrooms that foster children's creative growth have teachers who are accepting and caring, have high expectations, show genuine interest in children's activities, and provide materials that capture and sustain children's interest and imagination. Think about a kindergarten classroom that has a camping theme as its conceptual unit. The kindergarten teacher reads several camping stories, such as *Maisy Goes Camping* (by Lucy Cousins), to help children elaborate on their ideas during dramatic play. The children brainstorm ideas about camping and suggest categories of where to camp (backyard, state park, lake, campground), how to get there (walk, car, trailer, truck), where to sleep (camper, tents, sleeping bags), what to eat (trail mix, hot dogs), and things to do (swim, tell stories, hike). The teacher clears a corner of the room so that the children can develop the camping theme, and she leaves it in place for as long as children's interests allow. The children also use, make, or bring in various props to represent a campfire, trees, a lake, trails, and wildlife. Following a few days of play and enactment, the teacher adds some new materials and props, and asks some new questions to spur the children's creative expression.

Teaching for creative growth requires tapping into children's potential, helping them learn new skills, and developing their intrinsic motivation (Lynch & Harris 2001). The features of a kindergarten classroom are critical to fostering children's creativity. The box opposite describes and provides examples of four key features.

What makes a learning experience creative?

The first and most fundamental criterion in determining the value of creative activities in kindergarten is whether they have meaning for the children. Not all learning experiences even have the potential to tap into children's creative processes. Experiences with the *most potential* for creative expression require the least amount of teacher direction and control but do require guidance and scaffolding. An activity such as imagining various foods springing to life after hearing the classic Gingerbread Man story can easily satisfy children, does not require a great deal of skill, and focuses on expression rather than on the use of the materials. Experiences that maximize creative potential should be an essential daily part of the kindergarten curriculum.

Mary Renck Jalongo and Joan Packer Isenberg

Classroom features that promote creativity

Teaching/learning environment

Provides a predictable environment with clear expectations and a climate that encourages children to "feel" creativity

Accommodates different instructional strategies, nurtures creative work by promoting independence, and allows children unrestricted access to centers, books, media, and other materials without disrupting the work of others

Offers a comfortable space, lighting, temperature, and aesthetics

Is characterized by productive noise, a hum of activity, and on-task behavior

Possesses an inviting atmosphere

Includes a private space for creative work to be done, such as a loft or an upholstered chair, with a clipboard and crayons

Offers a large supply of open-ended materials, such as recyclable materials, dress-ups for dramatic play, and plastic containers of assorted sizes and shapes, for children to explore

Teacher

Is warm, genuine, and respectful when working with, observing, and listening to children

Responds to children's work in concrete, specific, and personal ways, such as "I can see that you were drawing people with different kinds of hair— straight, curly, short, and long. Which kind of hair do I have?"

Has a "Let's try this" or "Why not?" attitude that sends the message of openness to suggestions from the children and a willingness to venture with them as they explore creative media

Invites possibilities from the materials offered

Offers choices of open-ended, friendly materials, such as markers, crayons, colored pencils, pastels, or paint, a drama center that can be transformed into several different settings, and blocks, sand, and water

Encourages children to imagine in all domains, such as thinking up a solution to a conflict, building a long train, or moving like a tiger

Avoids evaluating children's work, and does not ask, "What is it?" or remark, "It doesn't look like an elephant"

Children

Are able to talk directly to one another, rather than only to the teacher, in response to specific questions as they explore possible ideas

Experience daily opportunities with creative expression

Have opportunities to explain what they mean by illustrating their ideas graphically, enacting them, or singing about them

Have opportunities to engage in the creative process with a variety of available materials and tools without focusing on the final product

Ask and answer questions of teachers and peers

Have opportunities to demonstrate or explain their projects and activities to others

Choose from overlapping, simultaneous learner-centered activities

Children's work

Is handled and transported home with respect (paint and glue are allowed to dry first, clay creations are carried home in a clean, empty milk carton)

Is displayed in different ways (on bulletin boards, with signs, on shelves, in the hallways, in display cases, hanging from the ceiling, framed)

Reveals that children are encouraged to revisit work and refine it rather than being rushed to the final product (for example, a writing/drawing portfolio includes drafts of stories and illustrations for a picture book)

Provides information about processes and products as part of student work displays

Includes projects that show evidence of collaboration with peers

Sources: Crawford 2004; Hendrick 2003; Kohn 1996; Lynch & Harris 2000

Experiences with *potential* for creative expression generally require more skill on the part of the children and more instruction by the teacher, tend to have a definite focus and direction even without the use of a model, and allow for individual expression. An example here might be decorating a pumpkin or making spring flowers. Experiences with the *least potential* for creative expression—copying, coloring in the lines, using stencils, filling out worksheets, following a model—may teach specific skills but are not creative (Hendrick 2003).

Learning experiences that stimulate creativity, curiosity, and problem solving are the vehicles through which we teach what kindergarten children need. Such experiences connect to standards across all disciplines and require children to tinker and experiment, visualize and model, brainstorm and role play, inquire and problem solve, as well as to paint, draw, dramatize, act, and dance their understandings (Isenberg & Jalongo 2006). The following five questions can help teachers promote kindergartners' creative thought (Crawford 2004; Jensen & Kiley 2005):

1. Does the activity make content more accessible? There are curricular standards that kindergarten children everywhere are expected to meet. The key is to make that content individually and age-appropriate for kindergartners so they can understand and use the knowledge and skills expected of them. The box on the next page summarizes a kindergarten unit on seeds, showing how its activities and experiences connect to multiple standards.

2. Does the activity encourage joyful, active learning? If a kindergartner chooses to draw a blue cat with orange ears and six legs and talks about a "silly animal," will that child be allowed to relish the moment and find enjoyment and fun in learning? Children need to try new things without fear of making mistakes, looking silly, or feeling awkward. Consequently, joyful, active learning prompts creative expression.

3. Does the activity help children express their personal connections to the content? Five-year-old Haley was captivated by the story of *Perfect the Pig* (by Susan Jeschke), in which a homeless, flying piglet is found, loved, and cared for by a young woman who decides to name him Perfect. Perfect is stolen and abused by a man who operates a carnival sideshow, then is happily

---

What kindergarten children need to develop creatively

Because kindergarten children tend to explore and play . . . They need activities that capitalize on their interests and passions, allow them to set the pace and take the lead, and respect their different levels of development.

Because kindergarten children tend to be curious and ask questions . . . They need support as they use the processes of exploring, selecting, combining, and refining a form, as well as the chance to pursue questions they generate themselves, questions posed by peers, and questions framed by adults.

Because kindergarten children tend to make guesses and pursue new challenges . . . They need to formulate hypotheses and try things out to test their ideas.

Because kindergarten children tend to approach learning holistically . . . They need to engage in activities that use multidisciplinary approaches that orient children to the creative-thinking processes that are common and unique to different subject areas.

Because kindergarten children seek to make sense out of their world . . . They need activities that are relevant and understandable to them as learners as they pursue a line of inquiry.

Because kindergarten children tend to seek competence . . . They need to engage in long-term, open-ended projects and pursue a narrower range of ideas and materials in greater depth so that they can acquire skill in self-evaluation.

Sources: Isenberg & Jalongo 2006; Stanko 2001

Mary Renck Jalongo and Joan Packer Isenberg

Addressing standards in the arts and other domains: A unit on seeds

Learning experiences	Standards in the arts and other domains	
Mathematics		
Sort, count, and make patterns using three or more different types of beans. Use instruments or improvised sounds to compose a song by assigning a different sound for each seed in their bean pattern. Sing their songs and have their classmates identify the pattern.	**Music:** Performing on instruments, alone and with others, a varied repertoire of music Improvising melodies, variations, and accompaniments Composing and arranging music within specified guidelines Understanding relationships between music, the other arts, and disciplines outside the arts	**NCTM:** Number and Operations; Data Analysis; Reasoning and Proof; Communication **NSTA:** Life Science
Language arts		
Listen to the story *The Tiny Seed* and depict their own seed adventure using torn paper to imitate Eric Carle's collage technique. Share their collage and seed adventure.	**Visual arts:** Understanding and applying media, techniques, and processes Choosing and evaluating a range of subject matter, symbols, and ideas Making connections between the visual arts and other disciplines	**NCTE:** Reading for Perspective; Evaluation Strategies **NSTA:** Life Science
Science		
Through guided imagery and movement activity, learn how sun, air, water, and soil help seeds grow into healthy plants. Dance the plant cycle using basic story elements of beginning, middle, and end.	**Dance:** Identifying and demonstrating movement elements and skills in performing dance Understanding choreographic principles, processes, and structures Understanding dance as a way to create and communicate meaning Making connections between dance and other disciplines	**NCTE:** Communication Strategies **NSTA:** Life Science
Social studies/economics		
Design a garden shop and engage in dramatic play using pretend money to buy goods and distinguish between wants and needs.	**Drama:** Acting by assuming roles and interacting in improvisations Designing by visualizing and arranging environments for classroom dramatizations	**NCSS:** Production, Distribution, and Consumption **NSTA:** Life Science **NCTM:** Measurement; Connections; Communication

Key: NCTM (National Council of Teachers of Mathematics), NSTA (National Science Teachers Association), NCTE (National Council of Teachers of English), NCSS (National Council for the Social Studies) reunited with the woman when a judge awards her custody. After hearing this story, Haley pretends to be Perfect, experiencing the feelings and thoughts of the pig. She also decides which props ("I'll need wings") and behaviors ("This is how he oinks when he needs help") she needs to enact that role.

4. Does the activity help children understand and express symbolic concepts? For children to understand and represent ideas symbolically, they must first experience them concretely. Using the book *Car Washing Street* (by Denise Lewis Patrick), kindergarten children can experience the concept of neighbors and a neighborhood. They envision their own neighborhoods with what they see in their minds (sidewalk, buildings, houses, trees) and represent these images through painting and color. They then can begin to think about how to represent the areas around their homes after a book such as *Mapping Penny's World* (by Loreen Leedy) has stimulated their thinking. All children's images and rudimentary maps can be displayed in a visible and attractive place in the classroom.

> By kindergarten, children enjoy illustrating their own stories and can even create their own books.

5. Does the activity help children develop collaborative work skills? Children's deepest, longest-lasting learning comes when they are working with others. Collaborative creative endeavors create and sustain community and promote knowledge retention. Children working together creatively engage in intense social interaction, absorb and expand their learning, and often reach a level of imaginative expression and understanding that one student could not achieve alone. In a collaborative mural project, for example, kindergartners must pay careful attention to one another's work. Music also provides a wonderful opportunity for collaboration, with harmonies, rounds, and call-and-response songs and chants.

Creative learning experiences contain a variety of opportunities for children to express themselves with both peers and adults. When teachers are open to children's creative efforts and provide rich activities, they build the foundation for a meaningful curriculum. Thus, teachers exert a powerful influence over children's creative expression.

How can teachers foster creativity while meeting standards?

Standards in the expressive arts are not strictures preventing creativity but signposts guiding teachers to create meaningful experiences for children. The traditional subject areas in the expressive arts are visual arts (such as drawing, painting, and sculpture), music, movement, dance, and drama. In 1994, content standards for the arts were developed by the Consortium of National Arts Education Associations, comprising major arts organizations such as the National Art Education Association, the National Association for Music Education, and the Educational Theatre Association. These standards describe what children in K–12 programs should know and be able to do in the arts. They are accessible online at www.ed.gov/pubs/ArtsStandards.html.

In the visual arts, standards include such topics as the examination and exploration of a variety of materials, experimentation with tools and processes, obtaining an appreciation for works of art and an understanding of how professional artists work, and the use of artistic processes and techniques for individual expression. Some of the best arts activities for kindergartners are those that integrate different subject domains while encouraging children's creative expression. For example, in the early years there is a high degree of overlap between drawing and writing—in fact, early writing emerges from children's experiments with drawing and mark-making (Schickedanz 1999). By kindergarten, children enjoy illustrating their own stories and can even create their own books. There is also ample opportunity to integrate arts and mathematics learning, such as learning about patterns or creating designs using symmetry and geometric shapes.

Many of the content standards associated with music, movement, dance, and drama involve encouraging children to involve their bodies in

Mary Renck Jalongo and Joan Packer Isenberg

creative expression, which may or may not include performance. Related activities often involve more than one art form: children may sing a song about a tree blowing in the wind while simultaneously acting this out through dance. Teachers also will find that the physical arts are an excellent means to integrate a wide array of curricular material. For example, after reading the classic children's story *The Three Billy Goats Gruff*, children can reenact the story as a short play, complete with a counting song about goats, animal and troll masks made by the children, and painted scenery. This one activity combines literacy, mathematics, visual arts, and drama!

Kindergarten teachers should not have to justify including the creative arts in their classrooms. But with so much pressure on today's kindergarten curriculum, the arts are sometimes in danger of being marginalized. However, teachers who are knowledgeable about the content standards in all curriculum areas and understand how the arts can be used to integrate subject matter will find it easier to make the case for them.

What changes might kindergarten teachers need to make?

Studies show that teachers are constrained by at least four things that dilute the power of creative thought and expression through art (Bressler 1998): (1) time—choosing quick projects to conform to a certain time block; (2) materials—using inexpensive materials, since high-quality art materials are not supplied; (3) physical environment—being overly concerned about neatness and cleanup; and (4) presentation—having a lack of space and resources for appropriate display of children's art.

One simple, yet effective, improvement in the kindergarten curriculum is to reject assembly line tasks and ready-made crafts, recognizing that these pursuits are busywork disguised as art. The box beginning on the next page outlines children's needs, the research that supports creative expression, and practical ideas for teachers.

Two kindergarten teachers asked to speak with their first grade colleagues about a disturbance during recess: the first-graders were pressing their faces up against the windows of the kindergarten classroom, distracting the 5-year-olds and their teachers. When the first grade teachers asked their students about these incidents, the children's responses were surprising. One child said wistfully, "Remember when we used to play?" Another remarked, "I wish I could play in the home life center again." And a third asked, "Why do we have to work so much in first grade?"

Kindergarten teachers today are under constant pressure to completely disregard the Froebelian origins of the kindergarten in favor of a get-ready-for-the-harsh-realities-of-elementary-school approach. But creative expression and the arts should not be abandoned; they should be made more meaningful and forge a stronger connection with learning. Every activity done in the name of creativity should contribute to learning, not only during kindergarten but throughout life.

Creative expression and the arts are not the opposite of "the basics." Arguably, they are the ultimate basics, because they are the activities we spontaneously and voluntarily engage in. If we doubt that this is true, we need only open our eyes and look around to see the disaffected teenager who would not think of leaving home without an MP3 player, the baby boomers who are moved to tears as they watch an award-winning movie, and the seniors who enthusiastically enroll in art, crafts, and creative writing classes in order to acquire long wished-for abilities. Creative thought and expression is more like the root system of the tree of learning than the small leaves and twigs, for without creative thought, learning in any of the subject areas is stunted and cannot flourish.

(continued on p. 126)

Research findings on kindergarten children's developmental needs, and implications for practice

What the research says	What kindergarten teachers can do
Children need to develop:	
Accurate ideas about creativity and insights into their own creative thought processes	
Adults often incorrectly assume that a child demonstrating a behavior earlier than most peers *(precocity)* is creative, when this is not necessarily the case (Nicholson & Moran 1986).	Create a classroom climate that permits alternative solutions.
Many teachers do not realize that thinking "outside the box" is a key element of creative thought, and teachers often are intolerant of children who dare to be different (Craft 2000).	Serve as a model of creative thought by using a think-aloud strategy to demonstrate problem solving.
	Educate colleagues and the community about contemporary views of creative thought.
Strategies for developing ideas and pursuing them with intensity	
The child at play is the prototype for the creative adult's fluid-adaptive thinking that is simultaneously serious and playful (Rea 2001).	Offer high-quality materials and effective instruction that give children real choices, capitalize on their interests, and give them time to become fully engaged.
Research on creative thinking often describes an ability to focus with such intensity that a person becomes "lost" in the work and time flies by unnoticed (Kasdan & Finchham 2002).	Provide challenging and stimulating learning materials.
When children are pressured to dash something off to meet someone else's schedule, they learn to value the quantity of work produced over the quality of the finished product (Amabile 2001).	Offer opportunities to work with varied materials under different conditions.
Recognition and respect from adults for their creative efforts	
Adults need to be aware that play during early childhood is predictive of facility with divergent thinking later on (Russ, Robins, & Christiano 1999).	Enable self-directed work that allows for initiative, spontaneity, and experimentation.
Children learn to value creative responses when adults encourage and accept constructive nonconformist behavior, take children's questions seriously and tolerate "sensible" or bold errors, help students learn to cope with frustration and failure, and reward courage as much as getting the right answer (Clark 1996; Cropley 2001; Urban 1996).	Actively teach creative strategies.
	Foster intense concentration and task commitment through high motivation and interest in self-selected topics.

Mary Renck Jalongo and Joan Packer Isenberg

What the research says	What kindergarten teachers can do

Respect for different ways of thinking and responding creatively

A review of 62 studies concluded that arts education has particular advantages for the economically disadvantaged, yet this is the population least likely to have extensive opportunities and a wide variety of materials (Manzo 2002).

One study found that African American students tended to outperform their peers in fluency and flexibility of thought, yet these abilities often were overlooked or actively discouraged by teachers (Clasen, Middleton, & Connell 1994).

Advocate for school policies that promote equal access to creative expression and the arts.

Create organizational and structural conditions that allow open and flexible distribution of roles, themes, problems, and activities.

Teach children to interpret creative products by discussing what the work is, who produced it, why it was made, how was produced, and the contribution that the work made to the culture.

Work with programs that bring diverse artists and creative individuals from various fields to school.

Skills in self-assessment

Over-reliance on conspicuous rewards may actually diminish the desired behavior (Fawson & Moore 1999).

A child might settle on a less innovative response to avoid rejection or might become so distracted by the prize that it diverts attention from the task (Joussement & Koestner 1999).

Encourage rather than praise. In praise, the teacher passes judgment on the quality of the child's work ("That's a very good story") rather than acknowledging the child's efforts ("I noticed that you worked very hard to revise your story until it was ready to be published online").

Surprise students with recognition for creative processes and products, rather than announcing rewards and making everything into a contest.

Increase children's autonomy in learning by engaging them in self-evaluation of their efforts ("Which of your stories and drawings do you like the best? Why?").

Confidence in their own abilities to think creatively and express original ideas

Too much or too little structure can interfere with the development of creative expression (McLeod 1997); creativity flourishes in learning environments that offer a blend of high support and high expectations (Rea 2001).

Provide support and positive feedback for problem finding not just problem solving.

Tolerate ambiguity and accept alternative solutions.

Allow for humor and playfulness.

Make adaptations that focus on children's strengths, and adapt the environment to enable all children to participate.

References

Amabile, T.M. 2001. Beyond talent: John Irving and the passionate craft of creativity. *American Psychologist* 56: 333–36.

Bressler, L. 1998. "Child art," "fine art," and "art for children": The shaping of school practice and implications for change. *Arts Education and Policy Review* 100 (1): 3–10.

Clark, C. 1996. Working with able learners in regular classrooms. *Gifted and Talented International* 11: 34–38.

Clasen, D., J. Middleton, & T. Connell. 1994. Assessing artistic and problem-solving performance in minority and nonminority students using a nontraditional multidimensional approach. *Gifted Child Quarterly* 38: 27–32.

Craft, A. 2000. *Creativity across the primary curriculum: Framing and developing practice.* London: Routledge.

Crawford, L. 2004. *Lively learning: Using the arts to teach the K–8 curriculum.* Greenfield, MA: Northeast Foundation for Children.

Cropley, A.J. 2001. *Creativity in education and learning: A guide for teachers and educators.* London: Kogan Page.

Fawson, P.C., & S.A. Moore. 1999. Reading incentive programs: Beliefs and practices. *Reading Psychology* 20: 325–40.

Fishkin, A.S., & A.S. Johnson. 1998. Who is creative? Identifying children's creative abilities. *Roeper Review* 21 (1): 40–46.

Hendrick, J. 2003. *Total learning: Developmental curriculum for the young child.* 6th ed. Upper Saddle River, NJ: Merrill/Prentice Hall.

Isenberg, J.P., & M.R. Jalongo. 2006. *Creative thinking and arts-based learning: Preschool through fourth grade.* 4th ed. Upper Saddle River, NJ: Merrill/Prentice Hall.

Isenberg, J.P., & N. Quisenberry. 2002. Play: Essential for all children. Position paper for the Association for Childhood Education International. *Childhood Education* 79 (1): 33–39.

Jalongo, M.R. 2003. The child's right to creative thought and expression. International position paper of the Association for Childhood Education International. *Childhood Education* 79 (4): 218–28.

Jensen, R., & T. Kiley. 2005. *Teaching, leading and learning in pre K–8 settings.* 2d ed. Boston: Houghton Mifflin.

Joussement, M., & R. Koestner. 1999. Effect of expected rewards on children's creativity. *Creativity Research Journal* 12 (4): 231–39.

Kashdan, T.B., & F.D. Fincham. 2002. Facilitating creativity by regulating curiosity. *American Psychologist* 57 (5): 373–74.

Kohn, A. 1996. What to look for in a classroom. *Educational Leadership* 54 (1): 54–55.

Lynch, M.D., & C.R. Harris. 2001. *Fostering creativity in children, K–8.* Boston: Allyn & Bacon.

Manzo, K.K. 2002. Arts programs enhance some skills, study says. *Education Week* 21 (36): 5.

McLeod, L. 1997. Children's metacognition: Do we know what they know? And if so, what do we do about it? *Australian Journal of Early Childhood* 22 (2): 6–11.

Nicholson, M.W., & J.D. Moran. 1986. Teachers' judgments of preschoolers' creativity. *Perceptual and Motor Skills* 63: 1211–16.

Rea, D. 2001. Maximizing the motivated mind for emergent giftedness. *Roeper Review* 23 (3): 157–64.

Russ, S.W., A.L. Robins, & B.A. Christiano. 1999. Pretend play: Longitudinal prediction of creativity and affect in fantasy in children. *Creativity Research Journal* 12 (2): 129–39.

Schickedanz, J.A. 1999. *Much more than the ABCs: The early stages of reading and writing.* Washington, DC: NAEYC.

Stanko, A.J. 2001. *Creativity in the classroom: Schools of curious delight.* Mahwah, NJ: Erlbaum.

Urban, K.K. 1996. Encouraging and nurturing creativity in school and workplace. In *Human Resource Development,* eds. U. Munander & C. Semiawan, 78–97. Jakarta: University of Indonesia Press.

Mary Renck Jalongo and Joan Packer Isenberg

Physical Education in Kindergarten

Stephen W. Sanders

For young children, movement is at the very center of their lives.

—David L. Gallahue (1995, 125)

Kindergarten is a time of discovery. At this age, children are fascinated with learning what their bodies can do—how fast they can run, how high they can jump, how skillfully they can move. They are becoming more sophisticated in their movements, more coordinated in their physical endeavors, and increasingly more competent in physical skills such as balance and eye-hand coordination. Kindergarten is also a crucial time when children begin to establish health and activity preferences and habits that will stay with them for a lifetime.

Young children have a natural interest in and enthusiasm for physical activity and play. They use movement to express their feelings, manipulate objects, and learn about their world. They also delight in physical accomplishment. Kindergarten educators have long understood that one of the ways in which young children learn is through their bodies. Learning through movement has always been a critical part of daily life in early childhood classrooms. But the importance of physical activity has taken on a new significance

today. We now understand that daily developmentally appropriate movement experiences in childhood can shape how physically active, competent, and healthy children will be throughout their lives.

In addition to giving children the opportunity to experience the joy and satisfaction inherent in movement, physical education should foster a positive attitude toward physical activity, self and body images, and physical skill competency. As classroom teachers, we play a significant role in helping kindergarten children understand the importance of learning through movement and participating daily in physical activity. Our enthusiasm, active support, and knowledge of child development are instrumental in increasing children's physical skills while helping them build a strong foundation of physical competency for the future.

Though physical activity has many different functions throughout our lifespan, one aspect remains constant: The ability to be physically active affects such quality-of-life issues as good physical health, positive mental health, and constructive social relationships. This chapter will review the current thinking about physical education and young children, what teachers should know about kindergarten physical education, and how to foster children's healthy development in this area.

Stephen W. Sanders is the director of the School of Physical Education, Wellness, and Sport Studies at the University of South Florida.

The basics

Empirical evidence clearly shows that movement is a fundamental function of life. Regular physical activity in childhood and adolescence improves strength and endurance, helps build healthy bones and muscles, helps control weight, reduces anxiety and stress, increases self-esteem, and may improve blood pressure and cholesterol levels (CDC 1996). Movement enhances social and emotional development by fostering cooperation and communication skills, and it promotes cognitive development as children learn to think about their actions and body movements (Sawyer 2001).

We know that in young children, all learning takes place in three interwoven domains—physical, cognitive, and social-emotional. Children acquire knowledge in all of these domains through play, experimentation, exploration, and discovery. Because facilitation of one domain can enhance learning in the others, links between physical education and other curriculum areas can better teach the whole child.

Physical education today has another important role—to fight childhood obesity. Consider Marcus:

> It's time for recess. Eight kindergarten boys and girls sprint to a large tree some 20 yards away across the playground. In this daily routine, Marcus always finishes last. In fact, by the time he reaches the tree—sweat dripping from his forehead—the others are already there, climbing and swinging. He's 5 years old and weighs close to 120 pounds. While the other children remain physically active throughout the playtime, Marcus spends the next 30 minutes sitting.

Though few children at age 5 are as overweight as Marcus, obesity in young children does pose a major health concern. A lack of daily physical activity is a major contributing factor. In 1970, the obesity rate in children was about 4 percent; it is now well over 20 percent and rising. If the trend continues, by the time today's kindergarten children reach age 40, more than 60 percent will be overweight (CDC 1996).

Both research and experience tell us that children who do not develop a foundation of basic motor skills are less likely to participate in physical activity on a daily basis—just as a lack of basic literacy skills would be a major reason for low reading rates. And we cannot assume that children will develop physical skills simply as they mature or in free play, no matter how vigorous (Gallahue & Ozmun 1995). In fact, kindergarten children need instruction and practice to develop the skills of throwing, catching, kicking, skipping, galloping, balancing, and so on.

The ideal time for children to develop these basic skills is from age 2 to 7—during their "fundamental movement phase" (Gallahue 1995). Most 2- and 3-year-olds attempt to throw, catch, or jump, but their movements are relatively crude and uncoordinated (the "initial" stage). By ages 4 and 5, most children have progressed by maturation to an "elementary" stage. They have greater control over their movements but still look awkward and their movements are not yet fluid. (Many adults never exit the elementary stage in basic activities such as throwing and catching.) By age 6 or 7 most children have the developmental potential to be at a "mature" stage in most fundamental movement skills. This means that they can integrate all the parts of a particular pattern of movement into a well-coordinated, mechanically correct act appropriate to the demands of the task.

In order to progress from the elementary stage to the mature stage, kindergartners need the guidance of interested and involved adults within an environment filled with developmentally appropriate equipment. They need to learn through exploration and guided discovery experiences. And they need plenty of encouragement as well as opportunities to practice the skills they are learning.

As with all areas of development, no two children are alike. Some kindergartners will come close to or reach the mature level for some skills, while others will need more guidance and practice. In general, girls tend to be more advanced than boys in fine motor skills and in gross motor skills that require precision such as hopping and skipping. Boys tend to do better with skills that require force and power such as running and jumping (Berk 1996).

Stephen W. Sanders

Building a developmentally appropriate program

Two documents, *Appropriate Practices in Movement Programs for Young Children* (NASPE 2000) and *Active Start: A Statement of Physical Activity Guidelines for Children Birth to Five Years* (NASPE 2002), help define a unified, profession-wide position on developmentally appropriate physical activity programs for all grade levels. They offer a roadmap to better educate young children and their families about the importance of regular physical education.

The National Association for Sport and Physical Education (NASPE), which published both documents, holds the position that all kindergarten children should take part in daily physical activity that fosters health-related fitness and the development of movement skills. NASPE promotes the development of these skills at an early age in ways that meet young children's unique developmental characteristics.

NASPE (2000) has developed the following principles to support the practice of developmentally appropriate physical education and learning:

Young children are not miniature adults. Youth sports and *movement programs* are not the same. Most young children are not developmentally ready for the skills and pressures associated with sports such as soccer or gymnastics. And "watered-down" adult activities can be both frustrating and unsafe for young children.

Kindergartners should not be asked to achieve a high level of competence in any one skill. At their age, it is better to introduce a variety of skills in structured ways and then provide plenty of unstructured time so they can practice and apply the skills in their play. For example, children need instruction in specific skills to learn to climb, throw a ball, or jump. Then they need practice opportunities over time and within many different contexts.

Activities should span a variety of developmental levels. As with any area of curriculum, teachers need to tailor activities to match children's varying developmental levels of ability.

Young children learn and develop in an integrated fashion. Because young children do not learn in a compartmentalized way, movement learning should encompass and connect to social-emotional and cognitive experiences. Learning to skip, for example, can be a social activity as children interact with friends, an emotional activity as they express their feelings through their movement, and a cognitive activity as they think about how their movement takes them through space.

NASPE recommendations for a quality program

In 2002, the National Association for Sport and Physical Education (www.aahperd.org/NASPE) made the following recommendations to effectively promote lifetime physical activity habits among kindergarten children:

1. Devote a total of at least 60 minutes daily to *structured* physical activity that promotes health-related fitness and movement skills. Breaking down the 60 minutes into smaller increments can make it easier to incorporate into the class schedule.

2. Devote a total of at least 60 minutes and up to several hours daily to *unstructured* physical activity.

3. Develop children's competence in movement skills that are the building blocks for more complex movement tasks. For example, help children learn to run, kick, balance, and throw, so they can eventually use all of these skills together while playing a complex game such as soccer.

4. Use indoor and outdoor areas that meet or exceed recommended safety standards for performing large-muscle activities.

5. Ensure that those working directly with children are aware of the importance of physical activity and able to facilitate children's movement skills.

6. Provide yearly in-service training for all early childhood teachers and administrators that is focused on developmentally appropriate physical activity for young children.

The skill themes

Locomotor skills
Body is transported horizontally or vertically

Walking	Leaping
Running	Climbing
Hopping	Crawling
Skipping	Chasing
Galloping	Fleeing
Sliding	

Stability skills
Body stays in one place but moves around its horizontal or vertical axis—also balancing against the force of gravity

Turning	Transferring weight
Twisting	Jumping and landing
Bending	Stretching
Stopping	Curling
Rolling	Swinging
Balancing	Swaying
	Dodging

Manipulative skills*
Vigorous movement that involves giving or receiving force from objects (gross motor)

Throwing	Volleying
Catching and collecting	Striking with rackets
Kicking	Striking with long-handled implements
Punting	
Dribbling	

*In addition to the gross motor skills listed above, this theme can also include fine motor skills used to handle objects (such as cutting with scissors or drawing with crayons).

Source: Adapted from G. Graham, S.A. Holt/Hale, & M. Parker, *Children Moving: A Reflective Approach to Teaching Physical Education,* 5th ed. (Mountain View, CA: Mayfield), 27. Reprinted with permission from McGraw-Hill.

Teachers are guides and facilitators who assess children's needs, abilities, and interests. They construct environments in which children are able to make choices, and they extend children's learning regarding specific skills.

A physical education curriculum framework

The physical education field recommends that the curriculum framework for kindergarten physical education include both **skill themes** and **movement concepts**. Skill themes are the actual physical movement skills that children need to learn and perform (Graham, Holt/Hale, & Parker 2001). The box on this page describes these *locomotor* skills, *stability* skills, and *manipulative* skills.

Movement concepts are the knowledge component of the physical education curriculum. These are *space awareness, body awareness,* and *effort awareness.* Space awareness refers to self and shared space, directions, levels, and pathways. Body awareness refers to the relationships the mover has with himself or herself and the environment—how a person's movement creates relationships to that person and to other movers and objects. Effort awareness refers to how the body moves in space—such as its use of time, force, and control. The box on the next page lists the many movement concepts.

Because children learn about movement concepts as they practice skill themes, their physical activities should incorporate both. For example, in a developmentally appropriate physical education program, a kindergarten child might be asked to:

Throw a ball at a target (a manipulative skill theme) that has been placed at a *high* level (a space concept).

Balance (a stability skill theme) *on* a beam (a relationship concept).

Climb (a locomotor skill theme) *sideways* (a space concept) at a *slow* speed (an effort concept) *across* (a relationship concept) a playground structure.

Stephen W. Sanders

The movement concepts

Space awareness: "I am learning *where* my body moves"

Space	Directions	Levels	Pathways
Self space	Up/down	High	Straight
Shared space	Forward/backward	Middle	Curved
	Right/left	Low	Zigzag
	Sideways		
	Clockwise		
	Counterclockwise		

Body awareness: "I am learning about the *relationships* my body creates"

	With myself		With other movers and objects
Body parts	**Body shapes**	**Roles**	**Locations**
Head, neck, ears, eyes, nose, shoulder, knee, heel, arms, waist, chest, stomach, hips, leg, bottom, foot, spine, back, elbow, wrist, hand, fingers, ankle, toes	Big/small	Leading	Near to/far from
	Curved/straight	Following	Over/under
	Wide/narrow	Mirroring	In front/behind
	Twisted	Unison	On/off
	Like/unlike	Alternately	Together/apart
		Solo	Facing/side by side
		Partner	Around/through
		Group	

Effort awareness: "I am learning *how* my body moves"

Time		Force			Control
Speeds	**Rhythms**	**Degrees of force**	**Creating force**	**Absorbing force**	**Dimensions**
Slow	Beats	Strong	Starting	Stopping	Single movements
Medium	Cadence	Medium	Sustained	Receiving	Combinations of movements
Fast	Patterns	Light	Explosive	Stabilizing	Transitions
Accelerating			Gradual		

Source: From S.W. Sanders, *Active for Life: Developmentally appropriate movement programs for young children* (Washington, DC: NAEYC), 91.

What kindergartners should know and be able to do

Benchmarks describe behaviors that indicate progress toward the development of specific skills. The following sampling of benchmarks reflects the skills that kindergarten children need to be working toward. They can also be used to challenge children and to inform parents about their children's developmental skill levels.

By the end of the year, physically educated kindergarten children should be able to do the following (Gallahue 1995; Sanders 2002):

— Walk and run using mature form

— Demonstrate progress toward the mature form of other movement skills

— Travel in forward and sideways directions in a variety of patterns, and change direction quickly in response to a signal

— Demonstrate clear contrasts between slow and fast movement while traveling

— Identify fundamental movement patterns such as "skip" and "strike"

— Establish a beginning movement vocabulary (such as "personal space," "high/low levels," "fast/slow speed," "light/heavy weights," "balance," and "twist")

— Identify and use a variety of relationships with objects (such as over/under, behind, alongside, through)

— Apply appropriate concepts to the performance of a movement (perhaps change direction while running)

— Roll sideways without hesitating or stopping

— Toss a ball and catch it before it bounces twice

— Kick a stationary ball using a smooth continuous running step

— Maintain momentary stillness while bearing weight on a variety of body parts

— Participate regularly in vigorous physical activity

— Recognize that physical activity is good for personal well-being

— Select and participate in activities that require some physical exertion during unscheduled times

— Identify likes and dislikes connected with participation in physical activity

— Identify the physiological signs of moderate physical activity (such as a fast heart rate or heavy breathing)

— Apply, with teacher reinforcement, classroom rules and procedures and safe practices

— Share space and equipment with others

— Recognize the joy of shared play

— Interact positively with classmates regardless of personal differences (such as race, gender, or ability)

— Associate positive feelings with participation in physical activity

— Try new movements and skills

The kindergarten teacher's role

In this era of "No Child Left Behind," with its focus on school readiness and academics, fewer than 30 percent of kindergarten children attend daily physical education classes away from their regular classrooms. This means that classroom teachers play a more important role than ever in supporting young children's physical development. Some teachers are fortunate to have access to a physical education specialist (someone with a university credential to teach children's physical education), but many are not.

Either way, classroom teachers must keep essential considerations in mind. First, if children are going to enjoy participating in physical movement activities, now and as adults, they must develop a foundation of physical skills. Second, children need competent adults to help them learn these physical skills and build lifelong healthy habits. Young children do not necessarily develop physical skills through play (Manross 1994, 2000). In other words, sending children out to recess and encouraging them to participate in plenty of physical free play does not guarantee that they will develop physical skills and healthy attitudes, competencies, and habits. One of the challenges of working with kindergarten children is providing a structure to teach basic physical skills and then offer play-based opportunities so

Stephen W. Sanders

children can experiment and be creative with the skills they are learning.

A teacher's role as guide and facilitator must be both knowledgeable and proactive, and should include the following practices:

Link physical education activities to other curricular areas

Developmentally appropriate physical education programs do not isolate the teaching of movement skills from other parts of the curriculum. Rather, they improve children's depth of learning by helping them apply physical education concepts in different contexts and practice specific skills that incorporate other forms of learning.

Here are some examples: When children are learning to strike a balloon, a teacher can provide lots of different balloons so they can learn about color and size at the same time. Children can practice locomotor skills at the same time as they are developing spatial awareness by moving along a variety of pathways and in different directions.

Or children doing a project about newspapers might discuss how the papers are delivered, as a tie-in to a physical education activity. Giving the children a chance to try delivering papers themselves would be an occasion to teach the steps basic to throwing. After the teacher has taught the skills, children can have fun practicing tossing rolled-up newspapers (fastened with rubber bands) into a large box that they have built to look like someone's front porch (Sanders 2002).

Children can learn to use movement to solve classroom academic challenges, too. When they are learning to print the letters of the alphabet, encourage them to form the letters on the floor using a rope or their bodies. Or invite them to use their imaginations as they practice physical movements in a variety of musical and expressive dance experiences. And don't forget to talk about the importance of physical activity and fitness. For example, after a period of continuous movement, engage children in a discussion about what was happening to their bodies during the exercise and afterward.

Develop fine motor skills

The development of fine motor skills is an important part of every kindergartner's growth and competency. A child's attention span usually lengthens during kindergarten, and this can lead to a greater enjoyment of and involvement in fine motor activities. However, children's preschool experiences do not guarantee their great comfort and agility with fine motor work. Many young children struggle with tasks that require detail, patience, steadiness, and small-muscle coordination, such as writing, drawing, and cutting with precision.

Kindergartners still need and benefit from activities that develop hand muscles and fine motor skills—drawing and painting, working with playdough, and constructing with Legos. In developmentally appropriate environments, teachers include daily activities that foster fine motor skill development. As with gross motor activities, kindergartners need open-ended opportunities to experiment with and explore both materials and their abilities. These explorations may include sorting small objects; stringing beads; zipping, buttoning, and tying various articles of clothing; using scissors; pouring milk or juice at snack; or setting the table for snack.

> If children are going to enjoy participating in physical movement activities, now and as adults, they must develop a foundation of physical skills.

Children with disabilities can also practice fine motor skills, using assistive technology such as Velcro shoes and weighted bowls and utensils. When children are unable to use their hands to draw and build, assistive technologies such as modified keyboards, switches, point devices, and graphics programs can help.

Individualize for all children

A teacher should assess all children's development for information that will help her individualize instruction, plan appropriate lessons, identify children with special needs, and communicate with family members about children's progress. As with all best practices in education, expectations must be in sync with children's developmental readiness and tailored to meet each child's individual needs. Readiness resides within the child and cannot be rushed. Each child needs support and encouragement as he or she negotiates learning at a personal pace. For example, if a teacher has a five-step plan for teaching children to throw a ball correctly, she must remember that not every child will learn best by following that plan. One child may begin with step four. Still another may need to begin with step one, go to step two, and then return to step one for more practice.

However, physical educators believe that sequential skill development is at the center of young children's physical growth. No matter what the physical activity, a child cannot take part successfully if the essential fundamental movement skills basic to that activity have not been mastered (Gallahue 1995). Teachers are essential in this process.

Instill healthy habits

It's important for kindergarten children to begin to understand the relationship between physical activity and good nutrition. School is an ideal place for children to learn nutritious habits.

A teacher should model and teach nutrition in the classroom so that children understand the relationship between good nutrition and the phrase "physically active and healthy for life." She should guide them to discover a variety of nutritious foods, develop a willingness to taste new foods, and recognize that a variety of foods can help them grow and stay healthy. She can help develop their confidence, independence, and even the motor skills associated with preparing nutritious foods, as well as teach them the importance of cleanliness when working with foods. These are worthy lifelong habits.

Create appropriate environments

The role of kindergarten teachers in physical education is to create positive and success-based environments in which children can develop fundamental motor skills through play-based learning activities. Although a teacher may not be teaching

motor skills in an ideal situation, he (and the school) can strive to create an environment that includes the following:

- Inside and outside physical activity areas with adequate space for children to move freely and safely without bumping into each other
- Opportunities for daily, high-quality movement instruction with plenty of time for practice—exclusive of free play sessions
- Appropriate equipment so that each child benefits from maximum participation

The ideal environment offers children opportunities to develop both fine and gross motor skills. Children naturally learn and practice fine motor skills daily in classroom writing centers and with drawing activities, puzzles, and manipulatives. However, learning and practicing gross motor skills requires open space, such as a large room, a gym, or a spacious hallway or outdoor area, so that children can throw, kick, strike, run, and skip. There must also be enough equipment so that many children can participate in similar physical education activities at the same time (for example, every child has a ball to work on different ways to dribble, or every child has a jump rope to practice jumping). If space is a problem, setting up physical education stations (supervised by adults such as trained parent volunteers) can allow children to move from place to place to practice a variety of skills.

Another good idea is a physical education center, a semi-permanent space similar to a reading or science center. Here, small groups of children can practice developing a specific movement skill, deepen their understanding of movement and movement concepts, and use their physical education skills in ways that link to other areas of the curriculum. For example, in a center where children are learning about moving through space, they might plot a route on a map they have created, construct a miniature obstacle course using playdough and props, or measure various lengths of jumps and leaps using rope segments.

Engage children's families

Teachers should provide families with information about the physical skill development cur-

Stephen W. Sanders

riculum so that they can be involved. For instance, they should know when their children's clothes are preventing them from fully participating in physical education activities. Children's families also will benefit from information about the importance of their children developing physical skills, as well as the essential role good nutrition plays in physical health and in the ability to perform physical activities.

Develop skills of children with disabilities

Children with disabilities also need to develop skills and habits that foster positive body concepts, build self-confidence, promote good health, and support a physically active lifestyle. In fact, for some children with disabilities, becoming physically fit can prevent secondary or additional challenges that might make their special need more disabling.

When working with children who have disabilities, teachers should include them as much as possible in activities with the other children, concentrating on the same key strategies for success—offering opportunities to experience a wide-range of motor activities, teaching specific skills when appropriate, repeating activities, gradually making tasks more complicated, and providing plenty of practice time. When a child uses equipment such as a scooter board, a walker, or a wheelchair, the mobility device can be incorporated in the physical education activity. Therapists and family members are sources of other suggestions.

Some children with special needs may have limited endurance. Some children may have trouble mastering muscle coordination. Some may have increased tone or tighter muscles; others may have low muscle tone, making it hard to sustain long stretches of strenuous activity. However, this does not mean that these children cannot and do not need to participate in physical education activities. Rather, teachers, family members, and therapists can work together to figure out the best ways for individual children to participate and be successful.

Presenting motor development activities to children

Foster the growth of children's physical education skills in your classroom by using these developmentally appropriate instructional strategies:

Begin by focusing learning on large body movements such as throwing or kicking. In the big picture of development, children typically learn skills that require large movements that involve their entire bodies before they can focus on fine motor skills such as putting a peg in a hole or writing.

Design tasks for gradual and sequential learning. Keep in mind that tasks should be more general than specific. You could say, "Show me that you can throw the ball at the wall," rather than, "See if you can hit the four-inch target on the wall." Appropriate tasks should have a definite purpose, progress logically, and be structured to yield high rates of success. For example, tasks such as working on puzzles, learning to write with various implements, and perfecting cutting skills help develop better eye-hand coordination, which is connected to fine motor development. When children make progress with these tasks, they can then visually track a ball as it comes toward them in order to catch it or strike it with a bat; roll a ball successfully to another child; or learn to bounce a ball, then dribble.

Break down motor skills into small, "doable" actions. This way everyone can participate, even if it is partial participation for some. For instance, if a child cannot grasp a racket to strike a balloon, encourage her to strike the balloon with her hand.

Provide cues that help children refine specific skills, by observing their movements and physical activity and making helpful, concrete suggestions. Appropriate cues provide children with little steps that help them learn a skill more quickly and correctly and, at the same time, keep them from forming bad habits. For example, when children are learning to catch, some may benefit from the cue: "Keep your eye on the ball."

Offer fun choices and challenges to help maintain children's interest as they learn. Encourage children to choose their own partners, equipment, personal space, and activities. A fun challenge might be: "Try jumping over the rope and landing without falling five times in a row!" You can also help children use "timing" as a self-testing technique: "Can you hop on one foot for 10 seconds without touching both feet to the floor?"

Individualize. In a developmentally appropriate program, not all children should be performing the same task at the same time. Individualizing allows you to modify a task based on the abilities and interests of the children. For example, if a child is having difficulty with a particular task, such as throwing a ball into the air and attempting to catch the ball, individualize the activity by giving the child a larger rubber ball and asking him to bounce the ball and catch it. In other words, match the task to the skill level of the child.

Model and pinpoint. Many children have difficulties understanding verbal instruction. They may do better when they can watch someone practicing the skill they are being asked to do. To pinpoint, ask children to stop their activity for 10 to 15 seconds and watch two or three children demonstrate the skill. This is not to suggest that they copy a movement exactly; instead they are watching others to get ideas.

Present multiple skills. Rather than devote your entire physical education time to one activity, introduce children to a variety of skills in 5- to 7-minute segments. This approach of spending short periods of time on varied activities is appropriate for the developmental level of kindergarten children. It allows children to obtain a wide base of skills instead of developing only a few (Sanders 2002). In a 30-minute movement class, for example, you might start with locomotor activities and proceed to jumping, throwing, catching, and kicking—all for brief, 5- to 7-minute segments.

Promote success. Provide activities that enable children to succeed at high rates. For example, if your goal is to help children learn to hit a target using a beanbag, allow them to choose how far they will be from the target. As they practice, encourage them to readjust their distances. Research suggests that children need to practice skills at a success rate of approximately 70 to 80 percent. In other words, when a child can complete a task, such as hitting the target with the beanbag, 7 or 8 times out of 10, he is ready for a more difficult challenge such as moving farther away from the target.

Offer a variety of tasks, materials, and learning centers to help children practice specific skills and learn to use different types and sizes of equipment. For example, provide balls of all sizes,

---

Resources for providing physical education experiences

When a physical education specialist is not available for daily classes, a kindergarten classroom teacher might need help providing physical education experiences. Among the wide variety of resources available are these:

PE Central (www.pecentral.org) is a Web site for teachers and parents. It offers the latest information about developmentally appropriate physical education programs for children, including assessment of physical skills. Kindergarten teachers can log on to access thousands of free lesson activities for teaching motor skills. Kindergarten teachers who would like to share their own activities can submit them to PE Central for publication. (The author is this Web site's preschool section editor.)

Human Kinetics Publishers (www.humankinetics.com) offers books and educational materials in all areas of physical activity, including kindergarten, to help people worldwide lead healthier, more active lives.

SPARK Physical Education (www.sparkpe.org) began in 1989 as a federally funded program to create, implement, and evaluate physical education programs with the intent of developing a national model. SPARK (Sports, Play & Active Recreation for Kids!) is a research-based program that prepares classroom teachers to provide physical education activities to children. It offers schools an all-inclusive package that includes program evaluation, hands-on staff development, curriculum, and equipment.

Stephen W. Sanders

shapes, and weights in the form of beanbags, yarn balls, sock balls, and rubber and plastic balls. Then use different centers set up throughout the environment to allow children to practice throwing, bouncing, and rolling the balls in different ways.

Give positive feedback. No matter what a child's ability, express appropriate encouragement: "You held your hand out. That's great! Now move your hand to strike the balloon when it comes close. Ready?"

Whenever possible, make sure that movement and skill activities involve everyone in your class. Don't use activities such as Duck, Duck, Goose; Musical Chairs; or relay races that exclude children from participation or require children to hold still and watch others while waiting for a turn to participate. Individual activities where children have their own equipment and can participate at their own skill level are more appropriate. Be sure to choose activities that promote inclusion and cooperation rather than exclusion and competition. Strive to foster a sense of community, emphasizing that everyone can participate and that everyone has strengths. This will also help children learn to understand and respect others.

Remember to give children time to rest, particularly during strenuous activities.

Physical education can be a joy as well as a learning experience for both teachers and children. More important, it is a necessity. Through developmentally appropriate physical education, kindergarten students develop gross motor skills, build positive relationships with their bodies, grow socially, emotionally, and cognitively, and form essential healthy habits that can last them a lifetime.

This is an important time in the field of physical education—a time when educators at all levels are recognizing the impact that quality physical education programs can have on children. In direct correlation, it is also an important time in the early childhood field. Early childhood educators have always placed great importance on children's learning about and with their bodies through play. We now understand that, in the case of physical education, children also need to learn through instruction. And that is our responsibility.

References

Berk, L. 1996. *Infants and children: Prenatal through middle childhood.* 2d ed. Boston: Allyn & Bacon.

CDC (Centers for Disease Control). 1996. *Physical activity and health: A report of the Surgeon General.* Atlanta: U.S. Department of Health and Human Services.

Gallahue, D.A. 1995. Transforming physical education curriculum. In *Reaching potentials. Vol. 2: Transforming early childhood curriculum and assessment*, eds. S. Bredekamp & T. Rosegrant, 125–44). Washington, DC: NAEYC.

Gallahue, D.A., & J.C. Ozmun. 1995. *Understanding motor development: Infants, children, adolescents, adults.* Dubuque, IA: Brown and Benchmark.

Graham, G., S. Holt/Hale, & M. Parker. 2001. *Children moving: A reflective approach to teaching physical education.* Mountain View, CA: Mayfield.

Manross, M.A. 1994. What children think, feel, and know about the overhand throw. Master's thesis, Virginia Polytechnic Institute and State University.

Manross, M.A. 2000. Learning to throw in physical education class: Part 3. *Teaching Elementary Physical Education* 11 (3): 26–29.

NASPE (National Association for Sport and Physical Education). 1995. *Moving into the future: National standards for physical education.* St. Louis, MO: Mosby.

NASPE. 2000. Developmentally appropriate practice in movement programs for young children ages 3–5. Position statement of the Council on Physical Education for Children. Reston, VA: Author.

NASPE. 2002. *Active start: Physical activity for children birth to 5 years.* Reston, VA: Author.

NASPE. 2004. *Moving into the future: National standards for physical education.* 2d ed. Reston, VA: Author.

Sanders, S.W. 2002. *Active for life: Developmentally appropriate movement programs for young children.* Washington, DC: NAEYC.

Sawyer, R.K. 2001. Play as improvisational rehearsal. In *Children in play, story, and school*, eds. A. Göncü & E. L. Klein, 19–38. New York: Guilford.

Assessment in Kindergarten

13

Dominic F. Gullo

In today's climate of educational accountability, and especially with the enactment of the No Child Left Behind Act, assessment is on everybody's mind. In the early childhood field, there is ongoing debate about the role that assessment plays—or *should* play—in early education. Much of the focus is on elucidation; that is, on what types of assessments are appropriate for young children, and what uses and misuses can result from making decisions based on assessment outcomes. Children are being assessed more often and at younger ages, often with profound effects on their educational futures. This can be seen in the vignette below:

My grandson Nick had to take a test for admission to a kindergarten for 4-year-olds. The test consisted of recognizing a few shapes and some colors. As a faithful viewer of *Sesame Street,* Nick was able to do that, no problem. One day, after Nick had been attending the school for a few weeks, I bumped into his teacher. Introducing myself, I asked her why the school had decided to admit my grandson. "He passed the screening test," she said. But, I asked, what if Nick had confused blue and green or hadn't known a square from a circle that day? "In that case," she replied, "he would have failed the screening and not been accepted."

"But wouldn't it make more sense to admit the children who *don't* know their shapes and colors, and then *teach* them these things?" I pushed. The teacher looked at me as if I were leftover mashed potatoes. "Such tests help us determine who is *ready* to benefit from school and who is still too immature. Nick's score told us that he was definitely ready for kindergarten."

"So next year my grandson, who is already testing in your top half, will have had the added benefit of being in your school for a whole year. At 5, won't he then be even further ahead of that 4-year-old who failed your admission test and spent the year without the benefit of kindergarten? How will that child ever catch up?" The teacher didn't give me an answer . . . but I hadn't really expected one.

Sadly, it seems that the children taught best are those who need it least.

In this vignette, assessment results were used to decide which children got into kindergarten. But many children already in kindergarten programs are affected by assessment decisions, too. Whether the impact of these assessments is positive or negative depends a lot on the teacher's understanding of the assessment process. To assess appropriately and effectively, a teacher must understand at least when and how to use assessment; how a child's development can affect the assessment process; and the intersections among assessment, program evaluation, and curriculum and teaching. Some of this understanding

Dominic F. Gullo is a professor and deputy chair of the elementary and early childhood education department at Queens College, City University of New York.

is common sense, and some requires formal and deliberate learning by the teacher. Kindergarten offers unique opportunities and challenges for assessment. The most marked challenge is that of matching assessment procedures to the developmental capabilities of children at this age.

This chapter discusses five areas related to assessment and kindergarten. The first section defines assessment and describes its purposes. The second focuses on the vignette's topic of assessing "readiness." The third addresses the critical issue of child development. The fourth section focuses on various types of assessment, both formal and informal. The last section looks at assessment with regards to special populations of children. The importance of incorporating assessment into the kindergarten curriculum is highlighted in each section, as kindergarten offers unique opportunities for assessing children in multiple contexts and in multiple ways.

Definitions and purposes

Assessment is a procedure used to measure the degree to which an individual child possesses a particular attribute (Gullo 2005). According to Mindes, "Assessment is a process for gathering information to make decisions about young children" (2003, 10).

Formal or informal?

Assessments can either be *formal* or *informal* in nature. Formal assessments include readiness tests, developmental screening tests, achievement tests, and diagnostic tests. Formal assessments are typically *standardized*, and allow the performance of one child to be compared with that of another child or with the performance of groups of children with similar characteristics. Informal assessments include performance assessments, academic or developmental checklists, and anecdotal records. Often information about a child gleaned from both formal and informal assessments can be organized in a portfolio.

Why do we assess?

Assessment of children has three purposes (Boehm 1992). The first is to better understand their overall development. This is especially important for kindergartners, as they vary considerably in their development at this age. Development is best viewed as a byproduct of a child's maturational level and experiential background. Kindergarten children differ greatly in their levels of maturation. And any group of 5-year-olds (the typical age in kindergarten) enter kindergarten with very different types of past experiences. Some have been in school or child care; for others, kindergarten is their first group experience or exposure to formal academic content. As a result, the *developmental trajectories* (depictions of both rate and direction of development) of kindergarten children vary more than they will in subsequent school years. Due to differences in biological maturation and experiences prior to entering kindergarten, children in this age group vary significantly as compared with differences in groups of older children. Understanding differences in children's developmental trajectories is of utmost importance in kindergarten, as teachers must individualize and modify curriculum and instruction based on each child's developmental level.

A second purpose of assessment is to monitor children's progress through the curriculum. Teachers use assessment to gain an in-depth understanding of each child's unique learning style and strategies. A one-size-fits-all approach to teaching kindergarten is not appropriate. It is critical that teachers understand how *each* child uniquely processes information, constructs knowledge, and solves problems. This kind of monitoring is important for kindergarten children in order for them to get the greatest benefit from their curriculum experiences.

Finally, assessment is used to identify children who are at risk for academic failure or who may need special education services. Because kindergartners vary greatly in their levels of development, it can be hard to determine whether particular children are having academic difficulties due to immaturity (and just need more time) or to developmental delays that call for intervention. Ongoing assessment is critical in making academic decisions based on children's classroom performance. (See section five for more on this point.)

Readiness

Kindergarten and readiness are two ideas that have become inextricably linked. *Readiness* is a term used to describe how prepared children are to begin "formal schooling." For many children, kindergarten will be their first experience with school, and various kinds of assessments are used to determine whether to allow them to enter kindergarten. The term is not used in a consistent way, however. Views on what readiness means differ, and these views ultimately affect educational decisions made on behalf of kindergarten children.

> Young children often will respond with the first thing that comes to their mind, without reflecting on or considering alternative responses.

In the early 1990s, the National Governors Conference set goals that made readiness a primary focus of attention (U.S. Department of Education 1991). As Goal 1 set forth, "By the year 2000, all children will come to school ready to learn." From the beginning, this declaration was wrought with controversy. What the goal implied was that some children were *not* ready for kindergarten. The controversy stemmed from the implied relationship among readiness, assessment, and the kindergarten curriculum.

In one interpretation of readiness, children are assessed to determine whether they are ready for school. The implication here is that children must be at some predetermined level of development and in possession of certain skills and knowledge to be deemed "ready" for kindergarten. If all children who enter kindergarten must be at a predetermined level of concept and skill develop-

ment, then it is also implied that the kindergarten curriculum is predetermined and rigid. A number of detrimental educational decisions can be derived from this view of readiness:

• Children are denied entrance into kindergarten based on test results

• Children are required to attend "developmental" kindergarten prior to "regular" kindergarten

• Children are retained in kindergarten

• Children attend a transitional first grade following kindergarten and prior to "traditional" first grade (Gullo 1994)

In another interpretation of readiness, children are assessed to determine what kinds of educational experiences they are ready for. The implication here is that the assessment results will inform curriculum and instructional practices, so they can be modified to meet each child's developmental and educational needs. Unlike the first interpretation of readiness, this one is consistent with what we know about children's development. That is, readiness is determined by each child's development and reflects the knowledge that in their early years, children of similar ages do not necessarily develop at consistent rates or in similar ways. Accordingly, the position of the National Association of Early Childhood Specialists in State Departments of Education (NAECS/SDE 2000) is that children should be enrolled in kindergarten based on their legal right to enter.

Child development

A major problem with kindergarten assessments is that most do not meet usual standards for reliability and validity. Kindergarten children have a 50 percent chance of being misplaced when standardized assessment results alone are used for placement (NAECS/SDE 2000). Most kindergarten assessments are neither reliable nor valid due to the developmental variations and limitations unique to children of kindergarten age.

The developmental nature of the kindergarten child is the focus the Berk chapter in this volume, but it is important to understand here that children's level of social, language, cognitive, and physical development affects the assessment process, both in *assessing* children and in *interpreting* the results. This is true for individual children and for groups of children within a single developmental period. This section discusses those developmental characteristics of kindergarten children that can affect the assessment process.

Variable development. More than at any other school grade, kindergarten children's behavior is highly variable (NAECS/SDE 2000)—both from day to day in any one domain of development (what they know and can do today they may not know and do tomorrow), and between various domains (advanced in one, delayed or typical in others). Consequently, kindergarten teachers must understand that using an assessment procedure that gives a child just one chance to demonstrate a particular skill or knowledge might not give a result that accurately accounts for what the child truly knows or is capable of doing.

Developmental constraints. Kindergarten teachers must also recognize that many assessment procedures are a poor match for the developmental capabilities of children at this age. For example, an assessment may require 5-year-olds to respond using extremely controlled fine motor movements. However, because kindergarten children are typically physically incapable of such movements, they will not be able to demonstrate what they truly know or can do. Asking kindergarten children questions that they do not understand can make it appear as though they do not know the answers. Even if they know the answers, they may not be able to respond with their level of language development.

Impulsivity. Kindergartners can be very impulsive. This developmental trait can affect the reliability and validity of assessments. Impulsivity means that young children often will respond (verbally, emotionally, or physically) with the first thing that comes to their mind, without reflecting on or considering alternative responses. In assessment situations, children often respond in ways that are inconsistent with adult expectations. Assessments that use multiple-choice picture items are a good example: In many multiple-choice assessments, the child must look at a picture, and then circle in a following row a second picture that best matches the first picture. Test developers often start the response row with a "decoy"—that is, a picture that would be the best match if there were not a better choice offered later in the row. Kindergarten children are disadvantaged in this type of assessment. Their impulsivity often causes them to select the first picture they see that meets the requirements of the task, without waiting to consider the choices that follow.

Generalization of knowledge and skills. Kindergarten children are limited in their ability to generalize knowledge and skills from one situation to another. Just because children can appropriately use what they know and can do in one situation or context does not mean they can apply their knowledge or skills in *all* situations or contexts. This poses a particular problem for teachers if they teach concepts and skills in one manner, but assess them in a different manner. For example, if children are taught mathematics through manipulating concrete objects, then assessed through a paper-and-pencil task using representational symbols, they may not be able to demonstrate what they have learned.

Types of assessments

Assessments used in kindergarten can generally be categorized as formal or informal. Formal assessments are usually standardized, and allow teachers to compare one child's performance with that of other children who share similar characteristics such as age or grade level. In contrast, informal assessments are primarily used to gather unique information about individual children. The children are often assessed while they are engaged in curriculum activities.

Formal assessments

There are many reasons to use formal assessments in kindergarten. Whatever the reason, when teachers use formal assessments they must ensure that: the results benefit the child and the adults who teach them; they are used for the purposes for which they were designed; the results provide valid, reliable, and useful information; and they are both linguistically and culturally appropriate (Neimeyer & Scott-Little 2001).

The four types of formal assessments described below are typically used in kindergarten:

A **developmental screening assessment** is a brief procedure designed to identify children who—because of a possible learning problem or disability—should receive further diagnostic assessment (Meisels & Atkins-Burnett 2005). One of the greatest mistakes in developmental screening is using an instrument that is neither reliable nor valid. But even valid and reliable instruments have predictive validity of only two years—that is, while a good screening instrument can assess an individual child's *current* learning potential, no instrument can accurately predict what a child's school performance will look like beyond two years (Meisels, Wiske, & Tivnan 1984). For all these reasons, educational decisions should not be based on scores of a developmental screening assessment.

> Kindergarten offers teachers a unique opportunity to develop and engage in a regular, ongoing routine of informal assessment.

A **diagnostic assessment** is a process used to definitively identify those children who *do* have a disability or specific area of academic weakness (Meisels & Atkins-Burnett 2005). This assessment is used both to identify the disability or weakness and to suggest remediation strategies. A diagnostic assessment is typically administered by a highly trained professional who has special expertise in assessment and intervention.

A **readiness assessment** is a brief achievement test designed to determine a child's relative preparedness to participate in a particular classroom program (Meisels & Atkins-Burnett 2005). This test is often administered to children heading toward kindergarten (like Nick, in the opening vignette) or to kindergarten children heading toward first grade. A readiness assessment may measure a child's acquisition of certain kinds of knowledge and skills, but it does *not* measure that child's future learning potential—that is, it is not a good predictor of a child's future academic achievement. According to Meisels (1987), one of the primary misuses of a readiness test is confusing it with a developmental screening. Both are brief measures, but they have very different purposes. Accordingly, a readiness test is *product* oriented, measuring what children already know and can do; a developmental screening is *process* oriented, measuring children's potential to acquire new knowledge and skills.

An **achievement test** assesses the extent to which a child has acquired certain information or skills that are identified as curricular objectives (Wortham 2001). At the end of their kindergarten year, many children are given an achievement test to determine what they have learned, particularly in the areas of literacy and mathematics. With all young children, schools or school districts should follow some guidelines when planning to use achievement tests:

- Know the limitations of achievement testing (the younger the child, the more this is true).

- Be aware of the new types of achievement tests that emphasize problem solving and have items with multiple correct responses rather than just one right answer.

- Recognize that until about third grade, children do not have the reading and writing skills/capacity to remember the detail required by achievement tests.

- Prepare children in advance for the test by identifying and practicing appropriate test-taking strategies. These can include following directions, working within a time frame, and marking answers in the way the test requires (Aschbacher 2000).

These points are especially true for kindergartners, as they are unsophisticated test-takers.

Informal assessments

Kindergarten offers teachers a unique opportunity to develop and engage in a regular, ongoing routine of informal assessment that looks at children's learning and development in multiple ways and in multiple contexts. Informal assess-

Dominic F. Gullo

ments include interviews, questionnaires, rating scales and checklists, and rubrics, as well as examples of children's actual classroom work. In general, informal assessments are characterized by tasks requiring children to: demonstrate, construct, or generate knowledge and/or skills; use critical-thinking and problem-solving skills; and be engaged in meaningful tasks within a meaningful context (Herman, Aschbacher, & Winters 1992).

Informal assessments can provide teachers with valuable information about children and curriculum. One distinct advantage of informal assessments is that they are derived directly from the curriculum and the teacher's instructional objectives (Wortham 2001). They do not rely on what test publishers think is important to assess. Teachers can pick and choose among different approaches that they judge to be appropriate for a child or a particular situation. Thus, assessment is linked directly to curriculum.

Informal assessments offer a number of distinct advantages in the kindergarten classroom (Gullo 2006) by:

- Focusing on the developmental and achievement changes in children over time
- Focusing on the individual child rather than on groups of children
- Not relying on the "one chance" opportunity for the child to demonstrate competence
- Not interrupting the process of curriculum implementation
- Helping children better understand their own learning, as children reflect in conjunction with the teacher or other children
- Providing concrete information to share with families

The role of the teacher changes when informal assessment procedures are used (Cohen & Spenciner 1994). The teacher has a direct influence on the assessment process, and assessment and curriculum are linked. When a close relationship exists among curriculum content, instructional strategies, and assessment, then instructional goals, views of teaching, and theories of how children learn and develop are articulated and aligned (Herman, Aschbacher, & Winters 1992).

Assessing special populations

Today's kindergartners are not the homogeneous group they might have been 20 or more years ago, when their teachers were of kindergarten age. Cultural and linguistic diversity has increased dramatically. Nationally, white (non-Hispanic) children make up 63.5 percent of public school enrollment, blacks (non-Hispanic) 17 percent, Hispanics 14.4 percent, Asian/Pacific Islanders 3.9 percent, and American Indian/Alaskan Natives 1.2 percent (NCES 2002). This diversity brings new challenges for assessment, primary among them the need to properly identify children who require special education services. Yansen and Shulman (1996) report that among the children who are referred for such services, there is an overrepresentation of children from cultural and/or linguistic backgrounds that are different from the majority. Could this be due to the difficulties teachers have in assessing this population of children?

In addition to the increase in cultural and linguistic diversity, more kindergarten children identified as having special educational needs are being included in regular classrooms (Cohen & Spenciner 2003). This is primarily due to changes in the law and improvements in identifying children with special needs at earlier ages. Again, these changes bring challenges for the kindergarten teacher, especially in using assessment to inform curriculum and teaching.

Cultural and linguistic diversity

"Children's backgrounds have a profound influence on their knowledge, vocabulary, and skills" (McAfee & Leong 2002, 19). While this statement certainly applies to all children, it has special significance for children from cultural and/or linguistic backgrounds that differ from the backgrounds of the majority, the teacher, or peers. Assessment procedures need to account for these differences. To obtain valid and reliable results, assessments must be free from linguistic or cultural biases. Assessment instruments and procedures must be chosen with care.

It is important to ask whether the assessment has built-in safeguards to ensure that its instrument or procedure is sensitive to cultural and linguistic diversity. Can it distinguish a result caused by cultural and/or linguistic factors in the child's development and learning versus a result that denotes a learning difficulty or developmental delay (McLean 2000)? The Division for Early Childhood of the Council for Exceptional Children (DEC/CEC) recommends that:

- Professionals first gather information to determine whether the child should be referred for assessment for special education, or whether the child's patterns of development and behavior can be explained by language or cultural difference

- During assessment, appropriate procedures be followed to determine which language should be used to assess the child, and to understand the impact of second-language acquisition on the child's development and performance in the early childhood setting

- Appropriate assessment strategies be tailored to the individual child and family when culturally appropriate and nonbiased instruments cannot be identified (as reported in McLean 2000)

The Early Childhood Research Institute for Culturally and Linguistically Appropriate Services (CLAS) has also developed a set of guidelines for selecting assessments to be used with children from culturally and linguistically diverse backgrounds (as reported by McLean 2000). They are as follows:

Scoring procedures. When an assessment has scoring or rating scales, note which cultural or linguistic groups were included in the design of the scales. In addition, note whether separate scoring or normative scales are offered for specific linguistic or cultural groups. Appropriate assessments are designed by involving different linguistic and cultural groups, and they have separate scoring scales for specific groups.

Specific cultural information. If an assessment indicates that it is appropriate for a particular cultural or linguistic group, note whether information about parenting practices and child development typical for that group is taken into account in the design and administration of the

assessment. This should be clearly stated in the administration and interpretation documentation.

Modifications. Suggestions for modifying the assessment for this population of children should be clearly stated in the examiner's manual. Children from different cultural or linguistic backgrounds do not necessarily behave or respond similarly to assessment questions. Such differences in behaviors may yield erroneous results unless modifications account for them.

Interpretation of findings. Specific procedures for interpreting the assessment results of children from various cultural or linguistic backgrounds should be clearly stated in the examiner's manual. These procedures for interpretation should reflect the preceding guidelines.

Special needs

Kindergarten teachers need to be particularly aware of the issues regarding assessment and identification of children with special needs. They are often the first to see these children in settings that may indicate a need for special services. While many of the assessment principles previously discussed also apply to children who are identified as having special educational needs, some differences result from mandated guidelines for the identification of and planning for such children. Wolery, Strain, and Bailey (1992) offer seven decision points related to assessment of special needs children. They are the determination of:

1. Whether to refer a child for special needs services and additional assessment; this usually results from information gleaned from developmental screening

2. Whether the child actually has a developmental delay, sensory disability, or health-related problem; a diagnostic assessment measure is typically used for this purpose, following developmental screening

3. Whether the child is eligible for special education services; this is accomplished by matching the findings of the diagnostic assessment results to the state's criteria for eligibility

Principles guiding assessment practices

The Early Childhood Assessments Resource Group was convened in response to National Education Goal 1. Its charge was to establish general principles for guiding assessment practices in early childhood education. Six principles of child assessment were developed (Shepard, Kagan, & Wurtz 1998):

Assessments should benefit children. They should lead to improvements in the quality of programming, in that assessment data should be used to modify curriculum and instruction such that each child benefits maximally.

Assessments should have a specific purpose and be reliable, valid, and appropriate for that purpose. Sadly, many assessment instruments used to determine academic readiness have no long-term predictive validity in identifying which children will be successful academically in kindergarten (Gullo 2005).

Assessments should recognize the developmental limitations of young children. Inappropriate assessments that do not account for the great variability among children of the same age can result in findings that do not reflect children's true abilities. Because kindergarten children vary considerably in their development, using uniform assessment procedures for all children can result in unreliable results.

Assessments should be age-appropriate, in both content and data-collection method. Any group of children vary in their development, but all 5-year-olds do share some characteristics. For example, because all kindergarten-age children are concrete learners, assessments that require an ab-

stract response would be inappropriate. Or, because all kindergarten-age children more reliably demonstrate what they know and can do when the context is familiar, assessments should be conducted in situations familiar to them.

Assessments should be linguistically appropriate. To some extent, all assessments are a measure of children's language proficiency—that is, how can a child follow directions if he does not understand them, or respond if she does not speak the assessor's language? Today's kindergartens enroll large numbers of children for whom English is not their first or dominant language. That teachers of these children understand this principle is of immense importance.

Assessments should value families. Kindergarten children's families should be considered an important source of assessment information. We know that for many children, kindergarten is the first experience they have outside of the home. Kindergarten teachers should build strong relationships with the families of their students. The links among the child, the school, and the family are often stronger in kindergarten than they are in other grade levels. These strong links have implications for assessment. Kindergarten teachers have to realize that families can provide insights into their child's behaviors that in-school assessments alone cannot provide. Conversely, families should be considered an integral part of their child's education and as such, kindergarten teachers must use assessment information to provide valuable information to families regarding their child's development, learning and achievement, and progress in school.

4. How the child should be taught within the program; that is, what types of adaptations need to be made to ensure that the child develops and learns optimally

5. Where the child should receive services and what types of services are needed; this is especially critical for kindergarten, in that most special needs kindergarten children are fully integrated into a regular classroom

6. Whether the child is making appropriate progress; this requires ongoing assessment by the kindergarten teacher

7. Whether and/or to what extent the child has achieved the educational and/or developmental outcomes desired

As can be seen from these seven guidelines, assessment plays an important part at the beginning, during, and at the end of the educative process. Teachers of kindergartners with special needs must incorporate assessment as a regular part of instruction in order to meet these guidelines.

Assessment is helpful in identifying children with special needs. However, there are some concerns, especially for very young children (DEC/CEC 2000; NAEYC 2003). First, labeling children as having special needs when they are too young can be detrimental for those children and their ability to reach their potential. Second, there is a shortage of adequate assessments for young children that are both valid and reliable measures of their learning potential and developmental status. Finally, some categories used to describe disabilities in young children that are also used to describe the special needs of older children may be inappropriate where young children are concerned. On this last point, consequently, states are permitted to use the term "developmental delay" when referring children between the ages of 3 and 9 for special education services. Developmental delay can be a temporary phenomenon; using that term rather than a diagnosis term identifying a particular or permanent special need, such as "ADHD" or "hearing impaired," reduces the chances of a child carrying an inaccurate label throughout his or her educational career.

Kindergarten holds a special place in early childhood education. It is often the first time children attend formal schooling and they experience more definite expectations for behavior. They learn and develop within a social setting in groups of peers of similar age, and are away from their family for extended periods of time. Likewise, children of kindergarten age are also special in that they challenge teachers with their vastly differing levels of development, prior experiences, and learning styles and trajectories. Proper assessment can help teachers understand the unique qualities of each child, as well as supply useful information to guide their planning. Recalling the last sentence of this chapter's opening vignette ("It seems the children taught best are those who need it least"), the hope is that assessment can be used to teach all children best, whether they need it least or most.

> Assessment plays an important part at the beginning, during, and at the end of the educative process.

References

Aschbacher, P.R. 2000. Developing indicators of classroom practice to monitor and support school reform. *CRESST Line,* Winter, pp. 6–8.

Boehm, A.E. 1992. Glossary of assessment terms. In *Encyclopedia of early childhood education,* eds. L.R. Williams & D.P. Fromberg, 293–300. New York: Garland.

Cohen, L.G., & L.J. Spenciner. 1994. *Assessment of young children.* New York: Longman.

Cohen, L.G., & L.J. Spenciner. 2003. *Assessment of children and youth with special needs.* Boston: Allyn & Bacon.

DEC/CEC (Division for Early Childhood, Council for Exceptional Children). 2000. *Developmental delay as an eligibility category.* Position statement. Missoula, MT: Author. Online: www.dec-sped.org/pdf/positionpapers/Position%20Dev%20Delay.pdf.

Gullo, D.F. 1994. *Understanding assessment and evaluation in early childhood education.* New York: Teachers College Press.

Gullo, D.F. 2005. *Understanding assessment and evaluation in early childhood education.* 2d ed. New York: Teachers College Press.

Gullo, D.F. 2006. Alternative means of assessing children's learning in early childhood classrooms. In *Handbook of research on*

Dominic F. Gullo

the education of young children, 2d ed., eds. B. Spodek & O.N. Saracho, 443–56. Mahwah, NJ: Erlbaum.

Herman, J.L., P.R. Aschbacher, & L. Winters. 1992. *A practical guide to alternative assessment.* Alexandria, VA: Association for Supervision and Curriculum Development.

McAfee, O., & D.J. Leong. 2002. *Assessing and guiding young children's development and learning.* 3d ed. Boston: Allyn & Bacon.

McLean, M. 1998. Assessing children for whom English is a second language. *Young Exceptional Children* 1 (3): 20–25.

McLean, M. 2000. *Conducting child assessments.* CLAS Technical Report No. 2. Champaign: University of Illinois at Urbana-Champaign, Early Childhood Research Institute on Culturally and Linguistically Appropriate Services.

Meisels, S.J. 1987. Uses and abuses of developmental screening and school readiness testing. *Young Children* 42 (2): 4–6, 68–73.

Meisels, S.J., & S. Atkins-Burnett. 2005. *Developmental screening in early childhood: A guide.* 5th ed. Washington, DC: NAEYC.

Meisels, S.J., M.S. Wiske, & T. Tivnan. 1984. Predicting school performance with the Early Screening Inventory. *Psychology in the Schools* 21 (1): 25–33.

Mindes, G. 2003. *Assessing young children.* 2d ed. Upper Saddle River, NJ: Merrill/Prentice Hall.

NAECS/SDE (National Association of Early Childhood Specialists in State Departments of Education). 2000. *Still! Unacceptable trends in kindergarten entry & placement.* Position statement. Chicago: Author. Online: http://naecs.crc.uiuc.edu/position/trends2000.html.

NAEYC. 2003. *Early childhood curriculum, assessment, and program evaluation: Building an effective, accountable system in programs for children birth through age 8.* Position statement. Washington, DC: Author. Online: www.naeyc.org/about/positions/cape.asp.

NCES (National Center for Education Statistics). 2002. *Digest of education statistics: 2001* (NCES 2002–031). Washington, DC: National Center for Education Statistics, U.S. Department of Education.

Niemeyer, J.A., & C. Scott-Little. 2001. *Assessing kindergarten children: A compendium of assessment instruments.* Tallahassee, FL: SERVE.

Shepard, L.A., S.L. Kagan, & E. Wurtz, eds. 1998. *Principles and recommendations for early childhood assessments.* Report of the National Education Goals Panel. Washington, DC: U.S. Government Printing Office.

U.S. Department of Education. 1991. *America 2000: An educational strategy source book.* Washington, DC: Author.

Wolery, M., P.S. Strain, & D.B. Bailey. 1992. Reaching potentials of children with special needs. In *Reaching potentials. Vol. 1: Appropriate curriculum and assessment for young children,* eds. S. Bredekamp & T. Rosegrant, 92–112. Washington, DC: NAEYC.

Wortham, S.C. 2001. *Assessment in early childhood education.* Upper Saddle River, NJ: Merrill/Prentice Hall.

Yansen, E., & E. Shulman. 1996. Language assessment: Multicultural considerations. In *The handbook of multicultural assessment,* eds. L. Suzuki, P. Meller, & J. Ponterotto, 353–93. San Francisco: Jossey-Bass.

Part IV

Kindergarten in a Policy Context

Transition from Kindergarten to First Grade

14

Jason Downer, Kate Driscoll, & Robert Pianta

The kindergarten to first grade (K–1) transition is an important developmental period for children. Their adjustment during this time can have long-lasting effects on their success in school (Entwisle & Alexander 1998). Although many factors contribute to a child's experience in this shift, kindergarten teachers play an invaluable role in fostering smooth transitions. Consider the following:

June: Mary attends full-day kindergarten at the same elementary school where she will attend first grade. Her kindergarten teacher, Ms. Jones, speaks with her parents each month about what Mary is learning in the classroom and what they can do at home to extend this learning. Mary experiences a kindergarten curriculum that is well matched with the first grade curriculum; in fact, Ms. Jones regularly talks with other kindergarten and first grade teachers about integration of her classroom curriculum with the first grade curriculum. Mary's school district generates class lists in May, so she already knows which of the other kindergartners in her class will accompany her to first grade. Ms. Jones and a first grade teacher arranged joint field trips throughout the year and provided regular opportunities for Mary and her peers to visit first grade classrooms.

Jason Downer is a research scientist in the Center for Advanced Study of Teaching and Learning (CASTL), Kate Driscoll is a doctoral student in clinical psychology, and Robert Pianta is a professor and the director of CASTL, all at the University of Virginia.

August: Mary's parents attend a K–1 transition night where they meet her new first grade teacher, socialize with other parents of first-graders, and obtain information about supporting Mary as she transitions to first grade.

September: Mary shows up for her first day of first grade and knows exactly where to go. Her new teacher greets her by name at the door, and inside she sees many familiar faces in her peer group. Mary settles into the routine of the first grade classroom quickly, because last year Ms. Jones made explicit efforts to introduce selected first grade routines such as attendance taking into the kindergarten experience.

October: Mary's father picks her up at school each day. He feels welcome and comfortable in the school building because he has spoken with Mary's first grade teacher and other school personnel on several occasions—including the summer K–1 transition night, a first grade family potluck, and a recent Back-to-School Night.

Mary made a successful K–1 transition, thanks to a thoughtful plan implemented by her teachers and the school system. She had the opportunity to develop relationships with first grade teachers during her kindergarten year, enter the first grade classroom surrounded by familiar peers, and witness the connection between her parents and teachers. Mary's parents formed a proactive, collaborative partnership with her kindergarten teacher, which provided them with information about what Mary needed to learn in preparation for first grade. The established relationship between her family and school made it more likely that her parents' involvement would continue throughout her school years.

Unfortunately, not all children experience as smooth a K–1 transition as Mary. Findings from surveying prekindergarten, kindergarten, and first grade teachers suggest that the typical transition for a child in the United States consists of contact with new classrooms that is too little, too late, and too impersonal. Families feel disconnected from schools and lack useful information to help them plan for their child's transition (Epstein 2001; Pianta & Kraft-Sayre 2003). Relationships and information sharing among families, peers, schools, and teachers during the *transition period* (beginning early in the kindergarten year and lasting throughout first grade) tend to be missing for many young children today.

> What a young child knows and can do today may not be the same tomorrow, and may not be the same at home versus in the classroom.

A useful way to conceptualize the K–1 transition is as an organized system of interactions and transactions among people (families, teachers, children), settings (home, school), and institutions (community, governments) occurring over time—that is, as a transition *ecology* (Pianta & Walsh 1996). Just as a child's first blanket comforts and supports him during his early years, positive relationships between people in his life— such as his kindergarten and first grade teachers—and between places—such as home and school—knit together to serve a supportive role during his transition. As social connections are strengthened and more information is shared between people and settings, the yarns of this K–1 blanket become more finely intertwined.

This approach to easing the K–1 transition— the **developmental/ecological perspective**—is described in detail in this chapter. We believe this approach should guide thinking toward choosing and implementing effective transition practices.

Two approaches to K–1 transition

Teachers and school systems use a variety of approaches or conceptual models in addressing children's K–1 transition. Each model has different implications for the transition practices of teachers and schools (see Rimm-Kaufmann & Pianta 2000 for a full discussion of various models). Two widely used models are the skills-only approach and the developmental/ecological approach. Here is a brief comparison of each:

The *skills-only model* reduces the transition period to a focus on abilities and skills the child displays at a given time, such as the number of letters she can write at the end of kindergarten. This approach is the most commonly used, but also the most limited.

The *developmental/ecological model* describes a web of child, family, school, peer, and community factors that are interconnected and interdependent on one another throughout the transition period.

Under the skills-only model, a young child's adjustment during the transition period is understood in terms of the child's characteristics, such as readiness skills, chronological age, or level of maturation. The model does not look at ecological features (such as the quality of classroom instruction) or even at developmental features. In other words, the skills-only model imagines that when children go to school, they simply get on a bus and carry certain skills with them—ready or not.

In contrast, the developmental/ecological model acknowledges evidence that children's social and academic skills are remarkably unstable during the early school years (La Paro & Pianta 2001)—that is, what a young child knows and can do today may not be the same tomorrow, and may not be the same at home versus in the classroom. The developmental/ecological model takes into account the stability of relationships among the child, school, family, and community as the child moves from kindergarten into first grade. Perhaps most important, it considers information sharing and connections among children, parents, and schools to be critical supports for children.

Jason Downer, Kate Driscoll, and Robert Pianta

The kindergarten teacher in this vignette uses the developmental/ecological approach:

Mrs. Jenkins knows that her student Michael has difficulty following multi-step instructions and needs visual cues to focus his attention. She shares this information with Michael's future first grade teacher, so when he moves to the first grade room, he can continue to receive the support he needs to learn.

Mrs. Jenkins pays attention to Michael's individual needs, and communicates this information to his next teacher to help ensure that his transition will be smooth. She views Michael's readiness for first grade as more than just his age and ability to follow instructions. Her actions help to form a fabric of relationships that will support him as he moves to first grade.

At a national level, some teachers and school systems have recognized the developmental/ecological approach as superior in promoting successful K–1 transitions. Initiatives at the prekindergarten and kindergarten levels inspired by the national "Ready Schools" movement focus on school policies and practices that relate to transition, including relationships between families and schools. The Ready Schools idea was drawn from the work of the National Education Goals Panel, which called attention to the importance of quality experiences for children in K–1 settings (Pianta & Walsh 1996; Rimm-Kaufmann & Pianta 2000).

But it is the skills-only model that predominantly influences transition policy and practice today (Rimm-Kaufman & Pianta 2000). Its prevalence is perhaps best illustrated by the recent adoption of child outcome accountability assessments in the federal government's Head Start initiative and by the use of standardized assessments and "benchmarks" for child performance in early elementary school. States and school systems operating under the skills-only model typically use testing or other forms of "readiness assessment" and then make decisions about young children's suitability for educational programs based on those assessments.

In focusing on academic standards and children's skills, the skills-only model gives scant attention to program quality, educational practices, or teacher-child relationships. The school district in the following example uses the skills-only approach:

Kindergartner Jill's school district considers only measurable skills when promoting students. Jill is automatically promoted to first grade because she meets reading achievement standards, though just barely. The school fails to take into account Jill's close relationship with her kindergarten teacher—who worked tirelessly to help her meet the reading standards—and it makes no special plan to help Jill with her transition.

While Jill's adjustment to first grade certainly will depend in part on her reading skills, an equally important piece will be her acclimation to a new teacher and the extent of the support that Jill receives from this teacher. The skills-only model does not address all aspects of a successful K–1 transition as defined by the developmental/ecological model.

Factors that influence a child's K–1 transition

A variety of factors can help or hinder a child's transition from kindergarten to first grade and subsequent success in school. Structural factors include class size, teacher credentials, and length of school day. Quality of instruction and practice are also significant factors. How teachers and school systems address these factors and their consistency between kindergarten and first grade are critical.

Teachers, families, and communities need to understand how young children's competencies (their listening skills, for example) collide with how school and communities choose to structure the resources they provide kindergartners in transitioning to first grade. The very nature of this period as a *transition* is due to this meshing of individual differences in children (and their families) with variations in the structures and relationships of their schools (and communities). Dealing with that discontinuity puts a stress on children's self-regulation and social skills, which can interfere with their capacity to learn.

Variation in K–1 structures

Class size and teacher credentials are structural factors that policy makers decide upon and regulate. These features can differ drastically among various kindergarten programs and from kindergarten to first grade, resulting in a discontinuity that challenges children making a K–1 transition. Other kindergarten policies such as mandatory attendance, compulsory age, and length of day are also inconsistent across the country. (For more on this inconsistency and other such policy matters, see the box in the Graue chapter and the Kagan/Kauerz chapter in this volume.) Kindergarten attendance is mandatory in some states and optional in others (ECS 2005). In some states, the kindergarten day lasts only 2½ hours, versus a full 6 or 7 hours (Vecchiotti 2003).

Frequently reported K–1 transition practices are teacher-to-teacher discussions of curriculum and group visits by kindergartners to first grade classrooms.

When children move from kindergarten to first grade, new structures provide new challenges. For example, a family whose child attended voluntary kindergarten may not understand that sending their child to first grade every day is mandatory. Longer school days, too, can make for difficult adjustments, because they put increased demands on children to focus their attention and sit still. Teachers and school systems can help prepare children for these changes by sharing information and maintaining strong relationships with families, strengthening the fabric of support that eases children's K–1 transition.

Variation in instructional quality and practices

State policies typically require educational programs for young children to be of high quality and to use appropriate practices (for examples, see Clifford et al. 2003; NCES 2003; National Educa-tion Goals Panel 1995; Ripple et al. 1999). However, instructional quality and practices inside, as well as between, kindergarten and first grade classrooms vary widely. Again, these differences provide for challenging K–1 transitions.

Several large-scale observational studies provide information about the types and quality of experiences children have today in K–1 classrooms. First, on average, the typical early school setting is not doing a good job at supplying the kind of interactions and stimulation children need for development (La Paro, Pianta, & Stuhlman 2004; NICHD ECCRN 2002). Second, the type of learning activities provided for children differ considerably from classroom to classroom (NICHD ECCRN 2002; Pianta et al. 2002; Stipek 2004). These studies show, for example, that the typical child in an early elementary classroom overwhelmingly receives instruction in a large group, rather than in a small group or individually. In some classrooms, however, children are never taught in a large group. And while literacy instruction is the most common activity offered to children in kindergarten and first grade, a substantial number of classrooms provide no literacy activities at all. Even with this exceptional variability across settings, these K–1 classrooms can still be characterized overall as socially positive but instructionally passive.

When these studies looked at the same children's experiences over time, variation in classroom quality remains the rule. For example, a child who had a "sensitive" teacher one year could not count on having a similar experience the following year (NICHD ECCRN 2004, 2005). Even in the same schools using the same curriculum, a child was unlikely to experience similar levels of instructional activities in reading or math from year to year (NICHD ECCRN 2005).

In sum, the average child is likely to experience a substantial change in instructional practices and support during the K–1 transition. Using the developmental/ecological approach, more information sharing and stronger connections among schools, teachers, and parents are necessary to provide the strong fabric of support children need during this period of change and stress.

Jason Downer, Kate Driscoll, and Robert Pianta

How teachers and schools can help smooth the K–1 transition

Typical transition practices used by teachers and schools across the country provide little consistency in children's instruction and relationships between kindergarten and first grade. This section identifies the shortcomings of some typical transition practices, and outlines how to choose effective practices that are in step with a developmental/ecological approach. These practices will align a child's social and instructional experiences *over time* (throughout the transition period) and *between settings* (home-school and classroom-classroom).

The current state of K–1 transition

One of the first national surveys of public and private school teachers' K–1 transition practices indicates that strategies used by teachers and schools across the country are missing the relationships and information exchanges children need to make a smooth transition (La Paro, Pianta, & Cox 2000).

The good news is that more than half of teachers surveyed indicated using some form of transition practice, with more extensive use found in private schools. Overwhelmingly, teachers in this study reported using transition practices that focus on teacher or group child activities rather than on activities that involve families and are sensitive to the needs of individual children. The two most frequently reported K–1 transition practices are teacher-to-teacher discussions of curriculum and group visits by kindergartners to first grade classrooms. These are good practices, but they are insufficient when no other strategies are used.

Effective transition strategies in action

The developmental/ecological approach embraces the idea that school transition is an ongoing, relationship-building process at multiple levels: families with teachers and other school staff, children with peers and teachers, and kindergarten teachers with their first grade counterparts. Active collaboration among the key players in the transition process—teachers, directors and principals, and families—is fundamental in ensuring a successful transition for kindergartners. The following classroom examples illustrate several specific transition strategies in action (an extended list of strategies is offered in the box beginning on the next page). Consider the types of linkages that occur in each vignette and the players involved in building connections:

As one component of a comprehensive transition program, kindergarten and first grade teachers at Washington Elementary School collaborate to host a K–1 family transition night. Families receive information about similarities and differences between kindergarten and first grade, and kindergarten and first grade teachers are available to answer their questions.

✳

In April, veteran kindergarten teacher Mrs. Winters takes her students on a tour of first grade classrooms and introduces them to first grade teachers. In May, she invites first grade students to share a picnic with her class. Mrs. Winters encourages her kindergartners to ask the first grade students any questions they may have about first grade.

✳

Each spring, Ms. Bailey begins incorporating first grade routines into her kindergarten classroom. With her students, Ms. Bailey practices a reading ritual once a week that is practiced daily in first grade classrooms. Because first grade students must leave the classroom to use the bathroom located at the end of the hallway, she asks her students to practice walking down the hallway in a "first grade line."

✳

Mr. Hinton makes an effort to introduce his kindergarten students to children from other kindergarten classrooms as frequently as possible, because he is aware that their peer groups will change with the transition to first grade. He assigns each child a "reading buddy" from another classroom; each pair gets together on Tuesday afternoons to share books. Mr. Hinton invites another kindergarten classroom to a class puppet show in May. He initiates a pen pal program with first-graders at the local elementary school (which is located in a different building); each week, Mr. Hinton and his aide help the kindergartners write letters.

(continued on p. 158)

Examples of K–1 transition practices

Activity	How	When
Family-school connections		
Contact families during the first few days of kindergarten and first grade	Telephone calls, visits	First week of kindergarten
Maintain periodic contact with the family	Telephone calls, notes, newsletters, visits	Ongoing
Encourage family participation in home learning activities	Materials and/or instructions sent home	Ongoing, particularly during the summer between grades
Encourage family participation in the classroom and at school events	Telephone calls, notes, newsletters, visits	Ongoing, particularly at the start of the school year
Conduct regular family meetings at school	Lunches, family nights	Ongoing and at regular intervals
Conduct family meetings about transition issues	Family nights, workshops	During kindergarten spring, summer, and first grade fall
Coordinate information sharing about individual children between the families and teachers	Conferences	During kindergarten spring or summer
Create newsletters and resource materials	Transition packets, tips, handouts	Ongoing
Conduct parent orientation after the beginning of kindergarten and first grade	Back-to-school nights	First two weeks of kindergarten and first grade
Child-school connections		
Establish a connection between the kindergarten child and the first grade teacher	Visits to the first grade classroom by the child or visits by first grade teacher to the kindergarten classroom	During kindergarten spring
Create a connection between the child and the first grade using special school functions	School fairs, assemblies, playground parties	During kindergarten spring and summer

Jason Downer, Kate Driscoll, and Robert Pianta

Have children practice first grade rituals in kindergarten	Practice behaviors, sing songs, read stories	During kindergarten spring
Incorporate kindergarten activities into the first grade year	Read a favorite book, introduce similar activities	During first grade fall
Encourage kindergarten teachers to stay in contact with former students	Letters, school visits	During first grade fall
Peer connections		
Establish peer connections within the kindergarten class	Purposeful classroom assignments	During the summers before kindergarten and first grade
Establish peer connections outside of school	Play dates	Ongoing, particularly during the summer
Establish connections with peers who will be in first grade	Activities with other kindergartens	Ongoing, particularly during kindergarten spring and summer
Establish kindergarten peer connections with first grade peers	School visits, summer school	During kindergarten spring and summer
Classroom-classroom connections		
Share curriculum activities and classroom routines between kindergarten and first grade	Teachers observe each others' classrooms and hold regular meetings	Ongoing
Agree on a common assessment tool to describe individual children and their families	Meet to decide what information will be helpful to both teachers	Ongoing

Note: This table is intended to serve as a flexible menu from which teachers can pick and choose transition activities that fit their situation. In fact, teachers are encouraged to be creative and add their own ideas to this list as they build a developmentally and ecologically responsive transition plan.

Family-school connections. Healthy family-school relationships are critical in helping a child adjust to a new classroom and teacher during the transition period. A major objective of creating positive family-school connections is to increase each family's collaboration and involvement with the school so that information about their child's experiences at home and school can be shared within a trusting relationship. A family benefits from understanding what is expected of their child in the classroom, knowing about the types of learning experiences available at school, and hearing how their child is adjusting to the new setting once the child goes on to first grade.

Child-school connections. The K–1 transition will be smooth when children are involved in comfortable, supportive relationships with their kindergarten and first grade teachers. When kindergarten teachers provide opportunities for children to interact directly with the teachers they will have in first grade—during tours of their soon-to-be first grade classrooms and visits from the first grade teachers to the kindergarten classroom—the children will be more comfortable with the transition. A positive teacher-child connection can begin to form. In some school systems, kindergarten and first grade classrooms are located in different schools, making the logistics of a visit more difficult. Nevertheless, it is just as important, if not more so, for kindergartners to have the opportunity to familiarize themselves with their new school setting (in a class trip, for example).

Peer connections. Strong peer relationships also provide children with support throughout the transition. When children move from kindergarten into first grade with their friends, those connections can make them feel more comfortable with their new environment and provide social experiences that will feel predictable. Such peer connections are promoted inside and outside of the classroom when, with help from kindergarten teachers, families whose children will share a first grade teacher connect, and when sets of kindergartner peers visit their future first grade classroom together.

Classroom-classroom connections. Information sharing between kindergarten and first grade

---

Smoothing the PreK to K Transition, Too

The discontinuity between preschool and kindergarten can often be more pronounced than the K–1 transition:

- Almost half (48%) of parents surveyed in the 2000 U.S. Census reported that their 3- and 4-year-olds were not "in school"—that is, kindergarten will represent their first formal schooling experience.

- A preschool day can be as short as 2½ and as long as 10 hours, while kindergarten days are as variable.

- A child's kindergarten classroom is likely to be housed in a location different from the preschool classroom.

- PreK teachers typically have less education and training than elementary school teachers do.

- Substantial variability exists within and across preK–K classroom quality and practices.

- Parent-teacher contact is emphasized less and often decreases in frequency from preschool to kindergarten.

The developmental/ecological principles discussed in this chapter also apply to this preK–K transition. That is, kindergarten teachers are encouraged to form collaborative relationships with preschool teachers and parents to enhance preK–K continuity. For specific suggestions, see Pianta & Kraft-Sayre 2003.

---

teachers is an essential part of establishing continuity for children during the K–1 transition and beyond. As highlighted earlier, instructional practice and classroom quality vary strikingly across kindergarten classrooms and between kindergarten and first grade. In order to create a more consistent educational experience for children during their K–1 transition, it is critical that teachers

Jason Downer, Kate Driscoll, and Robert Pianta

communicate with one another. Schools or individual teachers can initiate such information sharing.

Redefining "success" in transition outcomes

The K–1 transition is best understood as a web of relationships among children, families, teachers, classrooms, schools, and communities that can enhance or deter young children's development and subsequent school success. Frequently, however, the definitions of "success" in K–1 transition only include the transmission of skills from kindergarten to first grade. These definitions favor a skills-only model of transition, rather than a developmental/ecological approach.

From a skills-only perspective, a child's successful transition from kindergarten is measured solely by her social and academic competence in a first grade classroom. But this competence may not be the only, or best, outcome measure of a successful transition from kindergarten. Factors such as continuity of instructional practices and family-school relationships are instrumental aspects of a coherent transition process and should be considered worthy outcomes in their own right. Current definitions of successful K–1 transition should be revised to include elements of the fabric of support described by the developmental/ecological approach.

Teachers and early childhood educators who take the responsibility to think about transition from a developmental/ecological perspective and make smooth transitions a priority will greatly benefit their students. These teacher efforts can also help create school cultures that focus on strengthening relationships and information sharing to serve as resources for children and families. Future K–1 transition efforts embedded in a developmental/ecological model hold promise for realizing a system of early schooling in which children's educational experiences are coherent, systematic, and effective.

Note

The work reported herein was supported in part under the Educational Research and Development Centers Program, PR/ Award Number R307A60004, as administered by the Office of Educational Research and Improvement, U.S. Department of Education to the National Center for Early Development and Learning. It was also supported by the National Institute of Child Health and Human Development (NICHD) to the NICHD Study of Early Child Care and Youth Development. The NICHD Study of Early Child Care and Youth Development is directed by a Steering Committee and supported by NICHD through a cooperative agreement (U10) that calls for a scientific collaboration between grantees and the NICHD staff. The contents do not necessarily represent the positions or policies of the National Institute on Early Childhood Development and Education, the Office of Educational Research and Improvement, the U.S. Department of Education, or the National Institute of Child Health and Human Development and endorsement by the federal government should not be assumed.

References

Clifford, R., O. Barbarin, F. Chang, D. Early, D. Bryant, C. Howes, M. Burchinal, & R. Pianta. 2003. What is pre-kindergarten? Trends in the development of a public system of pre-kindergarten services. Unpublished manuscript.

ECS (Education Commission of the States). 2005. State statutes regarding kindergarten. Online: www.ecs.org/html/educationissues/earlylearning/kdb_intro.asp.

Entwisle, D.R., & K.L. Alexander. 1993. Entry into schools: The beginning school transition and educational stratification in the United States. In *Annual Review of Sociology* 19: 401–23. Palo Alto, CA: Annual Reviews.

Entwisle, D.R., & K.L. Alexander. 1998. Facilitating the transition to first grade: The nature of transition and research on factors affecting it. *Elementary School Journal* 98 (4): 351–64.

Epstein, J.L. 2001. *School, family, and community partnerships.* Boulder, CO: Westview.

Foundation for Child Development. 2003. *Mapping the PK–3 continuum (MAP): PK–3 as the foundation of education reform.* New York: Author.

La Paro, K.M., & R.C. Pianta. 2001. Predicting children's competence in the early school years: A meta-analytic review. *Review of Educational Research* 70: 443–84.

La Paro, K.M., R. Pianta, & M. Cox. 2000. Kindergarten teachers' reported use of kindergarten to first grade practices. *The Elementary School Journal* 101 (1): 63–78.

La Paro, K.M., R.C. Pianta, & M. Stuhlman. 2004. Classroom Assessment Scoring System (CLASS): Findings from the pre-K year. *Elementary School Journal* 104 (5): 409–26.

NCES (National Center for Education Statistics). 2003. *Overview and inventory of state education reforms: 1990–2000.* Washington, DC: U.S. Department of Education, Institute of Education Sciences.

NCES. 2004. *Full-day and half-day kindergarten in the United States: Findings from the Early Childhood Longitudinal Study, kindergarten class of 1998–99.* Washington, DC: Author.

National Education Goals Panel. 1995. *National Education Goals report executive summary: Improving education through family-school-community partnerships.* Washington, DC: Author.

National Education Goals Panel. 1998. *Ready Schools.* Washington, DC: Author.

NICHD (National Institute of Child Health & Human Development) Early Child Care Research Network. 2002. The relation of global first grade classroom environment to structural classroom features, teacher, and student behaviors. *Elementary School Journal* 102 (5): 367–87.

NICHD Early Child Care Research Network. 2004. Does class size in first grade relate to changes in child academic and social performance or observed classroom processes? *Developmental Psychology* 40: 651–64.

NICHD Early Child Care Research Network. 2005. A day in third grade: A large-scale study of classroom quality and teacher and student behavior. *Elementary School Journal* 105 (3): 305–23.

Pianta, R.C., & M. Kraft-Sayre. 2003. *Successful kindergarten transition: Your guide to connecting children, families, & schools.* Baltimore: Brookes.

Pianta, R., K. La Paro, & B. Hamre. 2005. *Classroom Assessment Scoring System manual.* Charlottesville, VA: Authors.

Pianta, R.C., K.M. La Paro, C. Payne, M.J. Cox, & R. Bradley. 2002. The relation of kindergarten classroom environment to teacher, family, and school characteristics and child outcomes. *Elementary School Journal* 102 (3): 225–38.

Pianta, R.C., & D.J. Walsh. 1996. *High-risk children in schools: Constructing sustaining relationships.* New York: Routledge.

Rimm-Kaufman, S.E., & R.C. Pianta. 2000. An ecological perspective on the transition to kindergarten: A theoretical framework to guide empirical research. *Journal of Applied Developmental Psychology* 21 (5): 491–511.

Ripple, C.H., W.S. Gilliam, N. Chanana, & E. Zigler. 1999. Will fifty cooks spoil the broth? The debate over entrusting Head Start to the states. *American Psychologist* 54: 327–43.

Stipek, D. 2004. Teaching practices in kindergarten and first grade: Different strokes for different folks. *Early Childhood Research Quarterly* 19: 548–68.

Vecchiotti, S. 2003. Kindergarten: An overlooked educational policy priority. *Social Policy Report* 17 (2): 3–19.

Jason Downer, Kate Driscoll, and Robert Pianta

Making the Most of Kindergarten— Trends and Policy Issues

15

Sharon L. Kagan & Kristie Kauerz

Testifying before the National Education Goals Panel some years ago, a kindergarten teacher dramatically impressed and moved the assembled group of governors and legislators with her words: "I am a kindergarten teacher and I have the best job in the whole world. My kids and I love each other." She went on to tell how she scavenged junk from neighborhood vendors for the children's science and art projects because supplies at her inner-city school were lacking. Even more poignantly, she noted very real tensions: "I am pressured to be everything to everyone; I am caught between developmental and disciplinary approaches to pedagogy and curriculum; and I am tossed about between play and formal instruction." She closed her comments with a simple question: "How am I supposed to keep the hopes of my families and children alive when my own dreams for the possibilities of kindergarten are so diminished?"

Like this caring kindergarten teacher more than a decade ago, we are all desirous of reconciling the pressures on kindergarten today with our

Sharon L. Kagan is a professor of early childhood and family policy at Teachers College, Columbia University, and an adjunct professor at Yale University. Kristie Kauerz is a research fellow at Teachers College, Columbia University, and former program director of early learning at the Education Commission of the States.

knowledge of child development and early childhood pedagogy. We are all eager to make the kindergarten experience as rich and as contributory to young children's development as possible. We want this even as we recognize that, for many, kindergarten remains the overlooked year, overshadowed by the policy fanfare of prekindergarten and the domination of standards, testing, and the regularities of school. Stated differently, we all are desirous of retaining the uniqueness of kindergarten culture against a society demanding academic assimilation.

How do concerned educators and policy makers buck the tide, or at least reconcile it with the needs of today's young children? What is worth holding onto from kindergarten's past? How do we align the social constructions of children from that past with the genuine need to consider the deep-seated and historically underaddressed issues of inequity of access and inequality of service? How do we create environments for children that are culturally sensitive, are respectful of current realities, and transcend the vagaries of the kindergarten debate?

Simply said: *What is it we want kindergarten to be and do? And how do we achieve it?* These questions frame this chapter.

Perspectives on what kindergarten should be and do

To address these questions, we turn first to those who are invested in kindergarten:

The child—I'm 5 years old, and I want to feel welcome in my kindergarten. I want to be in a space where I feel respected and honored, no matter what my background or learning ability is. I want there to be nice children in my class who will become my friends.

I want a teacher who will be patient with me when I make mistakes, who will challenge me to be better than I am, and who will notice my special strengths, needs, and progress. That's not too much to ask for, is it?

*

The parent—I'm the parent of three children, and I see big changes in kindergarten from when my first child attended and now that my "baby" is here. I want to understand the reasons for all these changes. Sure, I want my child to learn and be ready for first grade. But I'm not sure how children this age really learn best.

I want a kindergarten where I will be welcome, and where I can learn, too. I want a kindergarten that will help make my child the best she can be. Mostly, I want kindergarten to be a place where my child feels—and is—safe and engaged in learning.

*

The teacher—I've been teaching for 20 years, so I've seen kindergarten curricula and fads come and go. I've lived through talking toys, computer wars, science kits, and math tools.

I want the public and policy makers to recognize the legitimacy of play as a means for young children to learn and to achieve standards. I want curiosity, motivation, creativity, socialization, and task persistence recognized not merely as legitimate but as the primary goals of kindergarten.

I want the freedom to create my own classroom dynamic and to be as unfettered as possible by extraneous paperwork and requirements. Finally, I want and need to work in an environment where my knowledge and credentials as an early childhood educator are recognized and respected.

*

The principal—I'm the principal of a K–6 school in an urban setting, and I want good teachers who understand the importance of kindergarten.

I want teachers who see parents and the community as rightful partners in children's education. I want a per diem funding allocation that treats kindergartners as full-fledged members of the school community and funds them on an equivalent basis to older children. I want full-day kindergartens, because the data are clear that full-day services not only promote children's performance but also ease the burden on teachers. I want kindergarten standards, curriculum, and assessments that are appropriate and aligned with those of preschool and first grade.

I want to create a learning community in my school where teachers have the opportunity and desire to grow and to lead.

*

The policy maker—I'm a state legislator, and I'm concerned about the growing achievement gaps among children in my state. I want kindergarten to be an indispensable means for improving achievement and preparing all children to be engaged citizens. I want our state to recognize and support kindergarten as a fully integrated part of the education system. I want every district in the state to ensure that every child—regardless of language, culture, or ability—has the opportunity to attend kindergarten.

I want the state to provide adequate funds for kindergarten; I don't want to hear from my constituents how kindergarten teachers are buying their own classroom supplies or how parents are being charged fees for their child to attend a full-day kindergarten program.

Sharon L. Kagan and Kristie Kauerz

Guiding principles for what kindergarten should be and do in the future

Drawing from the work of many scholars and practitioners, we offer the following guidelines:

Kindergarten must remain "special." Kindergarten is the repository for the hopes and dreams of children, parents, teachers, principals, and policy makers. As children are not miniature adults, kindergarten is not miniature school. For children (and their parents), it is the transition year when they feel they are entering the formal "school" system. For teachers, it is the time when they know children's critical learning patterns begin to be established. For principals and policy makers, it is a time they want to be fully integrated with, yet distinct from, the complete educational continuum. In the future, kindergarten must continue to be regarded as special.

Kindergarten must still keep the child front and center, even with the new emphasis on content. As the world globalizes, and pressures for performance and performance-accounting mount, the kindergarten curriculum must evolve. But it must never sacrifice the child's social, emotional, cognitive, and learning development. Kindergarten must prioritize the teaching and nurturing of *children,* not the teaching of *content.* Kindergarten must promote children's enthusiasm, initiative, and engagement in learning. This is not to diminish the importance of cognitive development, but instead to suggest that children's social and emotional well-being and eagerness to learn are prerequisites for their absorbing formally taught content.

Kindergarten must acknowledge and support differences in the needs of children and their families. One-size-fits-all does not work in education. Children have different learning needs and styles, and kindergarten must support and encourage *all* children. Similarly, parents have different needs, and the structure of kindergarten (full-day/half-day or public/private) must be sufficiently flexible to meet their needs, as well.

Kindergarten must foster relationships. For young children, relationships form the sturdy foundation they need as they embark on their journey into formal schooling and the public's high expectations for achievement and life success. Kindergarten provides a critical window of time during which positive relationships—between children and their teachers, between families and schools, and between schools and communities—can form and be made permanent. Kindergarten is an ideal time to build patterns of trust and communication to last lifetimes.

Changes in policy today for the kindergarten we need tomorrow

Policy must play a central role in order to fulfill the expectations of what kindergarten should be and do and to honor the guiding principles outlined above. Policy—at the federal, state, district, and school levels—helps ensure that desirable practices and behaviors are the norm rather than the exception.

At the most fundamental level, policy makers can ensure that kindergarten is universally *available* and *accessible* to all students regardless of their family's income level, geographic location, language, culture, or ability. However, most states do not currently require children to attend kindergarten; seven states currently do not even require their school districts to *offer* kindergarten (Kauerz 2005). (For more data, see the box in the Graue chapter in this volume.) Of those states that do require their school districts to offer kindergarten, only nine currently require a full-day option. In states that do not require or financially support full-day programs, school districts that do offer such programs are often forced to charge tuition or restrict access to limited populations of children (such as low-income families). Full-day kindergarten programs should be available—and affordable—to *all* children.

"I'm the parent of three children, and I see big changes in kindergarten from when my first child attended."

Kindergarten entrance age

Public schools typically allow children to enter kindergarten when they turn 5 during the autumn of the kindergarten year. But this cutoff date for turning age 5 varies from state to state and even between districts. As of the 2006–07 school year:

• Four states have entrance age cutoff dates between December 1 and January 1 of the kindergarten year. This practice leads to classrooms with a balanced mix of 4- and 5-year-old kindergartners.

• Thirty-six states have cutoff dates between August 31 and October 16 of the kindergarten year. This leads to a mix of 4- and 5-year-olds entering each fall, but fewer 4-year-olds.

• Five states have cutoff dates on or before August 15 preceding the kindergarten year that begins that fall. This more or less ensures that all children are 5 years old before they enter kindergarten.

• Six states leave the cutoff decision to local school districts.

—K.K.

Note: The total number of states listed here is 51. Ohio allows school districts to choose either August 1 or September 30 as the kindergarten entry date, and so is counted in two different categories. **Source:** Education Commission of the States (www.ecs.org/kindergarten).

To make kindergarten universally available and accessible to all children also means offering families kindergarten choices. Some families prefer full-day kindergarten programs; others prefer half-day. Some parents prefer a kindergarten located in a community early-learning center; others prefer a school-based kindergarten. To this end, policy makers need to model kindergarten after the early learning field, supporting and encouraging a mixed delivery system that embraces both public and private providers.

Once access to kindergarten is guaranteed, policy makers need to focus on improving the *quality* of kindergarten. The national focus on measuring achievement and school readiness, which has grown since the standards movement began in the late 1980s and intensified with the No Child Left Behind Act, puts kindergarten in a quality bind. On one hand, kindergarten is increasingly looked to as a critical year for preparing children to be successful learners. This has opened new policy dialogues and opportunities. But on the other hand, the pressure of high-stakes testing of third-graders in literacy and math has resulted in policy dialogues that are often narrow and academically limited. Stories of the academization of kindergarten abound. Many states have developed or are developing early learning standards for kindergarten, most often limited to literacy, mathematics, and other cognitive areas (Scott-Little, Kagan, & Frelow 2003). Such kindergarten standards are too narrow and do not embrace the full range of young children's developmental needs.

Wanting to ensure students' "success" in kindergarten, many policy makers look to the children themselves rather than consider changes to kindergarten programs. For example, under the assumption that just because children are older they are somehow more likely to succeed, many policy makers tinker with the kindergarten entrance age. Some policies allow parents to hold their children back one year before starting them in kindergarten, a practice known as "redshirting." In fact, 14 states have raised their kindergarten entrance age since 1984, trying to ensure that more children will be at least 5 years old when they enter. In reality, no matter when the cutoff date is set, kindergarten classrooms will always include children whose ages vary by as much as 12 months or more. Classrooms will always include children who are "well prepared" and not so well prepared to succeed.

Rather than trying to change the characteristics of children who enter kindergarten, policy makers should focus their time and energy on supporting schools and teachers to be prepared to nurture and support the learning and development of *all* the children in their kindergarten classrooms. Effectively targeting policy to improve kindergarten requires addressing pedagogy and curriculum, the preparedness of teachers, the

Sharon L. Kagan and Kristie Kauerz

involvement of families, and linkages to community services. The remaining sections of this chapter look at these areas to envision how policy could create the kindergarten we all desire for the future.

Policies related to kindergarten pedagogy and curriculum

In the field of education, pedagogy and content have historically been considered two distinct domains, with pedagogy consisting of *how* one teaches (the art and science of teaching) and content consisting of *what* is taught and learned (the substance or essential meaning). This division, more true as learners proceed from elementary to secondary to postsecondary education, has long been at the heart of the early childhood debate. To a greater extent than subsequent grades, early childhood education merges pedagogy and content in practice, though recognizing the distinction between them. *How* young children are taught is difficult to separate from *what* they are taught. Indeed, this link between the *what* and the *how* of early education (often characterized as "two sides of the same coin") has long fueled internal debates about the need for more attention to the content of early childhood curriculum (Bowman, Donovan, & Burns 2000; Spodek & Saracho 2002).

While we acknowledge these historical debates and the reality that the pedagogy/content separation may be less pronounced in early childhood education, we have divided the discussion in two for the purposes of this chapter.

The content of the curriculum

Though intertwined, the recommended content of kindergarten can be seen to comprise six distinct domains. They are development and learning in these areas: cognitive, social and emotional, physical, language, creative expression, and the disciplines of mathematics, science, and social studies, as reflected in the excellent chapters in this volume by Golbeck, Bronson, Sanders, Strickland, Jalongo and Isenberg, Sarama and Clements, Chalufour and Worth, and Mindes, re-

Full-day kindergarten funding

Like funding for grades 1–12, state funding for full-day kindergarten is established in policy as part of each state's K–12 education funding formula. An **explicit incentive** for districts to offer full-day kindergarten exists when the state provides more funding for full-day programs than for half-day kindergarten programs *and* this amount is equal to or greater than the amount of state funds provided for first grade.

When there is no difference between the funding for half-day versus full-day kindergarten, but the amount is greater than that provided for first grade, there is a kindergarten **incentive,** but not an explicit full-day incentive. States create a **disincentive** for districts to offer full-day kindergarten when there is no difference in the funding amount for half-day versus full-day *and* the funding level is lower than that provided for first grade. As of 2006:

• Seven states provide an explicit incentive to offer full-day kindergarten.

• Twenty-one states provide funding incentives for districts to offer kindergarten, but no explicit incentive for full-day.

• Nineteen states provide a disincentive to districts to offer full-day kindergarten.

—K.K.

Source: Education Commission of the States (www.ecs.org/kindergarten).

spectively. In the past, as in the future, *all* these domains are required to address the full content of early education. No one domain can serve as proxy for all; each is necessary.

Certainly the future will demand knowledge of all these domains. In addition, as the world becomes smaller and its citizens more global, the content of the kindergarten curriculum needs to become more robust, by including *more* domains such as approaches toward learning that foster creativity, task persistence, and motivation. Children increasingly engage new realms of learning: most communities are becoming more diverse, requiring greater resilience, understanding, and critical thinking from their members. Unlike children of even 10 years ago, for example, today's children grow up in a digital age that brings with it an abundance of information, new spaces for learning, and unprecedented contact with people and ideas from around the world. Any vision of the kindergarten of the future must include a focus on *technological literacy*—the ability to use with agility all forms of technology. Some early childhood educators are reluctant to incorporate computers into their classrooms; however, while recognizing that computers can be used inappropriately, appropriately incorporating computer skills into the repertoires of young children is essential.

> Any vision of the kindergarten of the future must include a focus on technological literacy.

Kindergartens of the future should adopt *bilingualism* as the norm. Debate about the appropriate language of instruction for English-language learners has gone on for decades. However, with only greater globalization in our future, clearly all kindergarten children should be exposed to and taught a second language, including native English speakers. The ability to communicate in both English and another language increases children's perspectives and experiences of linguistic and cultural diversity and prepares them for participation in the international community.

Finally, kindergartens of the future need to attend to children's *physical and mental health*. The domain of social-emotional development and learning is closely aligned with mental health, and the domain of physical development and learning is aligned with physical health. But the kindergarten curriculum is often inexplicit about the importance of self health-care. As America ages, as childhood obesity increases, and as health-care costs soar, the importance of teaching young children healthy skills and a commitment to healthy lifestyles calls for their systematic incorporation into curriculum.

Where content and pedagogy meet

Characterizing pedagogy and content as "two sides of the same coin" implies that something binds them together. What *is* this binding force, and how binding is it? Looking at the second question first, a review of the literature suggests that the rhetoric of linkage far outstrips its reality. Early childhood education offers durable documents from the field that address pedagogy but give limited attention to content/curriculum, and vice versa. Moreover, when we train teachers, the courses we offer in the content areas (such as the teaching of reading or mathematics) are often quite separate from the courses in pedagogy (such as observing and assessing children or organizing the early childhood classroom). In short, linkages between content and pedagogy need strengthening.

To truly act as two sides of the same coin, content and pedagogy need a common adhesive. For that glue, early childhood education today may well look to the development of *early learning standards*—specifications of what young children should know and be able to do. Well-developed and well-used early learning standards can be the basis of what and how teachers teach. So as not to encourage the over-academization of kindergarten, the standards should reflect all domains of young children's learning, not just the cognitive or subject-matter knowledge that children will encounter in first grade and beyond. Standards should include young children's physical development, social-emotional development, and their approaches to learning.

Clearly, standards—as specifications of our expectations for students' learning—should guide the development of the content/curriculum. If standards are not the backbone of curriculum, then our curriculum is teaching children what we deem less important or unimportant for them to learn. In addition, early learning standards should become the basis for our child assessments—that is, there should be direct links among what is expected (standards), what is taught (curriculum), and what is measured (assessment). Misalignment deprives children of an integrated approach to

Sharon L. Kagan and Kristie Kauerz

learning and falsifies the learning process. That standards, curriculum, and assessment should be aligned not only within each grade but also from grade to grade (such as from prekindergarten to kindergarten, and from kindergarten to first grade) is self-evident.

But how does pedagogy fit into this picture? In resolving that, early childhood educators are involved in nothing less than a conceptual conversion. Traditional early childhood pedagogy is interactive, with curriculum building on children's interests, not in a prescribed way but spontaneously. But the school standards movement is pressuring kindergarten to follow along with what's happening elsewhere—notably, to base instruction on adult-prescribed learning goals or standards that frame the curriculum, which in turn frames child assessment. Increasingly in schools, more sequenced planning and learning is the norm. With the starting point for curriculum shifting from the child to the adult, and with pedagogy more planned than spontaneous, how does kindergarten retain its special commitment to the child? How does it honor what we know about child development?

To have specified standards, curriculum, and assessment—even to have standards-driven instruction—does not mean that pedagogy must be didactic and structured or that pedagogy cannot be child-driven. Instead, it means that teachers must understand *why* they are teaching what they are teaching (what learning goals will be met by the daily activities they plan). In this way, their teaching will become more *intentional,* with student learning outcomes in mind. Kindergarten teachers must have clear goals, a repertoire of activities to meet those goals, and the ingenuity and flexibility to create learning experiences that maximize and blend those goals and activities.

In the future, kindergarten content and pedagogy must become even more blended, more intentional, and more child-inviting. But this will take talent, training, time, an investment of resources in those who teach kindergarten, and a commitment from policy makers to validate and support developmentally appropriate practices in kindergarten classrooms.

Policies related to kindergarten teachers

As parents and policy makers increasingly recognize the importance of the early learning years, they turn to kindergarten teachers not just for hope but to deliver child progress. It remains a challenge for early educators to meet these expectations without compromising their knowledge of child development. In a magnificent description of early childhood pedagogy in this volume, Heroman and Copple specify the talents and skills required of teachers, including the need to know children culturally, to be sensitive to cultural diversity, and to regard diversity as a strength. Beyond this, teachers must know child development, curriculum content, classroom and environmental management, diverse approaches to teaching and guidance, and pedagogy.

To meet the increasing demands being placed on kindergarten teachers, some of which contradict their professional beliefs and goals, it would seem clear that the first order of business is to review all kindergarten teacher-preparation programs. We must be certain they are not stuck in outdated, last-century theories and approaches. A curriculum scan should uncover the degree to which the programs include multicultural, technological, and global components. Further, it should ensure the preparation of capable pedagogical diagnosticians who fully understand and can use standards and assessments appropriately. In Gullo's elegant chapter and elsewhere in this volume, we see how critical the art and science of assessment is—both in gathering accurate information and in using that data to inform and revamp instructional practice.

Such preprofessional development is only the beginning. It must be supported by ongoing in-service support. Many programs of new-teacher support and mentoring by seasoned teachers are being launched throughout the nation; priority should go to supporting those teachers who are new to teaching at the kindergarten level, irrespective of their experience in other grades. Coaching and peer support must also be added to the regular repertoire of in-service professional development. Indeed, conventional in-service training needs to be rethought to embrace both hands and heads—that is, it should focus on the practical combined with the theoretical, especially as new ideas, strategies, and technologies emerge. In-service efforts that help teachers to better understand the nature of standards, curriculum, pedagogy, and assessment in the learning years prior and subsequent to kindergarten are also essential.

Policies related to families and communities

As Downer, Driscoll, and Pianta describe in this volume, it is critical to recognize that kindergarten children are interconnected and interdependent with their family, their school, their peers, and the community. To have healthy, enthusiastic, and engaged kindergartners, we need healthy, enthusiastic, and engaged families, schools, and peers, as well as communities geared toward supporting young children. As our third guiding principle in this chapter makes clear, kindergarten must foster relationships. It is the prime time in young children's lives to lay strong foundations for trusting, mutual relationships among their families, schools, and communities.

Supporting families

Families form the bedrock for children's learning and development. As Berk and Bronson richly describe in their chapters, secure family relationships are central to the young child's social and emotional development. The ability of families to nurture their children physically, emotionally, and intellectually increases the likelihood that those children will grow up to be healthy, loving, productive, responsible, creative, and self-confident. And yet, it is rarely recognized that entering kindergarten brings profound changes and new stresses. Indeed, kindergarten is not just an important transition year for young children, it is also a major transition year for their families. As Powell and Gerde point out in this volume, kindergarten presents unique opportunities to provide special attention and benefits to families.

To support *all* families, and to realize the kind of kindergartens we want for the future, policy makers must embrace old-fashioned ways of thinking about what it takes to support young children's learning and development. For centuries and across cultures, families have helped one another cope with day-to-day living. But the families of today's kindergartners are increasingly diverse (West, Denton, & Germino-Hausken 2000) and live in a high-tech, fast-paced world that exacerbates isolation, mobility, and stress.

To enable and empower families to support one another and, therefore, to support their young children, policy makers must commit to programs and services that connect families to one another; that affirm and strengthen families' ethnic, racial, and linguistic identities; and that are flexible and responsive to families' ever-changing needs. Furthermore, policy makers must champion the importance of strong home learning environments. A family is a child's most important teacher, and the kinds of learning experiences that children have at home greatly impact their approach to learning in school and in life. Flexible work schedules, timely and appropriate information on child development, and parent-education programs can all enhance home and family learning environments.

Strengthening relationships between families and schools

During the kindergarten year, family routines change as children's schedules, peers, and exposure to the world change. In the chapters on families and transition in this volume, the authors note that studies show that once children enter kindergarten, contact between their families and their teachers declines and shifts from being primarily home-initiated to school-initiated. This contact is increasingly negative (focusing on problems) as children advance through the grades. The relationships that are formed between families and schools in kindergarten often set the tone and intensity for such relationships throughout a child's educational path.

Traditionally, transition practices have helped both children and families understand, anticipate, and thrive during the changes inherent in the

Sharon L. Kagan and Kristie Kauerz

move from the child-centered world of early care and education into the more formal world of kindergarten and early elementary school. "Transition" is the buzzword for efforts bridging children's home and school experiences, and has traditionally been defined as one-time, short-term activities or practices that facilitate children's movement from one level of learning to another. But to build the kindergartens of the future, we must move away from transition as discrete events and toward the establishment of family-school partnerships. Schools should provide family outreach workers whose sole responsibility is to engage families in their children's learning environment at school. Schools should design transition activities to meet the needs of working families by offering meeting times and events that acknowledge the variety of schedules that families keep in order to balance work and home life.

Strengthening family-school relations also requires expanding the discussions of readiness to more fully address the concept of "Ready Schools." Even though the National Education Goals Panel included Ready Schools as part of its groundbreaking work in the late 1990s, only recently have policy makers begun to address the question of whether schools are ready to support and nurture the learning of young children. Ready Schools include more than just providing a smooth transition from home to school; they are also committed to the success of every child and every teacher; they alter practices that are not benefiting children; they take responsibility for results; and they have strong leaders who recognize the unique learning needs of young children (Shore 1998). Fully embracing the concept of Ready Schools requires assessing, supporting, and improving not just children's individual skills but also the interactions occurring within classrooms, schools, and communities.

Strengthening relationships between schools and communities

Kindergartners' success in the classroom is inextricably linked with their health and well-being. The physical and mental health status of children is a critical contributor to their overall readiness for school. From its inception, Head Start has recognized the importance of providing comprehensive services to young children. The kindergarten of the future should be no different. Strong links to physical-, mental-, and dental-health services should become a standard experience for kindergarten children. School-based health centers, mental-health consultants, and onsite dental clinics are only the beginning of the possibilities.

Beyond expanding the scope of services that can be identified and accessed from inside the schoolhouse doors, policy makers have a key role to play in ensuring that the communities outside those doors are ready to support their young children's learning and development. For kindergartners to become wholly exposed to the diverse people, ideas, and experiences that characterize the 21st century, they should engage in learning beyond the classroom walls. Learning can and should take place through all community-based institutions. Libraries, parks, museums, recreational facilities, civic venues, and other community assets provide invaluable opportunities for children and their families.

> Kindergarten is the prime time in young children's lives to lay strong foundations for trusting, mutual relationships among their families, schools, and communities.

Whatever its precise focus, each and every chapter in this volume has sounded similar themes: the importance of kindergarten, the need to rethink current practice and thinking, and the need to be policy-cognizant. In our chapter, we have tried to take this discourse one step further by dreaming about what an ideal kindergarten of the future should be and do. Yet these are the thoughts of the authors alone. Any re-visioning of kindergarten cannot and should not be so limited.

To that end, our final suggestion is that a national forum on kindergarten be established to examine the ideas presented in this volume with the goal of developing a 10-year plan for enhancing the quality of kindergarten programs. Such a plan could then serve to guide policy and practice so that advances undertaken are keyed to a broad-based, field-constructed vision of American kindergarten.

Said differently, "You have to have a dream before you have a dream come true!" Our mission, the mission of our leaders, and the mission of this volume is to dream the dreams that thousands of kindergarten teachers lament they are beginning to lose. We all need clarity of vision sprinkled with optimism and effort to fuel the hopes and aspirations of the children and families who cross our kindergarten thresholds.

References

Bowman, B.T., M.S. Donovan, & M.S. Burns, eds. 2000. *Eager to learn: Educating our preschoolers.* Washington, DC: National Academies Press.

Kauerz, K. 2005. *Full-day kindergarten: A study of state policies in the United States.* Denver, CO: Education Commission of the States.

Scott-Little, C., S.L. Kagan, & V.S. Frelow. 2003. *Standards for preschool children's learning and development: Who has standards, how were they developed, and how are they used? Executive summary.* Greensboro, NC: SERVE.

Shore, R. 1998. *Ready schools: A report of the Goal 1 Ready Schools Resource Group.* Washington, DC: National Education Goals Panel.

Spodek, B., & O.N. Saracho. 2002. *Contemporary perspectives on curriculum in early childhood education.* Greenwich, CT: Information Age Publishers.

West, J., K. Denton, & E. Germino-Hausken. 2000. *America's kindergartners: Findings from the Early Childhood Longitudinal Study, Kindergarten Class of 1998-99, fall 1998* (NCES 2000-070R). Washington, DC: National Center for Education Statistics, U.S. Department of Education.

Sharon L. Kagan and Kristie Kauerz

Index

Did you know...?

In her 1922 guide, America's first maven of manners, Emily Post, advised parents in a chapter called *The Kindergarten of Etiquette*:

"If [the child] shows talent as an artist, give him pencils or modeling wax in his playroom, but do not let him bite his slice of bread into the silhouette of an animal, or model figures in soft bread at the table. And do not allow him to construct a tent out of two forks, or an automobile chassis out of tumblers and knives. Food and table implements are not playthings, nor is the dining-room a playground."

"Did you know . . . ?" sources

From page iii (top to bottom):

R. Wollons. 2000. On the international diffusion, politics, and transformation of the kindergarten. In *Kindergartens & cultures,* ed. R. Wollons, 1–15. New Haven, CT: Yale University Press.

R. Shore. 1997. *Rethinking the brain.* New York: Families and Work Institute.

N. Paulu. 1993. *Helping your child get ready for school.* Washington, DC: U.S. Department of Education, Office of Educational Research and Improvement.

K. Worth. 2000. The power of children's thinking. In *Foundations: Inquiry Thoughts, Views and Strategies for the K–5 Classroom,* 15–24. Monographs of the National Science Foundation, no. 2. Arlington, VA: National Science Foundation.

S. Shaywitz. 2004. *Overcoming dyslexia: A new and complete science-based program for reading problems at any level.* New York: Random House.

J.A. Lackney. 2000. Learning environments in children's museums: Aesthetics, environmental preference, and creativity. Paper presented at meeting of the Association of Youth Museums & Institute for Civil Society, 11 May, Baltimore, MD.

S.M. Carlson. 2005. Imaginary companions and impersonated characters: Sex differences in children's fantasy play. *Merrill-Palmer Quarterly* 51 (1): 93–118.

S. Heaviside & E. Farris. 1993. *Public school kindergarten teachers' views on children's readiness for school* (NCES 93-410). Washington, DC: National Center for Education Statistics, U.S. Department of Education.

E.E. Werner & R.S. Smith. 1982. *Vulnerable but invincible: A study of resilient children.* New York: McGraw-Hill.

From page 171:

E. Post. 1922. *Etiquette in society, business, in politics and at home.* New York: Funk & Wagnalls.

Early years are learning years

Become a member of NAEYC, and help make them count!

Just as you help young children learn and grow, the National Association for the Education of Young Children—your professional organization—supports you in the work you love. NAEYC is the world's largest early childhood education organization, with a national network of local, state, and regional Affiliates. We are more than 100,000 members working together to bring high-quality early learning opportunities to all children from birth through age 8.

Since 1926, NAEYC has provided educational services and resources for people working with children, including:

• *Young Children*, the award-winning journal (six issues a year) for early childhood educators

• **Books, posters, brochures, and videos** to support your work with young children and families

• **The NAEYC Annual Conference**, which brings tens of thousands of people together from across the country and around the world to share their expertise and ideas on the education of young children

• **Insurance plans** for members and programs

• **A voluntary accreditation system** to help programs reach national standards for high-quality early childhood education

• **Young Children International** to promote global communication and information exchanges

• **www.naeyc.org**—a dynamic Web site with up-to-date information on all of our services and resources

To join NAEYC

To find a complete list of membership benefits and options or to join NAEYC online, visit **www.naeyc.org/membership.** Or you can mail this form to us.

(Membership must be for an individual, not a center or school.)

Name_____

Address_____

City_____ State_____ ZIP_____

E-mail _____

Phone (H)_____ (W)_____

❑ New member

❑ Renewal ID # _____

Affiliate name/number _____

To determine your dues, you must visit **www.naeyc.org/membership** or call 800-424-2460, ext. 2002.

Indicate your payment option

❑ VISA   ❑ MasterCard   ❑ AmEx   ❑ Discover

Card # _____

Exp. date _____

Cardholder's name _____

Signature _____

Note: By joining NAEYC you also become a member of your state and local Affiliates.

Send this form and payment to

NAEYC
PO Box 97156
Washington, DC 20090-7156